Praise for *Uneven Ground: Appalachia since 1945*

"Appalachia still weighs heavily on America's conscience and consciousness, as Ronald D Eller demonstrates with great insight and eloquence in his much-anticipated new study. *Uneven Ground* offers a clear and compelling portrait of the complexities and contradictions that characterize this vast and increasingly diverse region, burdened at once by growth and stagnation, by both its past and its future. This is essential reading for anyone seeking to understand the dynamics of poverty and progress, of power and powerlessness, in modern Appalachia and the discomforting disparities that still set it apart from the nation as a whole." —John C. Inscoe, author of *Race, War, and Remembrance in the Appalachian South*

"Ronald D Eller has written a provocative, compelling, and comprehensive account of the vast transformations in the Appalachian region from 1945 to the present. Against a backdrop of major economic and demographic trends such as deindustrialization, the spread of consumerism, and out-migration, Eller brilliantly analyzes politics and policy making, reform movements and citizen activism, and, above all else, the misplaced faith in economic development that has contributed more to inequality, impoverishment, and environmental ruin in the mountain region than to prosperity and well-being. A must read." —Dwight B. Billings, Professor of Sociology, University of Kentucky

"The reality and the idea of Appalachia have intrigued and frustrated outside observers for more than a century. Policy makers have long sought to transform—'modernize'—through social engineering. Eller provides a judicious, informed history. . . . Anyone interested in Appalachia should read this book." —John B. Boles, William P. Hobby Professor of History

"*Uneven Ground* is passionate, clear, concise, and at times profound. It represents in many ways the cumulative vision of decades of observation about, experience in, and research on Appalachia. Eller is astute to relate very early in the book how integral Appalachia was to the history of American development."—Chad Berry, author of *Southern Migrants, Northern Exiles*

"Makes important contributions to the fields of Appalachian history and the history of the United States' antipoverty public policy. A sweeping narrative that cuts across a half century of economic, political, and

Praise for *Uneven Ground: Appalachia since 1945,* continued

environmental themes, this book provides a synthesis of scholarship and commentary concerning the politics of economic development directed toward the southern mountains. It is a highly significant work that will serve as the standard reference for the foreseeable future."
—Robert S. Weise, author of *Grasping at Independence: Debt, Male Authority, and Mineral Rights in Appalachian Kentucky, 1850–1915*

"In *Uneven Ground,* Ronald D Eller masterfully integrates historical and public-policy analysis into a new and definitive history of modern Appalachia. No other observer has so skillfully located post–World War II Appalachia at the center of debates over social, political, and economic equity in America. Eller shows how competing interpretations of modernization, development, and reform have historically failed to address structural factors in global capitalism that have contributed to persistent class and cultural conflicts in the region."
—John C. Hennen, author of *The Americanization of West Virginia*

"*Uneven Ground* is a cogent, deeply informed narrative of the transformations and traditions that have made Appalachia what it is today. Drawing on an impressive range of historical knowledge as well as his own experiences as an activist, advocate, and policy advisor, Eller examines the often-conflicting ideas, attitudes, motivations, and especially the politics behind post–World War II efforts to 'modernize' the region—and the deep-seated problems of inequality, social and environmental exploitation, and outside corporate dominance that these efforts either exacerbated or failed to address. . . . The story of Appalachia, Eller makes clear, is an American story: of persistent, now rapidly growing disparities of wealth and political power; of the drive for growth and development at both human and environmental expense; of efforts to 'solve' poverty without addressing underlying inequities; of the quest to preserve cultural integrity against commercial exploitation. . . . Though transformed by economic development, Appalachia remains grounded in the traditions that continue to shape and inspire another American story: of the enduring struggle for economic and environmental democracy." —Alice O'Connor, author of *Poverty Knowledge: Social Science, Social Policy, and the Poor in Twentieth-Century U.S. History*

UNEVEN GROUND

UNEVEN GROUND

APPALACHIA SINCE 1945

Ronald D Eller

THE UNIVERSITY PRESS OF KENTUCKY

Ferm UKy 7/09 29.95

"How America Came to the Mountains," by Jim Wayne Miller, is reprinted from *The Brier Poems* by permission of Gnomon Press. Copyright © 1997 by The Estate of Jim Wayne Miller.

The University Press of Kentucky

Scholarly publisher for the Commonwealth, serving Bellarmine University, Berea College, Centre College of Kentucky, Eastern Kentucky University, The Filson Historical Society, Georgetown College, Kentucky Historical Society, Kentucky State University, Morehead State University, Murray State University, Northern Kentucky University, Transylvania University, University of Kentucky, University of Louisville, and Western Kentucky University.
All rights reserved.

Editorial and Sales Offices: The University Press of Kentucky
663 South Limestone Street, Lexington, Kentucky 40508-4008
www.kentuckypress.com

12 11 10 09 08   5 4 3 2 1

Library of Congress Cataloging-in-Publication Data
Eller, Ronald D, 1948-
  Uneven ground : Appalachia since 1945 / Ronald D Eller.
    p. cm.
  Includes bibliographical references and index.
  ISBN 978-0-8131-2523-7 (hardcover : alk. paper)
  1. Appalachian Region, Southern—Rural conditions. 2. Appalachian Region, Southern—Economic conditions. 3. Appalachian Region, Southern—Social conditions—20th century. 4. Appalachian Region, Southern—Social conditions—21st century. 5. Rural development—Appalachian Region, Southern—History. 6. Poverty—Appalachian Region, Southern—History. 7. Rural poor—Appalachian Region, Southern—History. I. Title.
  HN79.A127E55 2008
  307.1'4120975—dc22
                        2008027993

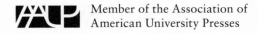

For Jane
and for the memory of our parents,
Elden Carl and Freda Jane Wilson
and
Oliver D and Virginia Ruth Eller

CONTENTS

Illustrations follow page 176

ABBREVIATIONS

AGSLP	Appalachian Group to Save the Land and People
ALCOR	Alice Lloyd College Outreach Reserves
	(later) Appalachian Leadership and Community Outreach
ARA	Area Redevelopment Administration
ARC	Appalachian Regional Commission
ARDA	Appalachian Regional Development Act
AV	Appalachian Volunteers
BLA	Black Lung Association
CAA	community action agency
CAP	Christian Appalachian Project
CSM	Council of the Southern Mountains
EOA	Economic Opportunity Act
EZ	empowerment zone
KFTC	Kentucky Fair Tax Coalition
	(later) Kentuckians for the Commonwealth
KHIC	Kentucky Highlands Investment Corporation
KUAC	Kentucky Un-American Activities Committee
MFD	Miners for Democracy
OEO	Office of Economic Opportunity
PARC	President's Appalachian Regional Commission
SCEF	Southern Conference Education Fund
SOK	Save Our Kentucky
TVA	Tennessee Valley Authority
UMWA	United Mine Workers of America
VISTA	Volunteers in Service to America

ACKNOWLEDGMENTS

Writing history is like piecing together a quilt. Separately the individual records of the past have little meaning until they are arranged by the historian. The remnants of historical evidence, cut from the context of their own time, are empowered to speak to a new generation by the scholar's pen, but that process of creating meaning from disparate facts is seldom a solitary effort. So it is with this book. The pages that follow are the product of a lifetime of living and learning in the place that I call home, but they are also the result of a growing body of scholarship, expanding archival collections, and the insights of countless students, friends, and teachers who have influenced my thinking over the years. Subsequent writers may rearrange the pieces of the historical record and reach different conclusions, but that is the beauty of books and quilts. They allow each generation to find meaning from the past that speaks again to the present and to the future.

I have spent over forty years teaching and writing about Appalachia. Much of that time I served as director of the University of Kentucky Appalachian Center, a multidisciplinary research center designed to link the resources of the university to the public policy needs of the Appalachian region in areas ranging from education to health care, civic leadership to economic development. In that capacity I worked with journalists, administrators, citizens' organizations, and public policy makers at the community, state, and national levels, including appointments to head several gubernatorial commissions. At the University of Kentucky, and earlier during a decade of teaching at a small mountain college in North Carolina, I attempted to apply my knowledge as a historian to the challenges and issues facing the region, serving on county planning boards, civic groups, and regional organizations and completing a two-year term as the scholar in residence at the Appalachian Regional Commission. The knowledge I gained from my participation in the public process informs my narrative just as much as do the hours of research in historical documents, archives, and books.

Some of my colleagues would call me a "presentist historian." I study the past from the perspective of the present to gain insight about those challenges that confront contemporary society. For me, the past is a window to present problems that plague Appalachia and a guidepost for building a more just and sustainable society in a part of the United States that has seen too much inequality, cultural loss, and environmental destruction. My people have lived in the region for more than two hundred years, surviving as farmers, coal miners, mill hands, musicians, preachers, and factory workers. Like other rural Americans, they developed close ties to the land, to family, to their religion, and to their local communities, and they have followed the rest of the nation into the age of consumption. I participated in the great out-migration from Appalachia during the 1950s, the War on Poverty of the 1960s, and the Appalachian renaissance of the 1970s, and I have sat at the table with policy makers as they distributed public funds for the development of the region. In recent years, scholars have gained a much better understanding of the political and economic history of the mountains, but too often we have ignored the lessons of that history, and we, citizens and leaders alike, have continued to abuse each other and the land in our continuing quest for progress. History speaks to us only when we listen.

Like most books, this one is the culmination of years of research and reflects the contributions of dozens of librarians, archivists, statisticians, students, activists, and scholars throughout the region. The staffs at the University of Kentucky Special Collections Library (especially Kate Black), the Berea College Special Collections and Archives, the West Virginia University West Virginia and Regional History Collection, the West Virginia State Archives, the Appalachian Regional Commission in Washington DC, and the Lyndon Baines Johnson Library and Museum in Austin deserve special thanks. Over the years graduate students attending my seminars and serving as research assistants at the Appalachian Center have provided data analysis and criticism through their own work. Among the many students to whom I am indebted are Glenna Graves, Nyoka Hawkins, Tim Collins, Tom Kiffmeyer, Glenn Taul, Phil Jenks, Carrie Celia Mullins, Jim White, Debbie Auer, Tom Riley, John Burch, Jerry Napier, Carlye Thacker, Lori Copeland, Margaret Brown, Roy Salmons, and Jodi Mullins. Several colleagues and friends read early drafts of this manuscript, including Dwight Billings, Rudy Abramson, Ron Formisano, Robert Weise, and Chad Berry. I deeply appreciate their insight and kindness, even though I did not always take their advice. I am, moreover, indebted to the University of Kentucky College of Arts and Sciences for a sabbatical leave, to the Appalachian Regional Commission for a term as its John Whisman scholar, and to the National Endowment for the Humanities for a summer research stipend. Finally, I want to thank my stepdaughter, Sarah Jane Herbener, for many hours of editing a much too long manuscript. Her critical eye and way with words have added immeasurable clarity to my academic prose.

One person is, however, more responsible for this book than any other, my wife Jane Wilson Eller. Without her steady support, encouragement, and gentle prodding, this manuscript might not have been completed. She alone understands my love for the mountains. After all, this is her story too.

How America Came
to the Mountains

Jim Wayne Miller

The way the Brier remembers it, folks weren't sure
at first what was coming. The air felt strange,
and smelled of blasting powder, carbide, diesel fumes.

A hen crowed and a witty prophecied
eight lanes of fogged-in asphalt filled with headlights.
Most people hadn't gone to bed that evening,
believing an awful storm was coming to the mountains.

And come it did. At first, the Brier remembers,
it sounded like a train whistle far off in the night.
They felt it shake the ground as it came roaring.
Then it was big trucks roaring down an interstate,
a singing like a circle saw in oak,
a roil of every kind of noise, factory
whistles, cows bellowing, a caravan
of camper trucks bearing down
blowing their horns and playing loud tapedecks.

He recollects it followed creeks and roadbeds
and when it hit, it blew the tops off houses,
shook people out of bed, exposing them
to a sudden black sky wide as eight lanes of asphalt,
and dropped a hail of beer cans, buckets
and bottles clattering on their sleepy heads.
Children were sucked up and never seen again.

HOW AMERICA CAME TO THE MOUNTAINS

The Brier remembers the sky full of trucks
and flying radios, bicycles and tv sets, whirling
log chains, red wagons, new shoes and tangerines.
Others told him they saw it coming like a wave
of tumbling dirt and rocks and carbodies
rolling before the blade of a bulldozer,
saw it pass on by, leaving a wake
of singing commercials, leaving ditches
full of spray cans and junk cars, canned
biscuit containers, tinfoil pie plates.
Some told him it felt like a flooding creek
that leaves ribbons of polyethylene
hanging from willow trees along the bank
and rusty cardoors half silted over on sandbars.

It was that storm that dropped beat-up cars
all up and down the hollers, out in fields
just like a tornado that tears tin sheets
off tops of barns and drapes them like scarves
on trees in quiet fields two miles from any settlement.

And that's why now so many old barn doors
up and down the mountains hang by one hinge
and gravel in the creek is broken glass.

That's how the Brier remembers America coming
to the mountains. He was just a little feller
but he recollects how his Mama got
all of the younguns out of bed, recalls
being scared of the dark and the coming roar
and trying to put both feet into one leg
of his overalls.

    They left the mountains fast
and lived in Is, Illinois, for a while
but found it dull country and moved back.
The Brier has lived in As If, Kentucky, ever since.

INTRODUCTION

A mericans have an enduring faith in the power of development to improve the quality of our lives. At least since the late nineteenth century, we have associated progress toward the attainment of a better society with measures of industrial production, urbanization, consumption, technology, and the adoption of modern education and cultural values. Early in the twentieth century, we assumed that movement along the road to the good life was best left to the engine of private enterprise, but after the Great Depression and World War II, government played a larger role in assuring economic growth and incorporating minorities into the new American dream. Areas such as Appalachia were deemed to be backward and underdeveloped because they lacked the statistical measures of progress, both material and cultural, that had become the benchmarks of success in a modern world. For policy makers of the 1950s and 1960s, convinced of the appropriateness of the American path to development, those backwater places needed to be energized and brought into the supposed mainstream.

Appalachia has long played an ironic role in the drama of American development. Discovered or, more accurately, created by urban journalists in the years following the Civil War, the idea of Appalachia provided a counterpoint to emerging definitions of progress at the turn of the twentieth century. Those writers who disliked modernity saw in the region a remnant of frontier life, the reflection of a simpler, less complicated time that ought to be preserved and protected. Those who found advancement in the growth of material production, consumption, and technology decried what they considered the isolation and backwardness of the place and sought to uplift the mountain people

1

through education and industrialization. The perceived economic and cultural deficiencies of Appalachia allowed entrepreneurs a free hand to tap the region's natural resources in the name of development, but by midcentury the dream of industrial prosperity had produced the opposite in the mountains. Persistent unemployment and poverty set Appalachia off as a social and economic problem area long before social critic Michael Harrington drew attention to the region as part of the "other America" in 1962.[1]

As the United States matured into a global economic power in the late twentieth century, the effort to spread the development faith at home and abroad once again focused the nation's attention on the region. The migration of millions of young whites from Appalachia and young blacks from the Deep South into the cities of the Midwest added to the congestion and poverty of urban ghettoes, and the shocking scenes of rural blight captured by the media during John F. Kennedy's 1960 presidential primary campaign in West Virginia contradicted popular notions of an affluent America. The rediscovery of Appalachia as a cultural and economic problem area was an embarrassment and a challenge to a generation confident of its ability to shape a better world. Attempting to eliminate the disparities between mainstream America and Appalachia, government made the region a domestic testing ground for strategies to promote economic growth, and social scientists used it as a laboratory for experimentation in human behavior modification.

Government and private programs launched during the 1960s eventually transformed the mountains, stirring both hope and resistance among mountain residents. The short-lived War on Poverty and the more lasting Appalachian Regional Commission fueled a new cultural identity in the region and spawned a multitude of new roads, schools, retail centers, and other symbols of the consumer society. Appalachia was swept up in another round of modernization that reshaped the physical landscape and permanently altered the way of life for most of the region's residents. Even so, the transformation begun by the War on Poverty failed to eliminate the perception of Appalachian otherness, and the new Appalachia that emerged from the special development programs continued to reflect the social inequalities and environmental exploitation that had burdened the region for decades. By the turn of the twenty-first century, growth and government-sponsored initiatives to promote change had altered the outward appearance of Appalachia, but development had done little to correct the structural problems of land abuse, political corruption, economic shortsightedness, and the loss of community and culture. Despite the rise and fall of national attention and resources, no other region within the United States has presented a greater challenge to policy makers or a greater test of modern notions of development. The idea of Appalachia survives in the popular mind, and the heart of the region continues to lag behind the rest of the country as an area of persistent economic and social distress.

Appalachia endures as a paradox in American society in part because it plays a critical role in the discourse of national identity but also because the region's struggle with modernity reflects a deeper American failure to define progress in the first place. For more than a century, Appalachia has provided a challenge to modern conceptions of the American dream. It has appeared as a place of cultural backwardness in a nation of progressive values, a region of poverty in an affluent society, and a rural landscape in an increasingly urban nation. We *know* Appalachia exists because we need it to exist in order to define what we are not. It is the "other America" because the very idea of Appalachia convinces us of the righteousness of our own lives. The notion of Appalachia as a separate place, a region set off from mainstream culture and history, has allowed us to distance ourselves from the uncomfortable dilemmas that the story of Appalachia raises about our own lives and about the larger society. However, Appalachia is more than just an intellectual idea. It is also a real place where public policies designed to achieve a healthy society, the objective of development itself, have played out with mixed results. As a venue for development, Appalachia provides a stage for the larger political debates over the meaning of progress, over who wins and who loses as a result of change, and over the role of government in assuring the good life.

I have spent much of the past four decades observing, participating in, and writing about the process of development in the mountains. My family has lived in the southern mountains since the 1790s, and we have witnessed many of the changes that have swept the region in the name of progress and modernization. We have survived as farmers, coal miners, mill hands, and ministers, and we have fought the nation's wars and enriched the larger culture with our music. As a college student in West Virginia during the War on Poverty, I served as a part-time caseworker in child welfare. I was told by my professors and field supervisors that the problems of poverty in my community were the result of cultural deficiencies, antiquated values, and low expectations; my responsibility as an educated person was to serve as a role model for my less advantaged clients. Uncomfortable with those assumptions, I became a historian, teacher, and activist, determined not only to gain a better understanding of my land and my people but to translate that knowledge into the national conversation about Appalachia.

My first book, *Miners, Millhands, and Mountaineers: The Industrialization of the Appalachian South, 1880–1930*, rejected the notion that the problems of the region were the product of a peculiar mountain culture and a different history and found instead that the region's distress was rooted deeply in the very process of private industrial development that had created modern America. As director of the University of Kentucky Appalachian Center for sixteen years, I worked with local leaders, state policy makers, and national planners to transfer the lessons of that development history into public policy affecting the region. Too often, however, I found not only that research and experience were ignored in the drama of political decision making (a fact that should come as no surprise to historians) but that the assumptions about change that guided policy toward Appalachia were based on a limited range of alternatives and visions of the good life. Appalachia was not different from the rest of America; it was in fact a mirror of what the nation was becoming. To challenge those assumptions was in some circles almost un-American.

This book therefore examines the politics of development in Appalachia since 1945 with an eye toward exploring the idea of progress as it has evolved in modern America itself. The story of Appalachia's struggle to overcome poverty, to live in harmony with the land, and to respect the diversity of cultures and the value of community is an American story. Since World War II, during my lifetime, Appalachia has undergone dramatic change. The long lines of unemployed men at government commodity distribution centers have given way to lines of commuters in Wal-Mart superstores acquiring the latest consumer products of a world economy. The dilapidated schools, poor housing, and inadequate health care that led my parents to briefly leave the mountains in the 1950s for a better life in northern cities have been replaced by modern facilities and services that provide access to the latest technology and knowledge within fifty miles of every mountain resident. Superhighways make it easier to get into and out of the region, and bustling suburban centers have emerged throughout the mountains, looking much like their retail-based counterparts elsewhere in America. Yet, as in the nation as a whole, these changes have come at a tremendous cost to the environment, at the displacement of millions of rural residents, and at the loss of traditional values and cultures. The diversity that is modern Appalachia belies a growing gap between the rich and the poor, and it ignores the continuing sacrifice of Appalachian resources and people for the comfort and prosperity of the rest of the nation.

Much of the change that has come to Appalachia is the result of well-intentioned government planning to promote growth and assimilation. Programs such as the War on Poverty and the Appalachian Regional Development Act reflect broadly held attitudes about progress within and outside the region, attitudes that are grounded in the received assumptions about development that have limited the dialogue and potential for alternative paths and outcomes. Too often, for example, we have mistaken growth for development, change for progress. Indeed, growth has become central to the American idea of development. Attainment of the good life, we assume, is dependent upon the continued expansion of markets, transportation and communication networks, mass culture, urban centers, and consumer demand. Economic growth may indeed generate employment opportunities, but if those jobs provide low wages and few health benefits, they can reinforce conditions of dependence and powerlessness. New highways may increase commerce and access to services for some communities, but other communities, bypassed by the transportation improvements, can suffer displacement and decline. Expansion of mining and other extractive industries may produce short-term employment but, if unregulated, can leave environmental damage that may threaten the sustainability of communities and ecosystems for generations to come. Investments in some areas of the economy can benefit a small number of individuals or places at the expense of others, and lifestyle enhancements for a few people may cause hardship and loss of meaning for other people.

Since World War II, moreover, we have assumed that the scientific management of growth could achieve progress in the mountains without requiring structural change in the distribution of wealth, the ownership and use of the land, or the control of the political system. Poverty could be eliminated by changing individual behavior and by tying people more directly to the market rather than confronting existing social and economic inequalities. This faith in the ability of technology and education to lift all boats has produced public institutions in Appalachia that look much like those in the rest of the nation, but those institutions continue to reflect regional disparities in social capital and political power. Since the goal of growth was a society that mirrored suburban, consumer America, development strategies in Appalachia further fragmented mountain society through the centralization of public services and retail facilities, the creation of class-segregated communities, and the generation of material symbols of individual success. The modernization of the mountains required the further integration of the region into the global marketplace and the subsequent weakening of local, producer-based economies. Although some aspects of local cultures were packaged and commodified for export, local community ties gave way to new, market-oriented identities, and in some places local residents themselves were displaced by newcomers tied to the land only by aesthetic and consumer values.

The mixed legacy of growth in Appalachia has also left its mark on the land and on human connections to the land. As a result of the rapid expansion of modern technologies after World War II, difficult terrain could be breached to promote commerce with the larger world. Streams could be relocated, rivers dammed, and hillsides developed for housing, recreation, and business use. Most of all, entire mountains and ranges of mountains could be leveled to extract their mineral resources and to create a landscape more suitable for manufacturing and retail expansion. Appalachian residents had always used the land for survival, and their knowledge of and intimacy with the land were based upon their use of it. Although some mountain residents may have developed a spiritual relationship to the land and an appreciation for the natural environment, their connection with the place was more often linked to family and community ties rather than recognition of the relationship between their way of life and the landscape around them. Like other Americans, most Appalachians were quick to turn to more convenient lifestyles when the products of a modern economy expanded their choices. The growth-based economy, however, forever altered the landscape itself and physically separated families from the old intimacy with the land that had provided sustenance and meaning to life. Having failed to learn the environmental lessons of resource overdevelopment at the turn of the twentieth century, we continued to see the mountains (just as we saw mountain culture) as a barrier to progress, something to be overcome and its resources tapped in the name of growth.

The tendency to blame the land, environment, and culture of the mountains for the problems of Appalachia obscures our ability to understand the complexity of political and economic struggles within the region and diminishes our national dialogue on the meaning of progress and the most appropriate path to development. Many popular images continue to set off Appalachia against the rest of America. In doing so, they deny the presence of class and ideological differences that divide Appalachian communities. Many public policies are still based on the naive assumptions that poverty can be seriously addressed without structural change, that growth is good for everyone, that urban lifestyles and institutions are to be emulated, and that local and regional markets are not important in a global economy. Such assumptions weaken the democratic conversation about the goal of government and the quality of our lives. Faith in the ability of growth-based development alone to eliminate poverty, moreover, effectively disfranchises poorer people and rural people and further displaces our collective responsibilities for the land and for each other onto the vagaries of the market and onto the best intentions of bureaucrats. The development process is a value-laden political act, complete with winners and losers. As such, it necessitates public debate, challenging the way we understand progress and the way we see ourselves.

Much of the story of Appalachia describes the exploitation of the region at the hands of outside economic interests. Considerable research since the 1960s has documented the extent of absentee landownership and corporate control of the Appalachian economy, but the development faith is not just something that has been imposed on the mountains from outside. As the pages that follow reveal, leaders from within Appalachia were among the first to call for government intervention programs to promote development and reduce poverty. Mountain residents themselves have been among the strongest advocates of growth, and they have engaged in some of the most callous exploitation of the land and of their fellow citizens that has befallen the region. If Appalachia's struggle with development has been uneven and has failed to meet our expectations and dreams, it is because Appalachia's problems are not those of Appalachia alone. They will not be solved in isolation from the dilemmas facing the rest of modern society. For that reason, we are all engaged in the struggle to define the good life in the mountains. We are all Appalachians.

1

RICH LAND—POOR PEOPLE

"What crops do they raise in this country?" the officer
asked. . . .
"Youngens," she said. . . . "Youngens fer th' wars and them
factories."
—Harriette Arnow, *The Dollmaker* (1954)

There was more than a little sarcasm in the reply of Harriette Arnow's fictional character to the soldier whose car she had stopped on a Kentucky mountain road during World War II. The upper Cumberland area, like most of Appalachia, was still an overwhelmingly rural place, rich in natural beauty and the cultural heritage of the frontier, but it had become a paradox on the American landscape, a rich land inhabited by a poor people. A region of small farms and scattered villages, Appalachia had been swept up by the tidal surge of industrialization that engulfed the United States in the years following the Civil War and had experienced unprecedented growth and economic change. Overwhelmed by an expanding market economy that altered land use patterns, social relationships, and the meaning of work, residents of the region were propelled into a new world of technology, science, and consumer capitalism. When the boom times gave way to depression, much of the old Appalachia survived, but much had fundamentally changed.

The great hillsides of hardwood timber, once among the most diverse and valuable forests in the world, had been cut over and denuded. The thick seams of coal, copper, mica, and other minerals had been sucked from the hills and shipped to the furnaces and factories of the urban Northeast. Exposed and gouged, the soil on the hillsides had eroded and washed down, and many of the streams, once clear and free flowing, were filled with sediment and the refuse of men and machines. As Appalachia's human and natural resources were tapped to feed the needs of a modernizing nation, the small mountain homesteads that once nurtured large families through diverse forest agriculture had given way to hundreds of little mining camps and mill villages, company towns fed by company stores and governed by company rules. Thousands of families left their farms and migrated to the new industrial camps or to textile towns in the foothills of the region. Along with other rural Americans, mountain people were drawn to the promise of a better way of life, but the new economic order proved to be a shallow cup. The wealth generated by growth and by what mountain people called "public work" largely flowed out of the region, leaving much of the land devastated and many of its inhabitants dependent and poor.[1]

Rural mountain residents had always been close to the land, although that closeness was reflected more in strong ties to family and place than to any ethic to preserve the land. Hard work and large families were important not only to survival on the land but to shaping a way of life around it. Preindustrial mountain farms were family farms run by cooperation and by a strong sense of responsibility to each other. As a result, the extended family became a key social institution in the mountains, affecting not only the traditional economy but almost every aspect of mountain culture as well. With industrialization, the family and the land became even more important to survival. Family linkages provided opportunities for employment, migration, and fellowship, and working with the land continued to provide the primary means of survival, even though the ownership and use of the land had changed considerably.

When the collapse of the first great industrial boom came in the late 1920s, unemployed miners and mill hands struggled to return to the land and to an earlier way of life. Displaced industrial workers moved in with kin on smaller, marginal farms that had been saved from outside buyers at the turn of the century. Never highly productive units, especially in a growing national market and without the productive use of the woodlands, these overcrowded homesteads were even less able to sustain the new population. In Knox County, Kentucky, for example, over a thousand families who had left earlier in the century to find jobs returned home in the 1930s, increasing the county's population by 30 percent.[2]

During the Depression, thousands of mountain families crowded together to subsist on poor land or to survive on the dole or on government work programs. Those who were able to return to the family farm were fortunate, for many who remained in the now neglected coal camps faced unemployment, hunger, and disease. Almost half of the mountain population laid claim to some kind of public assistance during the Depression, and Appalachia emerged as one of the most impoverished regions in the nation.[3] The Resettlement Administration estimated that about one-fourth of the rural relief cases in the United States in 1935 were in the Appalachian South.[4] Many mountain residents who had witnessed the arrival of the modern age and the transformation of the land and the economy faced the future with uncertainty and frustration. As one Tennessee mountain farmer lamented, "The real old mountaineer is a thing of the past, and what will finally take our place, God only knows."[5]

By 1940 a pattern of growth without development had settled over Appalachia. The region had experienced rapid expansion in jobs and in the capacity to extract its natural resources, but growth had come without the development of an internal capacity to sustain prosperity. With the outbreak of war in Europe and preparation for war at home, the demand for mountain labor rose again, and once more Appalachia's resources became vital to the nation. The expansion of war industries stimulated demand for Appalachian coal and timber, and the new aircraft plants, steel mills, ordnance factories, and uniform manufacturers clamored for additional workers. As early as 1938, coal production began to recover as operators reorganized and consolidated companies in anticipation of wartime markets. After the bombing of Pearl Harbor, a frenzy of production swept the industry as once idle mines were reopened and company towns reawakened.

The effect of war mobilization was to revive hope for a generation of mountain young people, a generation that had known only poverty and hard times. In rural areas farm prices recovered, and workers slowly returned to the mines and the mills, lessening the pressure on the land. Families and individuals migrated to defense jobs outside the mountains, and thousands of young men and women joined the armed forces. Sawmills that had not operated in years now hummed, turning out hardwood for building materials and military rifle stocks. New coal mines were opened and new sidetracks laid; abandoned tipples were repaired and painted and new mining equipment purchased. Company towns and county seats bustled with life, and a throng of mineral agents, timber buyers, and land developers invaded the region anew.

Much of the wartime boom was facilitated by government expenditures. Not only did federal contracts for ordnance and war materials stimulate production inside and outside the region, but government loans financed the expansion of critical industrial facilities. The Reconstruction Finance Corporation and other federal agencies, for example, helped to finance wartime conversion of the chemical industry in the Kanawha Valley of West Virginia and to underwrite the purchase of new mining machinery and loading equipment across the coalfields. The Tennessee Valley Authority (TVA) provided cheap electricity for the production of aluminum in east Tennessee and for making tents, uniforms, and blankets in North Carolina, Alabama, and Georgia. Throughout Appalachia the new public buildings and improved roads constructed by thousands of Works Progress Administration workers during the Depression provided critical infrastructure for the war effort.

The mountain population, moreover, responded to the call for national defense with enthusiasm. Even before the attack on Pearl Harbor, the attraction of military service and war industries jobs had begun to empty mountain public relief rolls of young men and mountain schools of some of their brightest students. Appalachian people had always been quick to serve their country in times of war, and enlistment rates in the region were among the highest in the nation during World War II. The war also provided an opportunity for escape from poverty and idleness. The promise of steady employment, higher wages, and better living conditions drew thousands into the armed services and into the defense plants of Chicago, Cincinnati, Dayton, Baltimore, and Norfolk. Companies from as far away as Michigan and

Massachusetts recruited employees, including teenage boys and girls, from mountain hollows and transported them to mills and assembly lines in urban centers. When asked how he liked the army, one mountain youth responded, "Anything is better than what I had at home." A year into the war, a mountain teacher reported, "The young manhood of our town has moved out almost en masse. . . . Never again can this section be the same."[6]

Those who remained in the region suddenly found employment opportunities where none had existed a short time before. The revived coal mines, sawmills, and chemical plants quickly experienced a labor shortage and were forced to depend on older workers when the young men of the area were drafted or volunteered for service. Men in their forties and fifties who had entered the mines during the heyday of the first boom found themselves heading once again belowground or into some other kind of public work.

War mobilization helped to redistribute population within the region and to launch an out-migration from Appalachia that would stream millions of mountaineers into the nation's urban centers over the next three decades. The movement of young people into the military and war industries and the return of families to the coal camps drained population from rural communities, renewing the process of decline that had begun at the turn of the century. Some rural agricultural areas experienced major difficulty in securing enough labor to sustain farm production, and many farmsteads were abandoned or only marginally maintained during the war.[7] As families migrated to jobs in neighboring industrial counties or to nearby urban communities such as Lexington, Kentucky, and Knoxville, Tennessee, the population of rural farm communities declined proportionately.

A study of wartime migration in eastern Kentucky estimated that more than eighty-five thousand persons, almost 19 percent of the population, left the area between 1940 and 1942 alone. The decrease in population exceeded the gain for the entire previous decade and took 40 percent of the men between the ages of fifteen and thirty-four. Most of the decline was accounted for by the loss of farm people, with about half of the loss attributed to entering the armed services and the remainder to leaving for industrial work in the Ohio Valley and Great Lakes. The study determined that the out-migration had been largely

13

one of young families and of individuals, especially young men. "Many heads of families," it concluded, "have left their wives and children to carry on the farm operations."[8]

While rural farm areas lost population, wartime recovery spurred unexpected growth in mountain county seats. These middle-class communities had stagnated during the Depression, but now local merchants, bankers, lawyers, and agents for outside companies flourished with the revival of activity in the outlying coal districts. Newly paved highways made possible by state and federal expenditures during the 1930s linked the county seats with each other and with the rapidly growing urban communities on the fringes of the mountains, and improved gravel roads constructed by the WPA stretched up the narrow valleys to the coal camps.[9] Automobiles, whose numbers had expanded even during the Depression, now shuttled goods and people back and forth from these commercial centers, reducing the isolation of the once rail-dependent coal towns.

The improved highways also gave rise to a new form of mining enterprise, the truck mine, which would become ubiquitous in the southern Appalachian coalfields after the war. Rising wartime markets for coal enticed many local residents to open small mines on family-owned land or to lease seams of coal on the secondary spurs that jutted from the main ridges. The larger mining companies deemed the coal in these secondary spurs, being thinner and more remote from the tipples and railroads, to be unrecoverable, but with better roads and a booming market, these seams provided an opportunity for indigenous entrepreneurs. With as little as a one-thousand-dollar investment, a man could open a seam of coal at the outcrop, construct a wooden bin down the hillside with which to load the coal into trucks, and transport it to regional markets or rail-side tipples. These small operations, which generally employed only five or six men, could produce eighty to a hundred tons of coal a day and realize profits of close to a dollar on the ton for their owners.[10]

The federal Office of War Mobilization encouraged the production of more coal as a patriotic duty, and thousands of small operators took advantage of the artificial demand to open new mines. During the war the growth of such mines was phenomenal throughout the coalfields, but nowhere was it as prevalent as in eastern Kentucky, where more than 4,200 truck mines opened in the 1940s, accounting for almost 38 percent of the state's production.[11] Most of these mines were nonunion and nonmechanized, utilizing human labor to cut and load the coal and ponies to haul it to the loading bins. Most paid wages significantly below the union scale, but even seven or eight dollars a day was welcomed by aging coal miners who had not worked steadily in years.

The war brought to the mountains a rush of activity that had not been seen since the early years of the century. Opportunities for jobs, business expansions, and the movement of young people into the war effort created a temporary respite from the hard times of the Depression, but this growth masked fundamental flaws in the region's development. Most of Appalachia's mineral and timber resources continued to be owned by outside corporations and controlled by nonresident interests. The value added from their extraction remained largely untaxed for local benefit. Moreover, a single-industry economy frustrated the diversification of local enterprises and tied most mountain communities to the vagaries of national and, increasingly, international markets. Local political leaders, many of whom benefited from their relationships to outside interests, continued to defend the status quo. The gap between traditional agricultural communities and rapidly modernizing urban centers beyond the region grew.

Although rising coal markets and expanding employment generated new sources of income, rationing and other austerity measures during the war prevented many consumer goods from reaching mountain residents. In the coal camps, company houses were simply patched and painted for the returning miners, and hospitals, schools, and other public facilities in the villages were left in disrepair. Even the spate of new truck mines placed additional burdens on public coffers to maintain the coal haul roads and contributed to the overexpansion of the industry itself. Overexpansion had plagued Appalachian coal mines in the 1920s, and following World War II it again led to instability and intense competition between the small mines and the larger producers. Since most of the truck mines were nonunion, miners in these smaller operations received lower wages and no benefits for their labor and were highly vulnerable to fluctuations in the coal market. Indeed, wartime demand and competition between the larger corporate mines and the new truck mines would increase the mechanization of the coal mining process, setting the stage for the eventual displacement of thousands of miners and their families.

The mechanization of the American coal industry was an evolutionary process, beginning as early as the 1890s, but new technology was slow to come to southern mines. Throughout the first half of the twentieth century, Appalachian coal mines depended primarily on the labor of men and boys to undercut and load their product for market. This was in part because of the lack of unionization and the availability of cheap labor, but it was also in part because of the expense and slow development of coal-loading technology. The introduction, for example, of mechanized undercutting equipment in larger mines early in the century actually increased the demand for workers to load coal and operate mechanical haulage systems. Undercutting machinery could produce many times more coal in an hour than the individual pick miner could blast "from the solid" in a day, but the technology required additional laborers to manage the equipment, to load the additional coal into gondolas, and to transport it to the surface. It was not until the introduction of mobile mechanical loaders on the eve of World War II that mechanization began to have a major impact on employment in the region, and only then as a by-product of union decisions and competition for postwar markets.

The end of the hand-loading era in Appalachia began during World War II, when a few larger mines introduced conveyor belts and new automatic loading machines into their pits to meet wartime contracts, but it was not until after the war that significant numbers of Appalachian mines began to utilize the new technology. Many of the region's mining operations had been unionized under the New Deal, and although owners were able to resist pressures from John L. Lewis and the United Mine Workers of America (UMWA) to drive up wages and benefits during the war, most operators anticipated rising labor costs with the return of peace. When the UMWA established its Health and Retirement Funds in 1946 and launched a series of annual strikes that increased levies on coal production to finance the funds, larger union mines turned increasingly to mechanization to reduce labor costs and to compete with the burgeoning nonunion truck mines. By 1950, 69 percent of the nation's coal was loaded by mechanical means, in comparison with 13 percent fifteen years earlier.[12]

The new mechanical loading equipment reduced the need for hand loading of coal just when large numbers of young men and women were returning home from the war with high expectations. This generation of mountain youth had grown up during the Depression and had been scattered across the globe by the war. They had experienced better housing, improved health care, and steady wages, and they had observed the comparative wealth of other parts of the country. Now they hoped for a brighter future for themselves and their children. Some expected to return to the mines. Others hoped for jobs as secretaries, welders, mechanics, and barbers, and still others planned to apply their GI benefits to acquire an education. Many returning veterans found the changes that had come to their communities overwhelming. "When I left here in 1941," observed one veteran, "everybody was stone broke and had just about run out of ambition to do anything except draw relief rations, piddle around on the WPA and loaf. But when I got back home the mines were goin' full blast and a lot of men who didn't even have a job in 1941 was runnin' two or three truck mines and had seventy five or a hundred thousand dollars in cash."[13]

At first it appeared that the veterans' hopes for a brighter future at home might be fulfilled, at least in some mountain communities. Although rural, agricultural areas continued to suffer economic decline, expectations remained high in the coal camps and other industrial centers. For a time, at least, the transition to peacetime production and the expansion of postwar markets sustained the coal boom. When Congress disbanded the wartime Office of Price Administration in 1946, coal prices soared, and a new flurry of mine openings swept the coalfields, fueling speculation that the good times would continue and temporarily disguising the inevitable consequences of mine mechanization.

By 1948, however, the postwar boom had run its course, and the demand for coal began to level off. The construction of new pipelines and refineries during the war increased the availability of oil and natural gas, and many of coal's traditional consumers began to convert to these alternative energy sources. Not only were these fuels cleaner, cheaper, and more efficient, but industrialists concerned with consis-

17

tent production had found them to be more reliable as well. A series of UMWA strikes following the war demonstrated Lewis's ability to shut down national coal supplies and further confirmed coal's reputation as a risky fuel because of the uncertainty of supplies. As homes, industries, railroads, and other consumers switched to oil, coal's dominance over American energy markets weakened.[14]

The first mines to feel the return of hard times were the truck mines, which generally sold their product on the "spot" market and were not protected by long-term contracts. As the price of coal plummeted at the railhead, hundreds of "dog hole" mines that had sprung up overnight closed almost as quickly as they had appeared. Thousands of miners were laid off, and the gilded prosperity of the coal camps and commercial towns faded again. Some small-time operators who had amassed minor fortunes during the boom years lost everything. Others took what remained of their wealth and moved away. All those whose incomes were tied to the volatile truck mine sector—truck drivers, mechanics, merchants—saw their livelihoods dwindle. Everywhere a decided gloom settled over the coalfields.

Then, in 1950, the UMWA and the nation's larger coal producers signed a labor contract that had monumental consequences in Appalachia. On the surface, the National Bituminous Coal Wage Agreement of March 5, 1950, appeared to be a major victory for union miners. The contract raised wages and benefits across the industry and restored royalties to the UMWA Health and Retirement Funds while assuring stable production for companies by eliminating the "willing and able" (right to strike) clause of earlier agreements. Unionized coal companies had stopped paying into the Health and Retirement Funds in 1949 in response to declining coal prices and rising competition from nonunion, primarily southern Appalachian, mines. In retaliation, Lewis called a brief strike and later ordered a production slowdown until a new contract could be negotiated. The slowdown precipitated a national crisis in coal reserves, and the UMWA leader, fearing a federal takeover of the mines, agreed to a settlement proposed by George H. Love, head of the Northern Coal Operators' Association. Despite opposition from the Southern Bituminous Coal Operators' Association, which represented most of the smaller producers in Kentucky, West Virginia, Tennessee, and Virginia, the contract was ratified and subsequently imposed across the industry.[15]

The 1950 wage agreement was the culmination of two decades of struggle by Lewis to increase wages and benefits for the nation's coal miners, and it reflected a vision for the industry that he had advocated since the 1920s. Believing that coal's persistent problems resulted from overexpansion within the industry, Lewis had long favored mechanization as a way to reduce the number of coal mines, stabilize production, and improve the health and welfare of working miners. He believed that a high wage scale would force operators to lower labor costs by introducing modern, labor-saving machinery, which would in turn increase production efficiency and lower coal prices to consumers. Smaller, inefficient (and nonunion) mines, which he saw as the source of overproduction, would be forced out of business, thus eliminating the problem of too many mines and too many miners. In Lewis's judgment, a high uniform wage rate and mechanization of the workplace would secure the health of the industry, and the two concepts would complement each other.[16]

Lewis recognized that the agreement would result in the displacement of thousands of coal miners, but he believed that high wages for actively employed miners and good benefits for retired workers were the long-term priorities for the union. By tying the growth of the union Health and Retirement Funds to increases in production and by agreeing to a no-strike clause to sustain those increases, Lewis provided incentives for larger mining companies to mechanize and for union miners to acquiesce in the practice. Unfortunately, the Lewis strategy worked to the disadvantage of southern producers, whose smaller operations and distance from markets made them more susceptible to rising labor costs. Soon after signing the 1950 agreement, the northern coal operators and the owners of larger captive mines formed the Bituminous Coal Operators' Association, which, along with the UMWA, set the standards for wages and benefits in the industry for the next three decades. Between 1950 and 1972, the nation experienced only three nationwide strikes by union miners, but this labor quiescence resulted in thousands of small and medium-size mines in Appalachia being sold or closed and an entire generation of miners being replaced by machines.

The impact of the 1950 wage agreement was especially dramatic in Appalachia. Between 1950 and 1970, the region's deep mines mechanized rapidly to increase productivity and reduce labor costs. The introduction of mobile Joy loaders and continuous miners permanently reduced the need for hand shoveling in the larger mines and increased pressure on smaller operations to mechanize. Introduced in 1948, the continuous miner revolutionized coal production. By integrating the work of undercutting, drilling, blasting, and loading into one process, the continuous miner made it possible for ten men to produce three times the tonnage mined by eighty-six miners loading coal by hand.[17] As the percentage of coal produced by machines increased, the number of actively employed miners declined proportionately. By 1960 fewer than half of the 475,000 miners in the region at the end of World War II still found work in the deep mines, and by 1970 that number had declined to 107,000.[18]

As hard times settled again over the coalfields, thousands of miners joined their rural neighbors in a massive exodus from the hills. Over the next two decades, the stream of young people that had poured from the mountains during World War II became a flood of displaced families. In one of the nation's largest internal migrations, over 3 million people left Appalachia between 1940 and 1970, seeking economic refuge in the cities of the Midwest.[19] Laboring beside other displaced populations—African Americans from the Deep South, Hispanics from Puerto Rico, Latinos from the Southwest, and second-generation immigrant families from southern and eastern Europe—Appalachians built the automobiles, washing machines, radios, and televisions that shaped the postwar consumer society of the United States. Mountain migrants brought their music and culture with them to the new world of the city, creating little Appalachian communities in the midst of urban centers and helping to bring national attention to the plight of communities back home.

Migration was not new to Appalachia. Mountain people had migrated for decades to find work, both within the region and outside it. After the Civil War, Appalachian families had moved to the West, especially to Texas and Missouri, in search of cheap land, and at the turn of the twentieth century, many more had filled the cotton textile mills of the southern Piedmont. Mountain farmers were accustomed to leaving home for seasonal jobs, transporting livestock to market, rafting logs to low-country sawmills, or finding occasional work in the coal mines. Indeed, during the heyday of the coal boom, mining families commonly moved from one mining camp to another in search of better wages, better schools, and better housing. Never before, however, had Appalachians migrated out of the region in such large numbers. When conditions at home forced them to seek opportunities in the North, they relied on old patterns of relocation and traditional support systems to ease their adjustment to urban life and to remain emotionally rooted in the hills.

Family and community were at the center of the migration experience. Family linkages provided the means for communication about jobs in cities as well as the support networks for relocation. "When mountain people migrate from the region," observed sociologists James Brown and Harry Schwarzweller, "they do not go because they have learned of attractive job opportunities through the efforts of the United States Employment Services or some private recruiting agency; they go because some relative 'out there' has written and told them, or has come back on a visit and told them that jobs are available."[20] Migration routes and urban destinations had been established during the war, and earlier migrants invited relatives to live with them until they could get jobs. Typically, breadwinners moved to the city for a short time to look for work before returning home to the mountains for their spouses and children. Other relatives followed later.

Often people from one community or hollow migrated to the same town in the North, providing an extended network of family and friends to ease the adjustment to urban life and to preserve cultural traditions. Northern employers utilized the kinship networks to recruit additional workers, establishing a steady pipeline of labor between particular mountain communities and specific northern cities. The Champion Paper Company in Hamilton, Ohio, for example, recruited heavily from eastern Kentucky and western North Carolina along U.S. 23, and the Cincinnati-Dayton area became a favorite destination for mountain migrants from these areas. By the end of the 1960s, one in three industrial workers in Ohio was from Appalachia.[21] Employees from one section of eastern Kentucky so dominated the labor force in one Ohio factory that a sign on the doorway between departments reportedly read "Leave Morgan County (KY) and enter Wolfe County."[22]

Migrants from Kentucky, Tennessee, and North Carolina tended to settle in Cincinnati, Dayton, Detroit, and Chicago, while migrants from West Virginia and Virginia moved to Akron, Canton, Columbus, Cleveland, and Baltimore. So many migrants poured into Akron, Ohio, that the Rubber City became known as the "capital of West Virginia," and for years the migrants held an annual West Virginia Day celebration that attracted more than thirty thousand former Mountain State residents.[23] Southern Appalachian migrants to Chicago tended to settle in the Uptown district; those in Cincinnati clustered in Little Price Hill. In Detroit, mountain migrants concentrated in an area known as Little Appalachia, where they established their own restaurants, stores, churches, and bars. Migrants to Baltimore settled primarily in Remington and Sparrows Point, near the booming Bethlehem Steel Mill.

As a result of these patterns of relocation, linkages between the mountains and urban migrants remained strong, and frequent weekend visits provided a web of support for both migrants and their families. It was not uncommon on Friday nights in the 1950s to find the highways flowing south from Akron, Dayton, Cincinnati, Detroit, and Chicago filled with Appalachian migrants heading to West Virginia, Kentucky, and Tennessee. Migrants quipped that the only things taught in mountain schools after World War II were the three Rs—reading, writing, and Route 23, or whatever the local highway to the North was. Steady work and higher wages in the cities soon enabled many young families to acquire new furniture, clothing, and better cars, which they proudly displayed for relatives during their weekend trips home. This in turn encouraged others to get on the "hillbilly highway" to the cities.

A variety of factors motivated individuals to leave Appalachia. Most of the migrants were young, between the ages of eighteen and thirty-five, and while the emigration of single individuals continued, the pressure of rising unemployment after 1950 increased the number of families and children in the migration pool. Young couples were especially drawn to the opportunities for better education, better housing, and better health care for their children, but they also hoped to find financial security for themselves. Although the majority of migrants lacked high school diplomas, they were often among the more educated and ambitious youth in their communities. Despite having strong emotional ties to family and place, they saw little opportunity for themselves or their children in the depressed mountain economy. Like their parents before them, who had left the farm for the mines and mills of the first industrial boom, many post–World War II migrants expected to return to the mountains after a short period of work in the cities. Even after a decade or more of successful life in the North, southern Appalachian migrants still referred to Appalachia as home.

Often men were the first family members to leave for the city and the first to want to return home. Mountain men had always enjoyed relative freedom in the workplace, whether in the mines, in the woods, or on the farm, so the more disciplined and regimented environment of the factories and the strange, congested, and fast-paced lifestyle of the cities sometimes caused stress, frustration, and other difficulties with adjustment. Some men compensated for their situation by continuing to participate in traditional mountain male activities such as hunting, fishing, drinking, and gathering to tell stories and jokes, whereas others simply abandoned the city and returned home.

Women, on the other hand, often derived greater rewards from migration and were more reluctant to return to the hard life of the mountains. Unlike Gertie Nevels, the heroine of *The Dollmaker* who longed to return to nature and the land, many mountain women found their lives much easier as a result of the modern household appliances available in the city and the relative proximity of stores, schools, and neighbors. Not only did their children have greater opportunities for education and health care, they themselves had chances for employment unavailable in the mountains. For the first time in their lives, some mountain women found a degree of economic independence and security that was unknown in Appalachia.

Adjustment to life in the city, however, was not easy for many migrants. Living conditions varied from the cramped and decaying apartment buildings of the ghettos to the rows of working-class bungalows in industrial districts. New arrivals often crowded together with relatives until they could secure jobs and save enough money to set up housekeeping. Some inner-city landlords refused to rent to "hillbillies," and those who did charged high rents for poor accommodations. In the Uptown slums of Chicago's north side, for example, as many as seventy thousand Appalachians crowded together in deteriorating brick and gray stone apartment buildings that lined streets cluttered with abandoned cars and littered with trash and broken bottles.[24]

One West Virginia reporter described the "hostile world" that awaited mountain families in the Windy City. "Many migrants arrive in Chicago with only a worn out car," he wrote. Needing cash to pay the rent and buy food, they were forced to take jobs as day laborers for agencies that "keep 40 percent of their pay as a fee," and they had little choice but to seek housing in the most dilapidated buildings. A typical unit was home to a family that had recently moved to Chicago to find work: "Their halls, dirty and smelling of urine, are like dimly lit caves. Rotting wooden steps lead to the fourth floor, one bedroom apartment without window screens where a former Kanawha County woman, her husband and five children live." Such apartments, he added, rented for thirty dollars a week and were surrounded by "buildings with their windows boarded up (what miners called Eisenhower curtains)." Drawn to Chicago by the hope for employment, these families found only "an unfriendly world of disappointment."[25]

Those who were fortunate enough to find steady jobs often relocated to working-class neighborhoods near the factories where homes could be bought on a land contract with little money down. These communities were cleaner and less violent and offered a better environment to raise children. In these working-class neighborhoods, mountain migrants could listen to familiar music in hillbilly bars and attend revivals in evangelical churches that had followed their flocks to the North. Some of the middle-class and more educated migrants established formal social clubs that sponsored dinners, dances, and other activities. Usually named for the state from which the migrants had come, as in the cases of the West Virginia Society and the Eastern Kentucky Social Club, these clubs helped to ease assimilation into urban culture while preserving the memory of home.

Appalachian migrants everywhere met with resistance and prejudice from the local population. Pejorative stereotypes of Appalachia as a backward and degenerate place had become part of the national popular conception of the region since the turn of the century, and these negative images followed mountain migrants to the cities.[26] Urban dwellers were quick to identify the newcomers as "hillbillies," a term that they applied to anyone from the rural South, and they were threatened both by the ever growing numbers of migrants and by their apparent cultural differences. Convinced that Appalachians were ignorant, lazy, unclean, and sometimes immoral, community leaders bemoaned their arrival as "a sore to the city and a plague to themselves" and blamed them for rising crime, congestion, and a host of other urban maladies. "In my opinion they are worse than the colored," complained a Chicago police captain. "They are vicious and knife happy. . . . I can't say this publicly, but you'll never improve the neighborhood until you get rid of them."[27]

Using imagery similar to that applied to other migrant populations, especially African Americans from the Deep South, northerners developed a repertoire of ethnic hillbilly jokes that reflected deep-seated fears and a misunderstanding of mountain culture. Many of the jokes poked fun at the lack of education, sophistication, and resources of mountain migrants; others cruelly implied immorality and ignorance. One popular midwestern story, for example, involved a fundamentalist preacher who had moved to Cincinnati: "Did you know that the old country preacher was arrested? Yes, he was arrested for polluting the Ohio River. . . . He was baptizing hillbillies in the river."[28] Southern Appalachian migrants became known across the Midwest by a number of derogatory labels, including SAMs, hillbillies, snakes, briar hoppers, and ridge runners.

Though black migrants from the South experienced discrimination in part because of race and class, the predominantly white Appalachian migrants suffered discrimination primarily because of cultural differences—or at least what were perceived to be differences—that were rooted in class.[29] Speech patterns, clothing, diet, religious practices, and even the closeness of the Appalachian family seemed to set the migrants apart from other urbanites. Frequent trips back home slowed their assimilation into urban communities and reinforced the image that they were only temporary residents. Indeed, some migrants returned to the mountains as soon as they had earned enough money in the city to keep them going in the rural area for a few months, only to return again when that money was depleted.[30] Such patterns of movement frustrated landlords and employers alike and contributed to an image of the mountain migrants as irresponsible.

The values and cultural assumptions of many migrants conflicted with the modern definitions of success commonly found among the urban middle class. Describing migrants in Cincinnati in 1956, Roscoe Giffin observed, "There is reason to believe that the way of life of southern mountain people is marked by a strong tendency simply to accept one's environment as it is rather than to strive for mastery over it." This, he added, led to "a lack of strong identification with urban goals and standards of achievement."[31] According to commentators such as Giffin, Appalachian migrants tended to keep to themselves, to distrust public officials and government organizations, and to neglect education. They valued family and kinship ties over work and appeared to be less competitive, less anxious for advancement, and less aggressive than their northern neighbors.[32] "They don't consider work to be the fundamental purpose of their lives," observed one reporter. "They are as indifferent to politics as they are to making money."[33]

Nowhere were these cultural conflicts more apparent than in the schools. Opportunities for formal education were limited in the mountains, and there were few incentives for the children of coal miners to complete school. Consequently, some migrant families placed little value on school attendance and performance. In the mountains, children were given greater freedom to roam and play with friends, but in city streets and schools, such activities led to trouble and delinquency. Appalachian children often lagged behind fellow students in academic achievement and were shy and reticent in the classroom. Many urban teachers had difficulty understanding Appalachian dialects and knew little of mountain culture and heritage, except for popular stereotypes. Students were quick to recognize condescension toward themselves, their families, and their culture. Parents had little experience with bureaucracies and were reluctant to become involved in the schools and in community improvement organizations. It is not surprising that dropout rates were higher among Appalachian students than among other urban groups.[34]

Nevertheless, despite economic and cultural barriers, a majority of migrants eventually made successful transitions to urban life. Those same factors that made them different in the new setting—cultural traditions and strong family ties—also provided strength and support to overcome adversity. Migrants who brought higher levels of education or some technical skills to the city were among the first to achieve stable employment and upward mobility. In time, thousands of fellow migrants followed them into the middle-class suburbs, becoming part of a growing, invisible minority of urban Appalachians. A study of West Virginia migrants in Cleveland in the mid-1960s found more former mountain residents living in the suburbs than in the Appalachian ghetto.[35] Certainly the folks back home in the mountains were conscious of this success, since they continued to leave for the cities in growing numbers.

It was the inner-city ghettos, however, that attracted the attention of journalists and drew the concern of local officials and social welfare professionals to the plight of the Appalachian migrants. As early as the 1950s, some urban governments began to organize special study commissions and to hold workshops to address the problems created by the great migration. In 1954, for example, the Mayor's Friendly Relations Committee and the Social Service Association of Greater Cincinnati sponsored a special workshop that focused on migrants in that city. The workshop was attended by over two hundred social workers, teachers, personnel managers, city officials, and church and civic leaders and featured a lecture on the southern Appalachian people by a sociology professor from Berea College.[36]

Near the end of the decade, the Council of the Southern Mountains (CSM), a Berea-based association of educators and social workers, began to hold workshops in cities across the Midwest to help northern professionals "gain a better understanding of the mountain people and their background." With funding from the Ford Foundation, the council established a network of civic leaders from Chicago, Detroit, Cleveland, Akron, Columbus, Dayton, and Cincinnati who traveled to Berea for a three-week training course and a tour of the region. These efforts not only helped to organize programs to improve the "urban adjustment of southern Appalachian migrants" but increasingly drew national attention to the worsening economic crisis in the mountains.[37]

As larger numbers of families joined the exodus from Appalachia, community leaders, educators, and politicians in the region began to struggle with the loss of population and deteriorating economic conditions. The emigration of young adults that began during the war reached its peak in the 1950s, when more than a million people left the region. Rural communities throughout the mountains experienced population decline, but the losses in central Appalachia were especially severe. Eastern Kentucky suffered a loss of a quarter of a million residents in the 1940s, and West Virginia exceeded this number over the next decade with a net loss of more than 400,000 residents. Together the two states lost 1.2 million people between 1940 and 1960. The losses during the 1950s in Appalachian Kentucky accounted for almost 35 percent of the population in eastern Kentucky. The loss rate in West Virginia was more than 25 percent.[38]

The rates of population decline were even more alarming given the traditionally high birth rates in Appalachia and the expanding population in the rest of the country. Birth rates in the mountains had long exceeded the national average. Throughout most of the first half of the twentieth century, natural population increases had helped to balance emigration, but in 1957 birth rates in southern Appalachia began to decline. By 1960 migration out of the region exceeded the natural increase by more than 12 percent, and in Kentucky the figure was almost 50 percent. Nor was the population decline of the 1950s limited to rural areas, as it had been in the 1940s. Appalachian small towns and growth centers such as Huntington, Charleston, Knoxville, and Asheville also lost population during a decade when other metropolitan areas in the United States were growing and the national population increased by almost 20 percent.[39]

The movement of people out of Appalachia was a symptom of the deeper economic and social problems that had settled over the region in the years since the Depression. The mechanization of coal mining displaced thousands of families in the coalfields, but unemployment, poverty, and welfare dependence became a way of life in communities throughout the region. The decline of farming, for example, pushed families off the land across most of Appalachia. Mountain agriculture had languished since the turn of the century, when industrialization altered traditional land use practices and local market patterns. After the war, this decline continued at an even more rapid pace. Between 1950 and 1960, half of the farmers and farm laborers in Appalachia left the land. By the end of the decade, only about 6 percent of the mountain population was employed full time in agriculture.[40]

The loss of the farm population in the 1950s completed the region's transformation to public work that had begun at the turn of the century. The number of full-time farmers was drastically reduced as some people fled the region and others searched for part-time work off the farm. With the coming of consumer society and the emergence of national marketing networks, many of the familiar elements of the old family farm were replaced by symbols of the new age. Orchards and beehives, mules and milk cows gave way to store-bought goods, tractors, trucks, and automobiles. The once prominent livestock industry all but disappeared with the elimination of woodlands for pasturage as a result of mining, logging, and absentee land ownership. Now more dependent on row cropping, most mountain farms were unable to compete with larger, flatland farms for national markets.

In 1954 only one in three Appalachian farms had running water and indoor plumbing, but over half had access to an automobile, and 92 percent had electricity. Because the mountain terrain was less conducive to the operation of tractors and other modern farm machinery, only about a third of the farms had tractors. The primary cash crop in many mountain counties was tobacco, which was labor intensive and could be raised on an acre or two of bottomland, but even this crop was dependent on government quotas to maintain market prices. The average southern Appalachian farm at midcentury contained less than eighty-one acres, with only fifteen acres of productive cropland. In the more rugged areas, from southern West Virginia through western North Carolina, the average was less than fifty-five acres.[41]

In some counties the movement off the land in the 1950s was so profound that it almost eliminated farming altogether. Forty counties in eastern Kentucky and West Virginia lost more than 70 percent of their farm population. Leslie County, Kentucky, lost 98 percent of its farmers and was left with only 20 full-time farms at the end of the decade. Harlan County, Kentucky, with a population of 51,000, had only 112 farmers, a loss of 82 percent. Mingo County, West Virginia, was left with only 32 full-time farmers; McDowell County, West Virginia, with 40; and Logan County, West Virginia, with 66. Even heavily agricultural counties in the Blue Ridge suffered major losses of the farm population. Ashe and Madison counties in North Carolina lost more than 2,000 farms each, and the number of farmers in Swain County was reduced by 80 percent. Carter and Campbell counties in Tennessee each lost about 40 percent of their full-time farms.[42]

Many traditional forms of off-farm employment in Appalachia declined as well during the 1950s, including logging, furniture manufacturing, railroads, and textile production.[43] Although the number of manufacturing establishments increased in northern Alabama and in some metropolitan areas of Georgia and North Carolina, rural Appalachian counties as a whole did not benefit from the expanding national business climate of the Eisenhower years and fell even further behind the nation and the non-Appalachian portions of their states. Eastern Kentucky, for example, failed by a considerable margin to keep pace with manufacturing growth both in Kentucky and in the nation as a whole. Between 1950 and 1955, manufacturing employment increased by almost 20 percent in Kentucky but by only 2 percent in eastern Kentucky. Of the thirty-five counties in the eastern portion of Kentucky, only six employed five hundred persons or more in manufacturing, and more than half of all the manufacturing jobs in the region were located in the industrialized Ashland area.[44] The number of manufacturing establishments in West Virginia increased by only 8 percent in the 1950s, and in southwest Virginia (including the valley counties) by only 15 percent.[45]

As a result of the limited growth of manufacturing in the region and declining employment opportunities in the mines and mills, unemployment increased dramatically throughout Appalachia. Official unemployment rates for the region hovered at almost twice the national average, and in the coalfields rates of three and four times that of the rest of the nation were common. Eastern Kentucky averaged close to 20 percent unemployment throughout the decade, and this did not include the thousands of individuals who had used up their unemployment benefits and simply dropped out of the labor force. Many more worked part time or in jobs not covered by unemployment compensation.

Those who could find jobs often earned low wages and poor benefits. Annual per capita income in Appalachia averaged only $1,400 in 1960, more than a third lower than the national average, and many rural counties averaged less than $1,000. In Appalachian Kentucky the average annual per capita income was only $841. One in three families in Appalachia lived below the national poverty level of $3,000, in comparison with one in five families nationally. Almost 60 percent of families in Appalachian Kentucky, 42 percent of those in Appalachian Virginia, 40 percent of those in Appalachian North Carolina, and 39 percent of those in Appalachian Tennessee fell below the poverty level.[46]

Low per capita income reflected a labor force that was largely uneducated. Despite decades of industrial development, schools in Appalachia were among the poorest in the nation. Only one in three Appalachians in 1960 over the age of twenty-five had finished high school, and almost 47 percent had less than an eighth-grade education. Only 17 percent in Kentucky had completed high school, 23 percent in Virginia, and 29 percent in North Carolina.[47] Thousands of mountain children, especially in rural districts, were educated in graying, one- or two-room schoolhouses. Many lacked running water, central heat, and indoor toilets. School districts were often the largest employers in rural counties, and the schools became the political fiefdoms of local power brokers. Jobs as teachers, secretaries, and maintenance workers were doled out according to patronage rather than individual qualifications. Teachers were often uncertified, facilities allowed to deteriorate, and books and instructional materials scarce. Per pupil expenditures for education in Appalachia were about half those in the rest of the country.[48] Levies on local property provided the bulk of financial support for the schools, but per capita assessments on property in the mountains averaged 38 percent less than comparable national assessments.[49]

Joblessness, low income, and poor education were reflected in depressed living standards throughout the region. At a time when suburban middle-class families were enjoying new homes with washing machines, televisions, showers, telephones, and other modern conveniences, many Appalachian families survived in aging houses with few amenities in rural areas or deteriorating company towns. At least 26 percent of Appalachian homes surveyed in the 1960 census needed "major repairs," and 7.5 percent were "in such a dilapidated condition that they endangered the health and safety of the families," more than one and a half times the national average. The best housing conditions were to be found in the metropolitan areas of the region, and the worst in the rural areas and neglected coal camps. Here almost one out of four homes had basic deficiencies in construction and plumbing, and one out of ten was found to be dilapidated. Almost 60 percent of the housing units in eastern Kentucky lacked indoor plumbing, 57 percent in Appalachian Virginia, and nearly 50 percent in western North Carolina. The median value of such housing was 27.7 percent below the national average.[50]

At the turn of the century, mountain families had traded the simple but relatively independent life of the family farm for dependence on a wage income in mines, mill villages, and other forms of public work. When those jobs disappeared, that dependence shifted to the state and federal governments as public welfare programs stepped in to prevent starvation and destitution. Federal relief programs of one kind or another supported almost half of the mountain population in the 1930s, but the deepening economic crisis of the 1950s further expanded welfare rolls and altered the fundamental character of dependence. During the Depression, public relief was viewed as a temporary measure that provided support until jobs opened again in the private sector. Except for Social Security, which extended benefits to the aged and disabled, the majority of New Deal relief strategies were work-related programs designed to provide assistance in return for labor on public projects. Most of these programs disappeared during the war, as war mobilization and an expanding national economy created new jobs.

By the 1950s, however, after three decades of declining job opportunities, many Appalachian families lost hope of ever finding work in their own communities, and an increasing number reluctantly turned to public assistance for survival. State governments attempted to respond to rising joblessness in their mountain counties by broadening qualifications for state-administered programs for the poor. Thousands of desperate families applied for disability benefits and Aid to Families with Dependent Children. In the coalfields retired union miners and their widows welcomed small pensions from the UMWA Health and Retirement Funds, while nonunion and middle-aged miners, unable to find employment anywhere, submitted disability claims for old injuries or new illnesses. On the first of each month, county seats and rural commodity distribution centers bustled with long lines of haggard men waiting to receive surplus food. A family of two adults and one or more children with a monthly income of $130 or less could receive twenty pounds of flour, ten pounds of cornmeal, nine pounds of rice, four pounds of butter, and ten pounds of cheese on which to sustain themselves.[51]

The new welfare system became a way of life for some mountain residents, who felt powerless to change their situation. A few justified their dependence by arguing that they had earned the benefits during earlier working years and were now entitled to the grants. Others were ashamed to be on the dole but believed that they had no other choice. Although government programs and handouts never reached most of the region's poor, the rush to claim public assistance gave rise to the image of the "welfare malingerer" who searched for ways to falsify symptoms of illness to qualify for assistance. But most welfare recipients were desperate, and they saw the government grants as just another way to survive. "Nothing in the history of the mountain people," wrote eastern Kentucky lawyer and historian Harry Caudill, "had conditioned them to receive such grants with gratitude or to use them with restraint. In a land in which huge corporations and their friends on judicial bench and in legislative hall had reduced the ordinary citizen to a status little better than that of a mere tenant-by-sufferance in his own home, the mountaineer had nurtured a cynicism toward government at all levels. The handouts were speedily recognized as a lode from which dollars could be mined more easily than from any coal seam."[52]

It was perhaps inevitable that such a system would feed the already corrupt and feudal political structure in the mountains. Poor people easily fell victim to local politicians who controlled the distribution of commodities and monthly welfare checks. Mountain politics had always been paternalistic and family oriented, and when the big coal and timber corporations injected greater economic self-interest into the system, the old ways simply blended with the new political order. Years of life in company towns left many mountain residents dependent on the companies for their income and housing and thus subservient to company interests at the polls. As the outside corporations abandoned direct involvement in local politics and lost interest in the company towns, power in these feudal counties reverted to local families and to the political machines that sustained them. New Deal work programs were a boon to the local elite, who used federal relief programs to ensure their control over county politics. Depression-era politicians throughout the region held out the promise of a public job in return for the votes of the applicant and his or her kin.

The expansion of welfare programs in the 1950s revived this powerful patronage system and helped to broaden the power of the political machines. Artful use of public funds could control not only who received food and income for their families but which truck mine operator received a new road up the hollow to his mine and who was employed as a schoolteacher, bus driver, cook, or janitor in the local school. With such economic power, the politicians increased their influence over local merchants, automobile dealers, contractors, and other small-business owners, creating a network of political and economic interests where a few individuals controlled the meager resources available to the entire community. In rural counties where a single family gained control of the county school board and the county government, domination was virtually complete.

The mountain political structure fed on the poverty and dependent relationships that had emerged in the region and choked efforts at long-range planning and community development. Civic participation was low and usually limited to the voting process itself. Especially in the coalfields, mountain residents had little experience in public decision making or in managing public affairs. When the large corporations withdrew from direct involvement in local matters—except to maintain low taxes on their land and mineral resources—local leaders had little incentive to change existing economic and political relationships. As long as their decisions did not threaten the interests of the external landlords, and in the absence of any opposition, the local machines were able to use public funds and programs to perpetuate their power.

Everywhere in the region, the intertwining of economic self-interest and political influence worked to maintain the status quo. This relationship was perhaps best revealed in the connections among mountain professionals, especially physicians, bankers, land developers, and lawyers. Mountain physicians, for example, had long held influential positions in local politics and often were among the principal investors in local land development efforts. As pressures mounted to certify more and more unemployed men for disability benefits, some physicians were not averse to manipulating public assistance for their own political ends. The combination of a good word from the county judge executive and a certification of disability from the local doctor was almost certain to convince the Department of Social Welfare to approve a monthly check and to obligate the claimant to the local political machine as well. In a similar way, bankers benefited from their control over local credit and sometimes used their influence over home mortgages, automobile loans, and small-business loans to influence local politics. Not only did bankers manage the assets that passed through the county from the development of area resources, but they were a primary source of capital for new business development, including new mining and logging enterprises.

Often at the center of this feudal political system were the land developers, the real estate brokers, and the local lawyers who served as agents for absentee developers and who managed litigation, land and mineral titles, and other legal matters. Indigenous land developers had served as midwives to the industrialization of the region at the turn of the century by promoting and selling local timber and mineral resources to outside developers, and after World War II they reasserted their influence over the local economy. Purchasing tax-delinquent properties and buying blocks of coal camp housing from coal companies for resale to individual buyers, these mountain elite were intimately involved with county-wide political decisions, especially those affecting roads, public utilities, and taxation. Many of the most powerful land brokers were also engaged in banking and politics, and in the coalfields, they were often the force behind the expansion of new truck mines and small surface mining operations after 1950. Native coal operators controlled the political process in most coalfield counties. In Harlan County, Kentucky, for example, the secretary of the coal operators' association was the chair of the county Republican committee, while the president of the association was the head of the county Democratic committee.[53] These local entrepreneurs accumulated small fortunes in counties where the majority of their neighbors lived below the poverty level, and they were not opposed to using the political system to maintain their good fortune.[54]

This political and economic system formed the backdrop for the emergence of a new form of mining enterprise in the 1950s that would leave a deep and permanent mark on the politics and landscape of the region. Surface mining, or "strip" mining, as it was pejoratively called, was not feasible on a large scale in Appalachia before the war, but the development of diesel-powered earth-moving equipment, giant screwlike augers, and more powerful explosives made it possible to extract great quantities of coal from outside the mountain rather than penetrating the seam using traditional, deep mining methods. A local entrepreneur, backed by a loan from a supportive banker, could open a seam of coal with minimal investment and only a fraction of the labor costs of a deep mine. After paying the cost of trucking the coal to a nearby tipple, the strip operator could sell his product more cheaply than that produced by underground mining and, within a year or two, could pocket millions of dollars in profit.

During the 1950s, hundreds of small coal operators and a few larger companies cut into the outcroppings of mountainside coal seams utilizing the new technology. In flat country, surface mining simply involved making a series of parallel cuts into the earth to uncover the coal and dumping the surface dirt and rock back into the previous cut as the process moved along. In the mountains, however, surface miners were forced to follow the contour of the coal seam as it wound around the mountainside. Contour mining removed the soil and rock from above the seam, gauging a shelf around the hillside to get at the coal below. This process not only left a forty- to ninety-foot "highwall" exposed on the inside of the cut but pushed most of the dirt, rock, and tree stumps from above the coal over the hillsides along the outer edges of the seam. This "overburden" created a loose, unstable mass that oozed down the hillside and sometimes broke loose, roaring through the hollow with the first heavy rains and destroying everything in its path. The coal left in the seam underneath the highwall could be further exploited by using giant augers to drill horizontally into the hillside at regular intervals, leaving the mountain ringed by a series of ledges and holes. A seam that was located near the top of the ridge could be reached by removing the crest of the mountain, decapitating it and creating a huge mesa of barren, flat land.

Surface mining not only added to the competition in an already overexpanded industry, further stimulating mechanization and unemployment in the deep mines, but it left the mountains disfigured and the environment altered in ways previously unimagined in the region. The practice of contour mining cut into the hillsides ugly scars that ran for miles along the ridges. Mountaintop removal leveled thousands of acres, filling in the hollows between the hills and creating vast, inaccessible stretches of barren land. In a region once known for the purity of its water, surface mining altered water tables, polluted nearby creeks and streams, and contaminated local wells. When it rained, sulfur in the exposed coal produced sulfuric acid that filtered into the creeks, killing the fish and most plant life. "Gob piles" of mine waste clung to the hillsides, and huge rocks and tree stumps loosed by the mining process were sometimes sent flying down the hillside, destroying fields and gardens below and occasionally crashing through residences and barns.

Mining companies were required by law to replace the soil and to replant the ravaged hillsides, but small operators seldom took the time and expense to reclaim the land. Even where meager efforts at reclamation were undertaken, the absence of topsoil and the composition of the fill itself meant that little vegetation grew on the disturbed site. Given the need for jobs and the political power of the coal industry, state governments were slow to enforce existing regulations. As a result, the heavy mountain rains washed acres of rocks and topsoil into the streams each year, choking and silting over rivers and flooding the farms and communities below. One study by the U.S. Geological Survey found that in strip-mined areas, the rains washed away 27,000 tons of earth per square mile each year, in contrast to 1,900 tons in areas where strip mining had not occurred.[55]

The social cost of the new industry was as appalling as the cost to the land itself. In much of Appalachia, mineral rights had been severed from surface rights by the actions of mineral buyers at the turn of the century. For as little as twenty-five cents per acre, hundreds of thousands of acres of coal were sold to absentee land companies, whose intricate deeds granted them use of the timber on the surface for mining purposes and access to the coal at some future date. The ownership and use of the surface land remained with the mountain farm family. These "broad form" deeds, as they were known in eastern Kentucky, effectively transferred to the land company all of the mineral wealth and the right to remove it by whatever means necessary, leaving the original owners and their descendants the semblance of landownership and the responsibility for paying the taxes.[56]

With the advent of surface mining in the 1950s, however, these old deeds took on new meaning as the mining companies sought access to their mineral property without regard to the rights of the surface owners. Roads were cut across pastures, forests devastated, fields ruined, and water supplies polluted to get at the coal, and the state courts upheld the right of the miners to remove the coal "by any means convenient or necessary."[57] Increasingly, farm families found that they had little control over their own land and that their meager hopes for subsistence on it were destroyed. Many believed that they had no recourse but to abandon the farmstead to the mining company and to join the growing numbers of landless migrants and unemployed workers that roamed the region or left the mountains entirely.

Ironically, the human and environmental destruction levied on Appalachia by surface mining was fed by a public agency created during the Depression to conserve the land and to promote economic recovery. The energy development policies of the TVA in the 1950s spurred demand for cheaper coal at a time when surface-mined coal was just beginning to enter the market. The TVA was established in 1933 to coordinate flood control, reforestation, and economic development along the Tennessee River and its tributaries, but by World War II the agency had moved away from many of its initial efforts at human development, conservation, and regional planning in favor of a policy that concentrated on the generation of cheap electric power for domestic use and industrial expansion. Anticipating future power demands in growing urban centers along the river and pressed by the cold war concerns of the Atomic Energy Commission for more power to fuel the uranium enrichment plants at Oak Ridge and Paducah, the TVA constructed seven of the world's largest coal-fired power plants between 1949 and 1953 and created a huge market for cheap, locally produced coal.

The generation of electricity from coal rather than from hydroelectric facilities on TVA dams reflected the public utility's commitment to cheap power as the centerpiece of its survival strategy in the conservative political environment of the 1950s. Armed with the development of new technologies that allowed for the efficient burning of low-grade coal, the TVA turned to lower-quality, surface-mined coal to fire its new generators. Although dirtier and often higher in sulfur content, surface-mined coal from Appalachia and western Kentucky could be delivered to the TVA furnaces at a fraction of the cost of deep-mined coal, and agency buyers quickly signed long-term contracts with the small, nonunion, and independent coal firms that had begun to strip the hills. The TVA's cheap-power policy inspired other power companies to modernize their furnaces and to shift to the burning of low-cost coal rather than other fuels. This trend not only increased the amount of sulfur dioxide in the atmosphere, adding to future environmental problems from acid rain, but effectively revolutionized the steam coal market and further spurred the production of surface-mined coal throughout central Appalachia. By the end of the decade, the TVA itself had purchased the mining rights to almost 100,000 acres of coal in eastern Kentucky and east Tennessee, and power plants and other consumers across the Midwest had turned to burning cheap, surface-mined fuel.[58] Thus the agency that had been created to conserve the soil and improve quality of life through cooperative regional planning contributed both directly and indirectly to the further desolation of the mountains.

Evidence of the tragic consequences of the TVA's cheap-power policy came in 1957, when disastrous floods swept the central Appalachian coalfields. Following a week of almost steady rain, streams in southern West Virginia, eastern Kentucky, and southwest Virginia roared out of their banks on January 29–30, 1957, inundating houses, stores, churches, and schools and killing fourteen people. As much as three inches of rain fell on the area in a twenty-four-hour period. Damage was estimated in the millions of dollars, and President Eisenhower declared the region a federal disaster area. The town of Pound, Virginia, was overwhelmed by twenty feet of water, and in the cities of Pikeville and Hazard, Kentucky, water reached the ceilings of Main Street stores. Rescue boats sailed over the tops of city streetlights. Rural roads were washed away, and deposits of sediment and piles of rocks and splintered trees ruined bottomland fields.[59]

The mountains had witnessed winter and spring "tides" before, but never with the destruction and loss of life of the 1957 floods. Strip mining and logging had ravaged much of the countryside in the most severely devastated counties, and now there was little vegetation on the hillsides to absorb the water from heavy rains. Surface mining, for example, had shredded tens of thousands of acres of land in Buchanan County, Virginia. "A bird's-eye view of it," wrote Harry Caudill, "reveals marooned and isolated farmhouses perched disconsolately on high pillars of dirt and stone. Towering high walls make access to them impossible. Much of the county's total land surface has been stripped of vegetation and reduced to jumbles of stone and gullying spoil-banks."[60] Similar conditions existed in neighboring Wise County, Virginia, and Harlan, Letcher, Perry, and Pike counties in Kentucky. A subsequent assessment of the floods by the U.S. Forest Service blamed "poor logging practices" and the "effect of strip-mining" for the increased erosion and sedimentation that had caused the streams to clog and to "have less capacity to carry runoff." The effects of strip mining "were clearly evident during and after the storm," and in the future, the report warned, "the conditions of the area will continue to get worse."[61]

The winter floods of 1957 brought a growing clamor for solutions to the human and environmental tragedies in Appalachia. Journalists, educators, and state and local politicians had called for action to alleviate the economic plight of the region for years, but there was little consensus on the causes of Appalachia's poverty or on the resolution of its complex problems. For some, the region's "backwardness" was a result of geographic isolation and insufficient development of modern patterns of transportation and industry. For others, the problem lay in the culture of the mountain people themselves, a culture, they argued, that preserved anachronistic values and prevented people from lifting themselves out of poverty. One view looked to the development of the region's physical infrastructure, its highways, water systems, and industrial parks. The other sought to uplift mountain residents through education and job training. Both perspectives favored the further integration of Appalachia into the economy and society of the rest of the nation. Both tended to define Appalachia's problems as a lack of resources for development, either physical or cultural, rather than as the result of structural inequalities and the politics of development itself.

To resolve Appalachia's distress, many educators and human service professionals, like those associated with the regional CSM, favored a broad program of educational enrichment and job training to help attract industries to rural communities and to enhance the success of Appalachian migrants in the cities. Modernizing Appalachian culture had been a goal of missionaries and educators in the region for decades, and the annual conference of the CSM provided a venue for leaders from across Appalachia to discuss the need for better schools, health services, improved recreation, and economic growth. At the heart of the council's "program for the mountains" was the idea of "cooperative community development," a strategy that had underpinned much of the benevolent work of private foundations, settlement schools, and some other educational institutions in Appalachia since the turn of the century. Combining elements of the progressive faith in science, education, efficient planning, and public-private partnerships, this philosophy challenged regional leaders to develop the human capacity of the mountains and to work together to find collaborative solutions to community problems.

Under the leadership of Perley F. Ayer, a rural sociologist from New Hampshire who assumed the role of executive director in 1951, the CSM became the largest organization of human service professionals within Appalachia and the leading proponent of human and community development strategies for regional improvement. During the 1950s, the council held workshops for teachers and urban social workers, sponsored tours of the region, and, after the 1957 floods, pressed state leadership across the region to undertake assessment and strategic planning initiatives for their mountain counties. Throughout its work, the council emphasized the importance of education, the capacity of the individual to overcome cultural and social barriers, the value of volunteerism in the community, and the role of schools as community-building institutions.[62]

Whereas members of the CSM focused their efforts on regional cooperation and on improving education, state and local leaders usually advocated economic growth through the expansion of industry and the identification of new uses and new markets for coal, timber, and other natural resources. Many business leaders and local politicians believed that the mountains had been victimized by the underdevelopment of resources that could generate more wealth. As a result of geography and inadequate infrastructure, they reasoned, Appalachia lacked the physical structures to provide employment, raise living standards, and sustain growth in a modern economy. The construction of roads and industrial water systems and the preparation of manufacturing sites that might provide jobs were expensive in mountainous terrain, and, historically, low-country legislators had been reluctant to spend state revenues on internal improvement projects in the Appalachian portions of their states.

Business leaders in the coalfields, for example, complained that economic conditions in the mountains were primarily a consequence of the ill health of the coal industry. The high cost of production—including labor, as a result of UMWA contracts—unfavorable freight rates, and the inroads of competing fuels had forced massive layoffs, they argued, and had contributed to the general economic despair. They noted that postwar foreign policy decisions had increased the flow of foreign oil into the United States, and "waste oil" had taken a large part of the energy market, further adding to the industry's woes. Given the "almost unlimited reserves" of top-grade coal that still lay within the region, coal country leaders called for government investment in the infrastructure of the mountains: dredging the major rivers, constructing dams to regulate water flow, and building modern highways to transport coal more cheaply to market. The new facilities and highways, some reasoned, might also attract tourists to the region.[63]

For a few observers, however, the opportunities and resources available in Appalachia were simply insufficient to support a large population under any circumstances. Some economists and a few regional leaders favored a policy that encouraged migration out of the mountains and advocated government programs that disseminated job information to the unemployed and provided for the relocation of rural workers. Writing in 1958, economists B. H. Luebke and John Fraser Hart suggested that rural areas of Appalachia needed to "adjust the local economy to that of the nation" by encouraging the migration of individuals and communities to fill the labor needs of other areas of the country. "Economic betterment for the great majority of the people of the Southern Appalachians is not to be found in development of the meager resources of the local area," they wrote, "but in migration to other areas more richly endowed by nature and by man." The export of surplus labor to the mill villages of the Carolinas and the automobile plants of the North would benefit not only Appalachia but the nation as a whole, which would "profit from more efficient allocation and utilization of its manpower."[64]

The depopulation of the mountains had been advocated as early as the turn of the century as a means to "remake" the Appalachians by replacing the region's subsistence economy with a more "natural" system of timber culture. National leaders had defended the condemnation of mountain land for national forests after 1911, for national parks in the 1920s, and for TVA dams in the Great Depression as progressive steps that would help to eliminate the region's economic distress by forcing mountaineers to migrate to the cities and mill villages of the New South. Through relocation they would enjoy the advantages of social intercourse, school, and livelihood that village life afforded.[65] Government-sponsored relocation, however, was as unappealing to most mountain residents in the 1950s as it had been in earlier decades. Such strategies assumed the superiority of urban living, ignored generations of family attachments to land and place, and abnegated the argument that free markets would bring the benefits of modernization to rural areas as well as to urban communities.

In the cold war environment of the 1950s, the failure of the free market in places like Appalachia was an embarrassment to the nation, and regional advocates increasingly looked for national solutions to Appalachia's problems. The new generation of state leaders who had come of age during the Depression and World War II was confident of government's ability to alleviate want and to mobilize for action. More and more, they called for the application of science, technology, and the organizational skills of government to rehabilitate the mountains.

"There is nothing wrong with hillbillies . . . that a strong dose of equal opportunity wouldn't cure," wrote Charleston, West Virginia, journalist Harry Ernst and Berea College professor Charles Drake to the *Nation* in the spring of 1959. "What the Appalachian South desperately needs is a domestic Point Four program combining federal, state and local resources. Only with federal help—similar to the economic aid Uncle Sam sends to underdeveloped nations abroad—can the region receive its share of the national wealth."[66]

Harry Caudill was among those who recommended the creation of a modernized version of the TVA—a southern mountain authority—that would plan for the region's future and provide electric power for the rest of the country. Through "enlightened government intervention under the auspices of careful planners," Caudill declared, the hideous waste of the land and the cycle of poverty in Appalachia could be halted. He had little confidence in the ability of state and local political machines to produce significant changes on their own, since they were themselves allied with the interests that produced the problems. But an independent federal agency endowed with sufficient power and resources could set thousands of unemployed mountaineers to work reforesting the hills, building new consolidated schools, improving highways, and providing decent housing. If the United States could afford to subsidize autocratic but anti-Communist governments abroad, he asked, "Can we fail to spare the funds and efforts required to convert an island of destitution within our own country into a working, self-sustaining partner in the nation's freedom and progress?"[67]

The idea of a permanent organization to serve Appalachian development was not new. As early as 1951, George Mitchell of the CSM proposed the creation of an organization that would unite the mountain counties of eight southern states and represent their common interests in Congress.[68] Mitchell hoped that a representative body of mountain state legislators, members of Congress, or organization heads might be brought together in an annual meeting to coordinate a long-range plan for the region, but the national political environment in the 1950s was not ready for a regional development program. Liberal Democrats in Congress passed two "depressed areas" bills during the decade to provide redevelopment grants to counties hard hit by industrial unemployment, but these were both vetoed by President Eisenhower, who believed that economic development was best left to local governments and to the free market system.

When congressional efforts failed to provide funds for the recovery of depressed areas, regional leaders turned to the governors of the Appalachian states to act "individually and in concert" to develop solutions to the region's problems. In a resolution passed on February 7, 1959, the CSM petitioned the states of West Virginia, Tennessee, Kentucky, Virginia, North Carolina, Georgia, South Carolina, and Alabama to establish "an officially responsible interstate commission composed of citizen representatives" that would study the region as a whole and recommend common strategies to state planning and development boards.[69] With the help of the council and a $250,000 grant from the Ford Foundation, Berea College launched a comprehensive survey of life and culture in the southern Appalachian region. Under the leadership of Berea College assistant to the president Willis Weatherford Sr. and University of Kentucky sociologist Thomas Ford, the survey would provide a scholarly base of information on which regional policy makers, church leaders, and others concerned with regional development might draw.[70]

Indeed, at the end of the decade, state and local planning initiatives were already underway in many southern Appalachian states. Beginning in the mid-1950s, state economic development boards increased their programs to recruit industries to mountain counties, and as the problems of flooding, poverty, and unemployment rose, these state efforts took on additional urgency. Several states, including Maryland, Georgia, and North Carolina, launched new initiatives to coordinate area-wide zoning and planning, but perhaps the most extensive effort to focus specifically on the problems of the mountain districts was undertaken in Kentucky. No other part of Appalachia more consistently epitomized the history and tragedies of the region than eastern Kentucky, and none was so devastated by economic stagnation, out-migration, and environmental depredation in the postwar years. The patterns of development and the political struggles to control the direction of development in Appalachian Kentucky were mirrored in other states, but Kentucky provides the most aggressive

example of state-initiated development efforts. Events in the commonwealth helped to set the stage for the emergence of a nationally coordinated program for all of Appalachia in the 1960s.

Public response in the commonwealth to rising poverty levels in eastern Kentucky came from two arenas: state government and a loose
network of leaders from industry, higher education, civic organizations, and the CSM. As early as 1953, Governor Lawrence Wetherby
attempted to draw the TVA's attention to the "economic wreckage" of
eastern Kentucky, and his successor, A. B. "Happy" Chandler, campaigned on a promise to revive the region's economy by finding new
uses and new markets for coal, eliminating transportation barriers to
Kentucky coal, diversifying sources of employment in forestry and
tourism, and improving the road system.[71] In 1956 the Kentucky Agricultural and Industrial Development Board contracted with an Illinois
research firm to assess the condition of Kentucky's coal, timber, and
other resources and to recommend new possibilities for industrial
growth. After the disastrous floods in the winter of 1956–1957, the
state commissioned a Rhode Island firm to conduct the Eastern Kentucky Flood Rehabilitation Study to analyze the immediate problems
caused by the floods and to identify the long-term barriers to economic development. In the summer of 1957, the Kentucky Department
of Economic Development combined the recommendations of these
studies into a report identifying possible action programs for eastern
Kentucky.[72]

While the state was undertaking its analyses of the problems,
independent efforts were also underway to mobilize private sector
leadership. Berea College's Willis Weatherford convened an interde-
nominational meeting of church workers in 1956 to discuss collective
action to alleviate Appalachia's distress, and in the same year the Kentucky Junior Chamber of Commerce, or Jaycees, launched an initiative
designed to involve eastern Kentucky civic clubs in local community
development work. Jaycee president John D. Whisman hoped to revive
languishing chapters in the mountains while helping to improve economic and social conditions in his native region. After conducting an
inventory of community problems, each Jaycee chapter would undertake specific projects to address local needs. Whisman believed that

the severity of the problems demanded area cooperation in planning programs that would be implemented at the community level, and he called a joint meeting of Jaycee officers and regional leaders from business, government, and industry to advise local chapters on possible projects. In September 1956 this group formed the Eastern Kentucky Regional Development Council. Made up of representatives from the Jaycees, other civic organizations, business and industry, state development organizations, and state government agencies, the development council was designed to act as an advisory board to civic organizations in the region and to formulate a program of long-range development objectives.[73]

The efforts of state government officials and private leaders came together the following summer when the Kentucky Department of Economic Development released its Action Plan for Eastern Kentucky. One of the recommendations of the plan called for the creation of a permanent citizens' regional development commission, with objectives similar to those of the development council but with official status as an agency of state government. This commission was to advise state and local policy makers on comprehensive strategies for floodplain protection, the improvement of emergency relief services, and planning for transportation and infrastructure improvements. Following the 1957 floods, acting governor Harry Lee Waterfield, perhaps desiring to ingratiate himself with eastern Kentucky voters for the next election, appointed the nine-member Eastern Kentucky Regional Planning Commission and promised state support for staffing and program development.

The new commission was chaired by B. F. Reed, an eastern Kentucky coal operator, and included four representatives from the coal, oil, and gas industries, as well as a real estate developer, a newspaper editor, a physician, and one representative each from higher education and religion. All of the members of the commission had been active in Whisman's development council.[74] Although the new body included the two-hundred-member citizens' advisory committee, the commission itself was dominated by business and industry interests, especially those connected to coal and land development. Its initial agenda was to assist communities with applications for federal disaster relief, but the commissioners were also expected to recommend legislation to establish new county-wide and area planning authorities and to develop a long-term strategy for diversifying the mountain economy. After a slow start, the commission hired Whisman as its executive director in the spring of 1958. Whisman brought new energy to the commission and increasingly shifted its work from the immediate crises of flood relief and rising unemployment to long-term planning for "strategic area development."

Whisman and the Eastern Kentucky Regional Planning Commission represented a growing confidence in the ability of state government to foster economic development by encouraging public and private sector cooperation and planning. Drawing on his experiences during World War II and his successful efforts to organize a community development program for the Jaycees, Whisman envisioned a comprehensive, two-front campaign in eastern Kentucky that would integrate improvements in physical infrastructure (roads, water systems, and industrial sites) and progress in building human capacity (education, job training, and housing) into a strategy for "total development." By mobilizing all levels of government and increasing civic participation among community leaders, he believed, the new commission could create a planning process that would bring together the resources and energy necessary to overcome Appalachia's deficiencies. Whisman defined the plight of eastern Kentucky and the rest of Appalachia as that of an "underdeveloped region" where "unrealized potential [was] yet to be developed." Unlike other areas of the country that were temporarily depressed because of unemployment and current market trends, an underdeveloped region, he argued, was "a region in which economic facilities, such as roads and transportation systems, utilities, water control systems, schools, markets or industrial operations have not been sufficiently developed to serve its population or to allow its people to provide themselves with gainful employment or adequate standards of living." In Whisman's mind, Appalachia's problems were primarily resource deficiencies, both physical and human, that had resulted from isolation, and he called on regional leaders to collaborate and identify strategies that would build the facilities necessary to generate development.[75]

Given these assumptions, it is not surprising that improvements in roads and other physical infrastructure quickly became the priority for the commission. Whisman launched a series of town meetings with local officials to establish an agenda for action, and roads emerged as an overwhelming priority, followed by industrial sites and flood protection.[76] In September 1959 the commission issued a comprehensive plan for eastern Kentucky that it hoped would influence the candidates for governor in the campaign then underway and set developmental objectives for the next decade. Program 60, as the plan was called, outlined an integrated strategy of improvements in planning and zoning, education, housing, transportation, job training, health services, flood control, and economic diversification. The plan recommended "a range of action projects in various fields, suggesting something to do for federal, state and local government, organizations, firms and private citizens," but the heart of the proposal was the construction of a system of regional highways and water facilities that would provide a basic foundation for development.[77]

Whisman and the commission believed that highway construction would not only address long neglected regional transportation needs and provide immediate jobs but also strengthen public morale and increase public participation in other projects at the local level. If people believed that their community activities were related to larger accomplishments, he reasoned, they would maintain their enthusiasm for cooperation and local involvement. Thus highway projects would provide both the essential framework for economic development and a visible symbol of regional progress that would sustain enthusiasm for long-term planning. Mountain communities had always vied with each other for limited state highway construction funds, but Program 60 proposed a regional system of improved arterial roads connected to new limited-access highways that would provide outlets for mountain products and incentives for industrial expansion, tourism, and other development. In contrast to the traditional competition for local roads, a comprehensive "development highway system"—a network of roads designed specifically to foster development—would break down the region's isolation, increase cooperation, and open up the entire economy to expansion and growth. In addition to the construction of a developmental highway system and other forms of physical infrastructure, Program 60 called for changes in public policy and a new system of development organizations that would encourage cooperation in local, state, and federal programs for the region. Recognizing that eastern Kentucky's problems could be treated only within a comprehensive, long-term Appalachian regional development program, the commission joined the CSM in calling for the creation of an Appalachian state development authority that would work closely with a proposed new federal agency for regional development. At the local level, the report encouraged the establishment of multicounty area development councils that would bring together community leaders to cooperate in planning and project implementation.[78]

Unfortunately, the Eastern Kentucky Regional Planning Commission's ambitious proposals, like those in other states, quickly ran into a quagmire of bureaucratic and funding barriers. At first planners for the Kentucky Department of Highways, for example, were reluctant to endorse the idea of an Appalachian development highway system capable of carrying industrial and commercial traffic because state funds were inadequate to build the roads at the high standards set by federal and state engineering guidelines. As early as 1958, the Kentucky commissioner of highways informed the eastern Kentucky commission that significant federal funding would be needed to finance such a system, and when the highway department finally approved the recommendations and sent the mountain highways plan to the federal Bureau of Public Roads, the Washington agency rejected the plan as failing to comply with its standards.[79]

The challenge of acquiring federal funds for building a new network of mountain roads was complicated by both procedure and politics. Not only were roads in Appalachia more expensive to build, but the federal highway funding plan was unchangeable for the next three years. The federal interstate highway system that connected major urban centers all but bypassed distressed rural areas such as Appalachia, and the method of allocating funding for highway locations based on traffic count assured that Appalachia would have little likelihood of success, since the poor mountain roads thwarted high traffic volume. Increasingly Whisman and other mountain leaders recognized that if their plans for highway development were to be accomplished, they would have to find ways to circumvent federal criteria and come up with special federal aid not currently allocated to the Bureau of Public Roads.

The eastern Kentucky commission experienced similar frustration in attempting to implement its strategies in other areas. The commission found that existing federal programs in flood relief, small-business development, housing, and urban renewal were underutilized in Appalachia because local communities were unaware of the programs or lacked the technical assistance necessary to apply for them. Even when applications were forwarded to Washington and when federal officials and members of Congress sympathized with local needs, mountain communities often failed to meet the legal criteria for federal assistance. Most Appalachian counties, for example, were ineligible for assistance from federal housing and urban renewal programs because the programs were designed for urban areas. Other mountain communities were ineligible for federal aid to build water and sewer projects because they could not raise the necessary matching funds or could not meet the cost-benefit ratio for the construction of dams, flood walls, and highways.[80]

Whisman described the challenges facing Appalachian development efforts as a "revolving impossibility." The greatest need in the region, he noted, was for basic facilities for development, but the lack of development prevented access to the federal resources needed to build these facilities. The dilemma, he wrote, was like a mountain roundelay: "What east Kentucky needs is one good road to join us up with the rest of the country. . . . How do we justify the building of such a road? We know there is not enough traffic count now to justify the new road. But the roads we have are so poor the people won't drive them. Without people coming into our region, we have little commerce. Without commerce, we have no traffic on the road. Without traffic, we can't justify the new road. But the roads we have are poor."[81]

Increasingly frustrated by inadequate funding and bureaucratic barriers, Appalachian state leaders were convinced that special federal assistance was necessary to accomplish their goals for the region. Appalachia's problems, they argued, were severe and unique, and they were beyond the capacity of local communities and state governments alone. Even the federal policies being proposed by national Democrats to aid industrial communities distressed by unemployment promised little assistance to rural areas like Appalachia. The Area Redevelopment Act, which reappeared in Congress in 1959, targeted urban industrial communities hit hard by recession and unemployment rather than chronically depressed rural areas in need of the basic infrastructure for development. "The Douglas-Payne Bill," reported the *Louisville Courier-Journal* in February 1959, "would not, for an instance, make significant headway towards mitigating those all-important economic factors affecting Eastern Kentucky: lack of modern transportation networks, vulnerability to floods, and the decline of coal-mining."[82] Frustrated, Whisman and other leaders of the eastern Kentucky commission launched a campaign to change federal policies in favor of "underdeveloped areas" and to make government and industry leaders more aware of Appalachia's plight and potential.

As the 1950s drew to a close, efforts increased throughout Appalachia to focus the attention of state and national leaders on the burgeoning crises in the hills. Rising welfare rolls and unemployment placed heavy burdens on state resources and spurred even non-Appalachian legislators, journalists, and private citizens to join the call for action. In the elections of 1960, candidates for governor in almost every Appalachian state endorsed programs to reduce poverty in the mountain counties, and in Kentucky, mountain lawyer and gubernatorial candidate Bert Combs promised to implement the recommendations of the Eastern Kentucky Regional Planning Commission. But it would take a national rediscovery of poverty throughout affluent America and the unexpected victory of a New England senator in the 1960 presidential primary to draw the nation's attention to the need for federal assistance to the region. Even then there would be little agreement on the sources of Appalachia's problems or the solutions to its distress. For the post–World War II generation, confident in its ability to sustain growth and to build a better life for everyone, Appalachia remained an American enigma.

2

THE POLITICS OF POVERTY

I've been preachin' the gospel for 25 years, and I've never
seen a time so bad.
—Levi McGeorge, pastor of the Closplint Church of God,
Harlan County, Kentucky, February 1959

The winters of 1959 and 1960 were unusually harsh in Appalachia,
bringing additional burdens to an already hard-pressed land. The
destruction of the record flood of 1957 could still be seen in many
mountain communities, and a national recession only deepened the
economic crisis in the hills. Throughout central Appalachia, hundreds
of displaced coal miners faced the specter of expired unemployment
benefits and dwindling food supplies. Heavy snows and subfreezing
temperatures resulted in several deaths from starvation and exposure.
Kentucky governor Happy Chandler declared an emergency in eastern
Kentucky and initiated a modest relief effort, but state resources were
inadequate to meet the problem.[1]

Conditions were equally severe in West Virginia when Senator
John F. Kennedy of Massachusetts arrived to campaign in the 1960
Democratic presidential primary. Kennedy's subsequent victory in the
West Virginia primary would mark a turning point in his drive to the
presidency. Winning in the Mountain State settled the question of
whether a Catholic candidate could carry a predominantly Protestant
state and smoothed the senator's path to victory in other primaries.
For Appalachia, however, the 1960 primary was a watershed of another kind. Events in West Virginia drew the attention of the federal

government and national media to the economic despair that had settled over the region.

When Senator Kennedy came to West Virginia, mountain villages were still digging out from heavy snows and bitter cold, the coldest March on record and the most snowfall since 1914.[2] By April the campaign began to warm along with the weather, and the candidates carried their search for votes out of the urban areas and into the rural districts and coal camps of the southern part of the state. Political strategists expected that the issue of religion would dominate the campaign, as it had in other states, and Kennedy was prepared to confront religious bigotry head-on. But the crowds of unemployed coal miners who greeted the senator in places like Welch and Williamson and in dozens of other coal communities along Paint Creek, Cabin Creek, and the New River were less interested in the candidate's religion than in his plans to relieve their economic distress.

Senator Hubert Humphrey of Minnesota, the only candidate to challenge Kennedy in the Mountain State, had raised concerns about economic conditions in the coalfields as early as January 1960. In a speech before the West Virginia Legislature, Humphrey attacked poverty in affluent America as "a national scandal," but he failed to reach the people with his message, and he could not compete with the Kennedy money and political organization. Kennedy, who seemed genuinely stunned by the conditions he witnessed in the coal camps, turned the economic issue to his advantage, suggesting that he was the only candidate who could provide relief for the state, if West Virginians would send him to the White House. Tying himself to the memory of Franklin D. Roosevelt, the patron saint of Democrats who had brought the union and relief programs to the mountains during the Great Depression, Kennedy campaigned alongside Franklin D. Roosevelt Jr., who assured hungry coal miners that the Massachusetts senator would follow through on aid to depressed areas. On the eve of the May 10 primary, Kennedy went before television cameras and promised the people of West Virginia, "If I'm nominated and elected president, within sixty days of the start of my administration, I will introduce a program to the Congress for aid to West Virginia." The next day Senator Kennedy received over 60 percent of the votes of West Virginia

Democrats for their party's presidential nomination, and Senator Humphrey withdrew from the race.[3]

While Democrats campaigned in West Virginia, state and local leaders in other Appalachian states pressed for federal assistance to the region. In January 1960 newly elected governor Bert T. Combs of Kentucky endorsed Program 60's recommendations as priority objectives for his administration, including the call for a meeting of Appalachian governors. Later that spring, concerned with the special problems of Maryland's Appalachian counties, Governor Millard Tawes invited the governors and representatives of seven Appalachian states to convene in Annapolis to coordinate state development efforts across the region. The first Conference of Appalachian Governors met on May 20, 1960, only ten days after the West Virginia primary and a week after President Eisenhower vetoed another depressed areas bill sent to him by Congress. The governors reviewed a report on economic conditions and population trends in eleven Appalachian states prepared by the Maryland Department of Economic Development.[4] They resolved to push for further cooperation among the states, but they were unable to agree on support for federal action.

Democratic governors at the Annapolis meeting favored special legislation to assist the self-help programs being developed within the Appalachian states, but Republican governor Cecil Underwood of West Virginia defended the president's veto of the depressed areas bill. "The President was 1,000 percent right to veto this bill," he argued, "on the grounds that it sets up another federal agency. We already have enough departments in the federal government." Adding that the "magic" of depressed areas legislation was "not the answer," he complained that politicians and journalists who had publicized the plight of West Virginia during the recent primary had not given a balanced picture: "It is true that 20 per cent of our workforce has been displaced. But we still have a strong, vigorous economy. We are not as bad off as Michigan. We have not had to borrow for unemployment compensation as Pennsylvania has. We are still teetering on the brink of solvency."[5]

Despite his opposition to the depressed areas bill, Underwood supported the idea of interstate cooperation, and the group agreed to hold a second Conference of Appalachian Governors to be hosted by Governor Combs the following fall. Meeting in Lexington, Kentucky, on October 17–18, 1960, the governors of five states and the representatives of six others discussed mutual problems facing their Appalachian areas, especially the challenges of highway construction and water control. Present were Governors Luther Hodges of North Carolina, Buford Ellington of Tennessee, and Lindsey Almond of Virginia, as well as Combs of Kentucky and Tawes of Maryland. Also attending were representatives of several federal agencies; Willis Weatherford of Berea College, who outlined the goals of the Appalachian regional survey then underway; and Perley Ayer, director of the CSM, who pledged the support of his organization.

Again Governor Combs called for the passage of federal area redevelopment legislation that would help address the "acute problem of unemployment in the region," and he appointed a committee chaired by Governor Tawes to draft a "statement of principles" that might serve as a framework for cooperation and "might be able to get the interest—and possibly some commitments—from both the presidential candidates [Richard Nixon and Kennedy] and from candidates for Congress."[6] Notwithstanding the reluctance of representatives from Georgia, Alabama, South Carolina, and Virginia "to yield even a portion of state sovereignty" to any new federal program,[7] the governors approved the "Declaration for Action Regarding the Appalachian Region." The resolution pledged to form and continue a "voluntary association of the states" to advance "a special regional program of development," and it called for candidates for national office to support "appropriate federal participation" in the solutions to the region's problems.[8]

The conference and the declaration for action bore the distinct mark of John Whisman. Serving as aide to Governor Combs, Whisman had helped to organize the Annapolis meeting and had coordinated planning for the Lexington conference. The Lexington resolution drew extensively on Program 60 for both its language and its strategies for action. The resolution, for example, avoided the phrase "depressed area" that was popularly associated with urban redevelopment efforts and instead pointed to the "chronic condition of underdevelopment and severe unemployment" that existed in the region. "As a result [of underdevelopment]," the declaration read, "many people [of

Appalachia] are denied reasonable economic and cultural opportunities through no fault of their own. In addition, the productive force in both physical and human resources is severely limited in its contribution to the nation, while the costs of essential welfare services are steadily increasing."[9]

By characterizing Appalachia as an underdeveloped region rather than a depressed area, the governors hoped to draw attention to Appalachia's special problems and to distinguish the needs of the mountains from those of urban areas that had achieved development but were now suffering from temporary economic decline. "By underdevelopment, we mean that basic handicaps to development of adequate facilities involving transportation and water resources have in turn hindered the local ability to support necessary public services and private enterprise activity. Because of such basic deficiencies, the success of local development activity in all areas of life is severely handicapped." What Appalachia needed, the document suggested, was temporary public work and job training programs similar to those being proposed for the rest of the country and the creation of modern economic infrastructure such as key roads and major water control facilities. Planning for this basic infrastructure should be connected to a "comprehensive state and regional development program . . . in appropriate fields of activity, including forestry, agriculture, mineral resources and tourist travel, industrial and community development, education, health and welfare."[10] The declaration attempted to move policy discussions beyond relief programs and toward the use of federal resources for the comprehensive development of the region. Effectively, the Lexington resolution outlined the issues that would shape efforts to create a special Appalachian development program over the next five years. The conference also adopted a resolution endorsing an Appalachian development highway system and elected Governor Combs as chair. Whisman was designated to head a permanent staff committee to plan future meetings and actions.

The recommendations of the governors' conference in Lexington took on additional significance three weeks later, when John F. Kennedy was elected to the presidency of the United States. To prepare his domestic agenda, the president-elect immediately asked his brother-in-law, Sargent Shriver, to put together a series of twenty-nine teams that would meet to draft a legislative program for the new administration.[11] Fulfilling Kennedy's pledge to the people of West Virginia, one of the first teams created was the Task Force on Area Redevelopment, appointed to formulate specific recommendations to assist people in economically depressed areas. Generally the Kennedy task forces comprised academics, business leaders, congressional staff, and members of the Kennedy team, but the ten members appointed to the Task Force on Area Redevelopment included seven labor and industrial leaders from West Virginia, the secretary of labor and industry from Pennsylvania, and the assistant to the president of the UMWA in Washington. Kennedy asked Senator Paul Douglas of Illinois, who had led congressional efforts to enact depressed areas legislation throughout the 1950s, to serve as chair of the committee and, after a last-minute request from Governor Combs, added Whisman to the team.[12]

The West Virginia task force, as the Kennedy people called it, met initially in Charleston, West Virginia, on December 9, 1960, and within two weeks it issued a report recommending both a short-term package of immediate relief for those unemployed as a result of the recession and a broader strategy of area development to provide long-term job opportunities. The report called for the passage of area redevelopment legislation similar to that which had failed during the Eisenhower years, including the creation of an area redevelopment administration and programs in human resource development, natural resource development, and public works. Most of these proposals were designed to address unemployment problems in declining urban areas such as Philadelphia, Pittsburgh, and Chicago, but the final recommendation of the report—reflecting Whisman's influence—urged the establishment of a system of regional development commissions across the nation that would attack the special problems of distressed regions and carry out comprehensive development programs. As an immediate step, the committee recommended that the president appoint an Appalachian regional commission, based on the initiative of the Appalachian governors, that might serve as a pilot for similar efforts in other regions.[13]

The core recommendations of the task force became Senate bill 1 when the new Congress convened in January 1961, but the proposals for a national system of development commissions and a pilot Appalachian regional commission failed to make the final draft of the legislation. A parade of Appalachian members of Congress testified in favor of the bill during House and Senate hearings. Jennings Randolph and Robert Byrd of West Virginia, John Sherman Cooper and Carl Perkins of Kentucky, Estes Kefauver of Tennessee, and Hugh Scott of Pennsylvania described the critical economic conditions in their mountain counties that had led to official unemployment rates of 12 to 25 percent. Governors Tawes of Maryland, Ellington of Tennessee, and Combs of Kentucky all praised the bill but added that other measures were also needed, including a highway program, funds for natural resource development, and increased aid to education. Opponents of the Area Redevelopment Act complained that the legislation was not needed and objected to the federal government's interfering in the economic affairs of local areas, but Congress passed the legislation in late March 1961.[14]

The Area Redevelopment Act authorized the creation of the Area Redevelopment Administration (ARA) in the Department of Commerce and the expenditure of $394 million over a four-year period. Most of the funds were to provide low-interest industrial loans, grants to local governments for public facilities needed to attract businesses, and subsistence for worker training programs. Even ARA officials acknowledged that the act "essentially followed a 'trickle down' approach to poverty and unemployment, with most of the direct benefits going to businesses and not to unemployed people," but Appalachian political leaders hoped that the legislation would lead to broader efforts to assist the region.[15]

The act became law on May 1, 1961, and a week later the Conference of Appalachian Governors met in Washington with President Kennedy and the director of the new ARA to coordinate regional development strategies with the agency. In response to the governors' proposal to create an Appalachian commission, the president asked the ARA to establish a liaison with the governors to coordinate state and federal development strategies. The governors appointed a staff committee, chaired by Whisman, to work with the ARA liaison to channel recommendations to the agency. Later this informal arrangement became the federal interagency committee on the Appalachian region, but there were no special funds set aside for Appalachia, and the responsibility for drafting a comprehensive development plan for the region remained with the governors.[16]

Over the next two years, the Conference of Appalachian Governors (now called the Council of Appalachian Governors) continued to meet on a regular basis and to formulate proposals for an Appalachian highway program, water resource and forestry development, and education and job training programs, but the president proved unresponsive to the call for a state-federal Appalachian regional commission. Frustration also grew with the ARA and with the slow distribution of federal aid to distressed mountain communities. Not only was the ARA severely underfunded for its task, but fully one-third of the counties in the nation qualified for ARA benefits. Seventy-six percent of Appalachian counties qualified for the program, but the bulk of ARA resources flowed to private businesses located primarily in urban centers outside the region. Rural areas, like most of Appalachia, lacked the existing businesses and business prospects to make them eligible for assistance, and they lacked the professional staff necessary to prepare the overall economic development plans necessary for funding. Furthermore, ARA and other federal programs continued to require local matching funds that seriously depressed rural communities were unable to supply. ARA also provided no funds for education, health care, or other human resource development needs.[17]

Only West Virginia benefited significantly from ARA resources, and these were utilized primarily in the development of tourism projects. Over half of the ARA funds expended in Appalachia ($79 million) during its four-year existence went to the Mountain State, and much of that was allocated to the massive New River Gorge project designed to create a series of tourism attractions in Fayette and Raleigh counties. The bulk of business loans and grants were funneled to a handful of heavily industrialized valley counties in West Virginia and Pennsylvania. The Appalachian portions of three states (Maryland, North Carolina, and Ohio) received no public facilities dollars at all, while four other states (Pennsylvania, Tennessee, Virginia, and Georgia) received less than 7 percent of the funds. ARA job training programs were slow to get started, and the few training programs funded in Appalachia were not linked to specific business expansions.

Many of the trainees had to be shipped out of the region to find jobs.[18]

By 1962 disappointment with the ARA was widespread in the mountains. Harry Caudill wrote that the ARA had been launched with "the most laudable intentions" but had "accomplished little beyond a few small loans for minor business enterprises."[19] The *Louisville Courier-Journal* complained that the agency's efforts in eastern Kentucky were "as useless as oars on an airplane."[20] The annual report of the Eastern Kentucky Regional Planning Commission noted that ARA loans, grants, and training programs were "useful tools" but that these were "far less important" than the agency's "potential function—inadequately used to date—in providing technical assistance and in coordinating federal programs."[21]

The Appalachian governors and the CSM continued to lobby the president to create a separate Appalachian regional commission that could coordinate federal programs with the states and could administer supplemental and special federal benefits for regional development. Although the president's attention turned to other domestic and foreign policy concerns in 1962, intellectual and political currents were converging rapidly on a mainstream assault on poverty as part of a new national agenda. Events in the mountains would place Appalachia at the center of that effort.

Following the West Virginia presidential primary in 1960, national journalists had increasingly turned to Appalachia as a symbol of the growing disparity between poverty and affluence in the United States. The image of a rich, young New England senator being greeted by barefoot children and destitute coal miners fueled an escalating sense that two societies had emerged in postwar America. Despite the conspicuous wealth evident in new suburban housing projects, shopping centers, interstate highways, and other signs of an emerging consumer culture, many rural areas and inner-city communities in the 1960s still struggled to overcome the blight of depression and poverty.

Kennedy's visible alarm at conditions in the Mountain State and the attention given to economic issues in the presidential campaign lured dozens of journalists to the mountains in the months that followed the election. Stories of human tragedy, personal struggle, cruel injustice, and heroic perseverance abounded in Appalachia and provided grist for a growing media mill of articles about poverty in America. The region's natural beauty and romantic folk culture added mystery and curiosity to tales of personal adversity and hardship, and it was an easy progression from stories of individual tragedy to descriptions of Appalachia itself as a region apart from the rest of America, a poor place in an otherwise rich land. Embedded in the idea of Appalachia as a distressed region, moreover, were unsettling questions about the American economic system as a whole—who benefited from development and who didn't, and why entire regions of the country failed to share in the rewards of postwar growth.

For the second time in less than a century, Appalachia appeared at the heart of national debates about modernization and progress. Whereas a generation of writers after the Civil War had helped to define Appalachia in the popular mind as the antithesis of an emerging national culture, journalists in the 1960s concentrated their attention on images of Appalachia as a socioeconomic problem area. To a generation immersed in the cold war and confronted by the civil rights movement, Appalachia provided further evidence of the failure of the American promise for many whites as well as for blacks. The presence of widespread poverty in an old and predominantly white part of the nation's heartland challenged prevailing assumptions about technology, the free market, and the social responsibility of wealth. In the context of the 1960s, the region became a popular symbol of poverty and of weakness in the American economy itself.

The rediscovery of the region fed on old stereotypes and outdated images, but the new commentaries spoke as much to the anxieties confronting the larger society as they did to the political and economic problems of the mountains. Images of Appalachia as isolated and of Appalachians as a quaint and sometimes violent people persisted, but increasingly observers described Appalachian poverty not as a permanent condition but as something that could be alleviated by the application of modern resources to human problems. If Appalachia was a distressed region, they reasoned, it must not have experienced the same economic and cultural changes that had lifted the rest of the nation out of the Depression and placed it on the road to prosperity after World War II. Appalachia might once have been a cultural and geographic anomaly, but, thanks to advances in science and technology, these conditions could now be overcome.

Postwar confidence in the American path to modernization provided the solution to the conundrum of Appalachian poverty, just as American capitalism provided a light for third world progress, but Americans differed on how to put the region on the road to prosperity. For some, poverty was the result of individual character weaknesses that could be alleviated through technical education, job training, and the cultural adjustment to modern values. For others, poverty was the consequence of governmental neglect of the basic public infrastructure that moved societies through the stages of development and capitalist expansion—roads, water systems, and public facilities. Most assumed that raising the expectations of poor people and providing the goods of industrial production—that is, modernization—would bring poor regions into the mainstream. Few questioned the benefits of growth or associated poverty with systemic inequalities in political or economic structures.

As early as the 1950s, liberal politicians and scholars had begun to describe poverty as an anomaly, a minority condition within an otherwise prosperous nation. Early in the decade, Minnesota senator Hubert Humphrey called for the creation of a youth conservation corps to address what were believed to be growing problems of juvenile delinquency, idleness, and poverty in urban areas. Later, Governor Averell Harriman asked the New York legislature for funds to study the causes of poverty in the Empire State, and twice in the decade Illinois senator Paul Douglas, a professional economist, sponsored federal legislation to aid depressed areas. Most of these efforts saw poverty as a deviation from the American norm that could be corrected by government investment in public works projects and job programs, but these New Deal–style initiatives failed repeatedly to pass in the face of postwar Republican opposition.

In 1958 Harvard economist John Kenneth Galbraith confirmed American confidence in the arrival of a new age of mass prosperity with the publication of his best-selling book *The Affluent Society*. The economic crisis of the Great Depression, he suggested, had been overcome now for most Americans. Scarcity had been replaced by affluence except in a few unrelenting pockets of poverty that still demanded government attention. Galbraith saw the persistence of poverty as a national scandal, but as a Keynesian economist he was primarily interested in the growing gap between private opulence and the need for public sector investment in roads, schools, parks, and other infrastructure to sustain growth.[22]

Other writers, however, led by Michael Harrington, soon extended Galbraith's analysis and questioned the depth of the postwar economic miracle. In the July 1959 issue of *Commentary* magazine, Harrington estimated that as much as a third of the nation's people still lived at substandard levels and were permanently, not temporarily, distressed. It was a popular myth, Harrington argued, that the poor in the United States were a small and declining group, largely limited to nonwhites and rural southerners and protected from despair by the reforms of the New Deal. The facts, he suggested, presented "a different and far less pretty picture." Poverty had become a trap for many Americans, and he called for a "comprehensive assault on poverty . . . [in] America's rural and urban slums."[23]

The events of the West Virginia primary appeared to confirm Harrington's views, and, soon after Kennedy's victory in the Mountain State, *Washington Post* staff reporter Julius Duscha followed up on Harrington's critique of the American economy by touring Appalachia, "this country's worst blighted area." Duscha's August 1960 essay set the pattern for a generation of writers who would see the southern Appalachian Mountains as a region in need and mountain people as victims. "From the Blue Ridge Mountains of Virginia to the trail of the Cumberland Gap in Kentucky," he wrote, "tens of thousands of Americans live in appalling poverty. Live? No, they hardly exist." These once proud and independent mountain families—"many of them descendants of pioneer American families"—had been reduced to living on handouts of surplus food or what they could scratch from hillside gardens. According to William D. Gorman, a community leader in Hazard, Kentucky, things were so bad that some people in his church were no longer coming to worship services "because they didn't have clothes to wear or food to eat."

Duscha found evidence of misery throughout the half-ghost, half-coal towns of eastern Kentucky and southern West Virginia: "the gaunt, hungry faces; the unpainted, crumbling homes; the women who are pitifully old before their time, and the men who have nothing to do but sit and tell a grim story that needs no substantiation with figures." The decline of coal mining and the obsolescence of the small farm had caused this suffering, and the region needed "massive assistance of the kind that Government and industry have given to the underdeveloped countries of the world. For much of the Southern Appalachians is as underdeveloped, when compared with the affluence of the rest of America, as the newly independent countries of Africa." In light of American abundance, he concluded, the nation "should be able to provide a decent life for all persons, whether they live in a hollow, on a ridge, in a city or on a 500-acre Iowa farm."[24]

A host of other writers followed in the literary path opened by the *Washington Post* reporter. Over the next three years, a wave of articles, books, and television documentaries flooded the media with descriptions of Appalachian poverty. In 1961 David Grossman and Melvin Levin, New England–based planners who had prepared the reference materials for the Annapolis Conference of Appalachian Governors, published a report in the journal *Land Economics* that statistically defined Appalachia as a "national problem area." Grossman and Levin identified a number of obstacles to economic growth in the region, including the topography, tax policies, inadequate community facilities, "unfavorable psychological attitudes," and a "superannuated, unskilled" workforce.[25] In 1962 a group of nationally acclaimed scholars came to similar conclusions when they released *The Southern Appalachian Region: A Survey,* sponsored by the Ford Foundation. The study provided scientific analyses of the region's economy and social institutions, but it laid most of the blame for regional backwardness on the provincial culture of the mountain people.[26] Later that year Michael Harrington included Appalachia as part of the "other America" in his book of that title designed to stir the conscience of Americans to do something for the nation's poor.[27]

These and other essays fed a growing chorus of commentary among the intellectual elite on the political and economic dilemma of poverty,[28] but when *Look* magazine published a collection of photographs of Appalachia in December 1962, the face of poverty in the United States, at least for many middle-class Americans, became indelibly Appalachian. Part of a series of essays about American regions, the *Look* photographs avoided the old stereotypes of mountain residents as historical relics or degenerate rubes. Instead they captured images of solid American families surrounded by the trappings of modern life but caught in the web of economic deprivation. Abandoned appliances and disabled cars belied the gaunt beauty of a young mother or the hidden strength of an unemployed coal miner. In images that evoked middle-class values of family, religion, and hard work, the magazine connected Appalachia with readers' notions of mainstream America. The people of "Appalachia, U.S.A.," declared the accompanying text, lived in an underdeveloped country. "No less than Latin Americans or Africans, they can use more American aid. They are more entitled to it because they are our own people."[29]

The idea that Appalachia deserved special attention as an internal example of the third world received further validation the following year with the publication of Caudill's *Night Comes to the Cumberlands: A Biography of a Depressed Area*. Probably the most widely read book ever written about Appalachia, Caudill's passionate account of the human and environmental devastation wreaked by the coal industry on his native eastern Kentucky was a cry from the exploited heartland for government assistance to a desperate people. In a mixed narrative that combined images of cultural degeneracy and corporate abuse, Caudill decried the economic, political, and social blight that had settled over the mountains and called for the creation of a southern mountain authority, patterned after the TVA, to oversee regional development. "Idleness and waste are antipathetic to progress and growth," he wrote, "and, unless the Cumberland Plateau is to remain an anchor dragging behind the rest of America, it—and the rest of the Southern Appalachians—must be rescued while there is yet time."[30]

Caudill quickly became a popular and eloquent spokesperson for the region, spreading the story of Appalachian distress on television and before congressional committees. Journalists by the dozens visited his Whitesburg, Kentucky, home and, after absorbing the Caudill "treatment" over tea, were granted a personal tour of decaying coal camps and scarred hillsides. One Pulitzer Prize–winning reporter, Homer Bigart, wrote a moving series for the *New York Times* following his pilgrimage to Whitesburg that depicted a wasted landscape and a people so poor that children ate dirt out of the chinks of chimneys to ease their hunger.[31] The series caught the attention of President Kennedy and helped to seal his commitment to antipoverty legislation for the 1964 Congress.

By the end of 1963, the image of Appalachia as a region of endemic poverty had settled once again in the popular mind.[32] Regional scholars and policy makers alike utilized the image to build their cases for federal funding for uplift and development programs. Journalists and politicians outside the mountains exploited regional economic distress to gather public support for a national crusade on poverty. Ironically, within the mountains the idea of Appalachia as a problem region was not widely recognized except among academics and social reformers. The word "Appalachia" itself was seldom used by mountain residents, except in reference to the town of that name in southwest Virginia. Interestingly, as the region came to be identified with national poverty, many among the mountain middle class rejected the application of the term "Appalachia" to their own community, preferring to associate it with communities far removed from their own. For observers in the rest of the country, however, Appalachia was more than an embarrassment. It had become part of a national problem.

The swell of media attention on Appalachia in the early 1960s was part of a rising wave of concern for the country's economy. The boom times of the 1950s had begun to falter a bit in the last years of that decade. Although Senator Kennedy had promised to get the nation "moving again" during the presidential campaign, the country's economy continued to struggle throughout the first two years of the Kennedy administration. Unemployment remained unacceptably high, hovering around 7 percent, and in May 1962 the stock market fell to its lowest point since the inauguration. Unemployment and applications for public assistance continued to rise throughout Appalachia, where joblessness was twice the national average.

During the summer of 1962, desperate families in central Appalachia received an additional blow when the UMWA announced that it was revoking the cherished health cards on which many depended for medical care. The UMWA had established its Health and Retirement Funds to provide free health care and other benefits to miners and their families, and in 1954 the union had built ten state-of-the-art

Miners Memorial hospitals in southern West Virginia, Virginia, and eastern Kentucky that provided medical care for a large percentage of families in the area. Now, however, declining revenues in its Health and Retirement Funds made it impossible for the union to sustain benefits for miners whose companies were no longer paying royalties into the funds. Most of the operators who defaulted on their forty-cent-per-ton royalty payment to the funds were small truck mine owners who had signed "sweetheart contracts" with the UMWA, allowing them to pay wages below the national contract. Declining coal markets in the early 1960s and competition from larger mechanized mines, however, led many of the struggling truck mines to cease their contributions to the funds. Miners in eastern Kentucky had accepted lower wages, but the loss of their family health cards was too much. They responded with a time-honored "wildcat strike" despite the union's objections.

By September roving bands of pickets were moving from one small mine to another, attempting to shut down delinquent operations. When the UMWA announced in October that it intended to sell or close its hospitals in Kentucky and other Appalachian states, the frustration of out-of-work miners boiled over. The roving pickets movement soon degenerated into class warfare, with jobless families on one side and coal operators, businesspeople, and local government officials on the other. At times nearly five hundred miners caravanned to a small truck mine only to be dispersed by state police, armed company guards, and the local sheriff, who in Perry County was himself a coal operator. Arson, shootings, beatings, and the dynamiting of homes, trucks, tipples, and equipment soon forced Governor Combs to intervene in search of a truce, but only the heavy snow and icy roads of December quieted the violence.[33]

The lethargic national economy and rising labor unrest in the coalfields prompted President Kennedy to look for ways to stimulate business growth. A fiscal conservative who disliked deficit spending, the president settled on an across-the-board tax cut. Before announcing his decision, however, he asked Walter Heller, chair of his Council of Economic Advisors, to look into recent media estimates of the number of poor people in America. Kennedy anticipated opposition to tax reduction from liberal Democrats in Congress, and he was aware that a tax cut would leave him vulnerable to criticism that he was indifferent to poverty at a time of increasing popular concern for the poor. Prior to this time, poverty had not been a focal point for policy discussions in the Kennedy White House. Like many Americans, the president assumed that a rising economic tide would steadily reduce the size of the low-income population. The domestic programs of the New Frontier had concentrated on generating growth rather than on fighting poverty. As a tireless reader with a strong sense of social obligation to the disadvantaged, however, Kennedy was sensitive to the intellectual currents of his time, especially to suggestions that his administration was not meeting the country's problems.[34]

In January 1963 the president read Dwight MacDonald's lengthy review in the *New Yorker* of several recent studies of poverty, including Michael Harrington's *The Other America*. MacDonald found ample evidence of persistent poverty within the United States, and he lambasted the Kennedy administration for neglecting "our invisible poor." Ignoring the plight of the disadvantaged not only made us "feel uncomfortable," he chided, but also challenged the general prosperity of the nation. Hidden in the midst of an otherwise rich country, the very poor could no longer be helped by economic expansion alone but must have government assistance lest they become permanently alienated from the rest of the society.[35] Troubled by MacDonald's criticism, Kennedy encouraged Heller to begin to identify antipoverty strategies that might be included in the domestic agenda for his 1964 reelection campaign.

The president's tax cut languished in Congress during 1963, but his request to Heller generated considerable interest among a small group of Kennedy advisors. Heller invited other economists from the Council of Economic Advisors, including Robert Lampman and Kermit Gordon, to meet for informal Saturday discussions with colleagues from the Bureau of the Budget and the Labor, Justice, and Health, Education, and Welfare departments. Most of these advisors were economists like Heller, trained in the postwar Keynesian philosophy of government investment in the economy to sustain growth, but some, like Daniel Moynihan, were social scientists who believed in government intervention to rectify social distress.[36] Although Heller and his associates viewed poverty as a moral problem, they also assumed that an assault on poverty would have economic and political benefits for the administration in 1964. Not only would a limited antipoverty program help to boost the national economy, but, since poverty cut across race and geography, it would appeal to rural whites in the South as well as to blacks and suburban liberals.[37]

As the Heller group began its meetings in the White House, spring rains in the mountains once again brought Appalachia to national attention. In mid-March 1963 back-to-back floods once more struck the Cumberland Plateau, causing rivers to pour out of their banks and displacing twenty-five thousand people from their homes. Coming within eight days of each other, the heavy rains caused more than $80 million in damage across fifty counties in the heart of the region. Although the work of the informal interagency committee on Appalachia expedited flood rehabilitation efforts among federal agencies, editorials throughout the region criticized the inadequate federal response. "The floods that are tearing the economic life out of the mountains are the direct and inevitable result of fifty years of federal neglect," wrote the *Louisville Courier-Journal.* "Our people and our economy are tired, worn out, exhausted," lamented the *Whitesburg (KY) Mountain Eagle.* "We do not have the money, the energy, or the willpower to dig ourselves out."[38]

On March 29, 1963, Governor Bert Combs and his staff met with Ed McDermott, chief of the federal Office of Emergency Planning, and other White House aides to discuss specific actions on postflood problems. Along with a number of proposals for immediate action, Combs again emphasized the difficulty of "the dual emergency of Appalachia—the long standing economic emergency now compounded by the natural disaster emergency." He also pointed out the proposal of the Appalachian governors for a special, comprehensive, and long-term Appalachian regional development program. Later the same day, McDermott met with the president, who expressed interest in the idea of an Appalachian program and agreed to add the subject to the agenda of an April 9 cabinet meeting originally scheduled to review the ARA. As a result of the president's decision to include the special focus on the Appalachian problem, the Appalachian governors were invited to attend the cabinet meeting.[39]

Over the next week, John Whisman and Governor William Barron of West Virginia, who had succeeded Combs as chair of the Council of Appalachian Governors, coordinated arrangements for the meeting with the governors and their staffs. On the afternoon of April 9, five Appalachian governors—Combs of Kentucky, Barron of West Virginia, Tawes of Maryland, Frank Clement of Tennessee, and Albertis Harrison of Virginia—along with representatives of the governors of North Carolina and Pennsylvania, met with the president, his cabinet, and a number of agency heads in the Cabinet Room of the White House. Also in attendance were presidential aide Lee White, Walter Heller of the Council of Economic Advisors and the informal antipoverty discussion group, and Franklin D. Roosevelt Jr., undersecretary of commerce.[40]

The president was delayed by a ceremony in the Rose Garden granting honorary citizenship to Winston Churchill. As those assembled awaited his arrival, Commerce Secretary Luther Hodges asked the other cabinet secretaries to begin reporting on the effectiveness of their departments' programs in Appalachia. The theme was one that the governors had heard many times before. Labor Secretary William Wirts, for example, lamented the inability of job training programs under the Area Redevelopment Act and the Manpower Development and Training Act to alleviate the long-term problems of the region. Unless they could identify new kinds of businesses to receive trainees, he pointed out, Appalachian people would continue to be trained for jobs that were simply not there. Agriculture Secretary Orville Freeman added that overall regional planning was desperately needed, but he could offer no suggestions for developing a comprehensive regional plan.[41]

In the middle of Freeman's remarks, President Kennedy arrived and assumed leadership of the meeting. The president welcomed the governors and reemphasized his deep concern for the economic problems of the Appalachian region. He noted that it had been a primary goal of his administration to reduce the immediate distress in the mountains and to help "build a solid economic basis on which the region could prosper." But unemployment remained unacceptably high, and federal efforts through the ARA and other programs were "not making much progress in the sense of really biting into the long term unemployment." Consequently, the president announced, he would take the following actions: First, he would direct his department heads to speed up current programs affecting Appalachia and to include more programs for the Appalachian region in their fiscal year 1965 budgets. Second, he would establish within the Department of Commerce a joint federal-state committee on the Appalachian region to develop a comprehensive program for regional economic development that would report back to him by January 1, 1964. This program would include recommendations for improving transportation facilities; providing education and job training; conducting research; developing water, mineral, and forest resources; and attracting tourists. Finally, he would seek to create an Appalachian development institute to serve as a nonfederal center for research and training on the economic problems of the region.[42]

After completing his remarks, Kennedy moved to a chair directly across from Combs while members of the cabinet and the governors discussed his proposals. Secretary Freeman resumed his comments, but everyone was watching the president as he pulled a sheet of notepaper from the table and wrote something. He then folded the paper into a little airplane and sent it gliding toward Combs, landing in front of the governor. The note read, "Bert, what do you really want?" Combs seized the opportunity and, in his formal remarks to the group, commented that the creation of a permanent federal-state regional agency would be the most important product of the president's committee. "The more I come up here [to Washington]," he explained, "the more I believe we need a handle to work with. You cannot go to Commerce and then to Agriculture and then to HEW, and then go to all of these other agencies and get a great deal done unless you live up here. And I just don't have the time to stay up here." The other governors concurred.[43]

Kennedy's choice to head the joint federal-state committee, the President's Appalachian Regional Commission (PARC), was Franklin D. Roosevelt Jr., who had campaigned with the president in West Virginia during the crucial 1960 primary. Once informed of his appointment to chair the commission, Roosevelt outlined the steps that he would take to achieve his goal. He asked each governor and each cabinet secretary to appoint a representative to the commission, which would begin its work with a tour of the state capitals to gather information and ideas for the development of the region. To assist him in drafting the final report, he selected John L. Sweeney from the Department of Commerce as executive director of the commission and appointed John Whisman to represent the states as executive secretary. Interestingly, he invited no members of the informal White House antipoverty group to serve on the commission.

Under Roosevelt's leadership, PARC began immediately to gather ideas and program recommendations from state, federal, and academic leaders. The commission launched initial visits to seven state capitals, and Roosevelt appointed Benjamin Chinitz, a Harvard-trained economist and chair of the University of Pittsburgh Department of Economics, to undertake a study of regional conditions. Chinitz pulled together a task force of academic sociologists, economists, political scientists, and geographers to analyze data gathered by agency professionals from each of the Appalachian states. With the assistance of staff from fourteen federal agencies, the research team collected information on a wide assortment of chronic problems, including water resources, coal, electric power, finance, highways, education, and forestry.

Like Whisman, Chinitz considered the Appalachian region to be underdeveloped in the same sense that "poverty-ridden countries in Latin America are underdeveloped." An unfortunate history of resource extraction, he believed, had left the region without the "superstructure" (schools, factories, private enterprises, public services) on which to sustain a modern economy. In the absence of core infrastructure for development, human resources languished. "So there is no second and third wave of economic development," Chinitz wrote, "founded by an interested entrepreneurial society." Federal, state, and county governments alone had not been able to address the region's chronic needs, he wrote, but "federal-state-county governments working together can."[44]

Chinitz's opinion that Appalachia's problems resulted from a lag in the natural stages of development was consistent with contemporary academic theories of economic growth and paralleled the ideas that Whisman had incorporated into *Program 60* and the "Declaration for Action Regarding the Appalachian Region" issued by the Conference of Appalachian Governors. American intellectuals and business leaders in the post–World War II years, drawing on their experience in rebuilding Europe and Japan, were confident that the mobilization of government resources to build basic infrastructure could set an impoverished region on the road to development.

This confidence in the benefits of physical infrastructure development was reinforced by suggestions that PARC received from meetings with state officials and cooperating federal agencies. Department of Transportation officials, for example, were "only too willing to suggest a $1.2 billion program of regional and local-access roads to be financed largely by additional federal funds."[45] The states were clear that they wanted highways, resource development, and preferential treatment on federal grants. State and federal bureaucrats agreed that the problems of Appalachia resulted from a lack of basic infrastructure for development. In this manner, academic theories about the process of development came together with the professional interests of federal agency personnel and state political leadership to provide a common agenda for the region.

During the summer of 1963, Whisman and Sweeney organized PARC into five working teams, which began to draft recommendations on transportation, human resources, physical resources, water, and the organization of a permanent commission. In addition to Chinitz's academic advisors, more than three hundred individuals from various branches of government participated in the deliberations. At the end of October, a draft report was readied, and between November 12 and 20, the commission staff again toured the states, seeking responses to its preliminary recommendations. By this time the number of states to be included in the new program had increased to ten with the addition of Ohio and Georgia.

While PARC prepared to finalize its report, President Kennedy followed through on his commitment to tap existing federal programs for emergency relief in central Appalachia. Responding to Bigart's October *New York Times* article that exposed the hardships of Kentucky coal miners facing a "grim winter,"[46] the president informed Walter Heller that he planned to include antipoverty legislation in the agenda for the next Congress. He also ordered a special winter relief program for the mountain coalfields that would serve as an advance demonstration of the special Appalachian initiative. Announced on November 14, 1963, the winter program included grants for food relief, home repairs, education, and school lunch programs. The president also instructed the Army Corps of Engineers to accelerate work on a number of water projects to provide additional jobs, and he requested the Forest Service to redirect funds for timber stand improvement to hire unemployed youth. Finally, he asked the Department of Labor to create a special job training program for displaced coal miners.[47]

The following day, Kennedy telephoned his congratulations to the newly elected governor of Kentucky, Edward "Ned" Breathitt, and assured him that the White House would follow through on its commitment to Appalachia. PARC, he added, was about to complete its work, and Kennedy would be in touch with Governor Breathitt to set up a meeting on the Kentucky–West Virginia border to announce his support for an Appalachian commission. He would have his secretary, Evelyn Lincoln, call the governor's office with details shortly after he returned from a brief trip to Dallas, Texas.

The assassination of President Kennedy on November 22, 1963, however, suspended plans to announce the Appalachian program and raised serious questions about the future of that initiative as well as that of the parallel antipoverty program being discussed by the Heller committee. Some observers feared that the Appalachian effort might die along with the slain president, since relations between Vice President Lyndon Johnson and PARC chair Roosevelt were strained at best, and Johnson had no particular knowledge of the region. At an Executive Office Building gathering on the evening before Kennedy's funeral, though, Johnson assured the nation's governors that he intended to complete everything on Kennedy's legislative agenda. Later that evening, Governor Breathitt and former governor Combs met privately with the new president in Johnson's vice presidential office. Recalling his election day conversation with Kennedy, Breathitt praised the work of Combs and other governors on the Appalachian program. Johnson responded that if the commitment had been made, he would carry it out along with other Kennedy proposals.

The new president had learned about the antipoverty discussions the day after the assassination, when Heller briefed him on his predecessor's economic plans. Johnson quickly expressed interest in the initiative and instructed Heller to prepare a draft proposal. The informal Kennedy discussion group had evolved into an interdepartmental task force in October, but the conversations had produced little in the way of hard plans. Heller hurriedly pulled together a brief proposal for a small, experimental program of demonstration projects among carefully targeted groups, but when he and budget director Kermit Gordon presented the plan to the president in late December, Johnson declared it to be inadequate. The timid plan was not his kind of program. To the amazement of Heller and Gordon, the president wanted to put a poverty program in every community that wanted one and to bypass experimentation for direct action. The next day he announced to reporters that he would take up the fight against poverty in the next congressional session.[48]

Johnson's motivation for making the antipoverty initiative a centerpiece in his Great Society agenda was as complex as the president himself. An old New Dealer, Johnson believed in government action to solve problems, and he had a strong, personal, if paternalistic, commitment to help the disadvantaged. Never an intellectual, he was uncomfortable around the liberal academics that Kennedy had welcomed into the White House, but he valued their respect and wanted to assert an image of himself as heir to Franklin Roosevelt. Above all, Johnson was the ultimate politician, who recognized the need to establish his own agenda while appearing to fulfill that of the slain president. More than the Kennedy advisors, Johnson understood the political benefits of government investment in local poverty programs, especially in the South, where white leaders were resisting federal civil rights pressures. Since Kennedy had not publicly announced a crusade against poverty, Johnson could present it as his own program. On January 8, 1964, in his first State of the Union address, Johnson declared "unconditional war on poverty in America" and appointed Kennedy's brother-in-law, Sargent Shriver, to head a poverty task force to design a strategy for the campaign.

In the weeks following Kennedy's assassination, political leaders from Appalachia continued to urge the new president to follow through on the Appalachian program as well. Governor Wally Barron of West Virginia wrote to Johnson soon after the funeral to familiarize him with the goals of the Conference of Appalachian Governors and the work of PARC. U.S. Representative Carl Perkins wrote his old friend about the problems facing his district in eastern Kentucky and recommended a program of public works similar to that being proposed by the Roosevelt commission. On December 13 Governor Breathitt, former governor Combs, Whisman, and Representative Perkins met with the president, recounted their conversations with Kennedy, and emphasized the need for action. Governor Barron sent a telegram to the president requesting a meeting with the Appalachian governors as soon as possible. On each occasion Johnson renewed his commitment to the program, but by the end of the year he still had not been formally briefed on the Appalachian initiative.[49] John Sweeney, executive director of PARC, feared that these commitments still lacked "a passionate quality" rooted in Johnson's own political agenda and that Johnson was committed to them only as part of the ex-president's program.[50]

In the meantime PARC staff hurried to prepare the final draft of their report. A variety of special interest groups attempted to influence staff recommendations. Harry Caudill lobbied strongly for an organizational structure similar to that of the TVA and, along with the American Public Power Association, advocated the use of public funds to generate and sell electric power from water- and coal-powered generating plants that might be built in the region. The coal industry, upset with the relative paucity of attention given to coal resource development in early drafts, advocated greater infrastructure investment and the elimination of government policies it believed impeded the expansion of coal markets. The Forest Industries Council, while interested in making timber the centerpiece of Appalachian economic development, objected to recommendations that would establish cooperative timber development organizations in the region whose demonstration centers might compete with existing sawmills. Even the Bureau of the Budget objected to the proposed structure of the new commission, which it believed transferred too much authority to the states and impeded the president's power to exercise responsibilities vested in him by the Constitution. PARC, however, resisted most of these lobbying efforts, and the final report adopted the majority of the ideas and strategies for a comprehensive development program that had been advocated by the Conference of Appalachian Governors since 1960.[51]

Appalachia: A Report by the President's Appalachian Regional Commission was completed in February 1964, but political considerations delayed its release. Just as the Roosevelt commission was finishing its work, President Johnson and his aides were absorbed in planning for the 1964 presidential campaign, including preparations for the War on Poverty initiative. Sweeney and several Johnson advisors were concerned that the Appalachian program, now a holdover from the Kennedy administration, might appear to duplicate the new poverty program, and they favored delaying the release of the report until after the announcement of Johnson's poverty initiative. Indeed, these concerns contributed to a greater emphasis in the final report on highways and other infrastructure than on health care, job training, education, and other human service programs. Whisman and other early advocates of the Appalachian program believed that investment in both the physical and human capacities of the region was essential to comprehensive development, but to distinguish the Appalachian program from the War on Poverty, PARC staff emphasized the long-term role of the new Appalachian commission in building public facilities for development while leaving the immediate goal of alleviating individual hardship to the new poverty agency. The Appalachian program, they argued, would not abandon its comprehensive development strategies but would initially emphasize infrastructure needs while coordinating its human development programs with those of the national poverty effort.[52]

Scheduling a date for the release of the report also proved to be complicated. Sweeney and his staff believed that the announcement of the Appalachian program should come only after Johnson's declaration of the War on Poverty, and finding a day when the president, ten governors, and members of the commission could be present for the announcement was a challenge. The president's staff hoped to schedule a meeting at the White House during the second week of April, but this failed because Undersecretary Roosevelt planned to be in India at that time. With concern mounting among the governors that the Eighty-eighth Congress might adjourn in July before any action could be taken on Appalachian legislation, Roosevelt presented the report to the president on April 9, 1964, before leaving for India and without a formal ceremony.

The PARC report described Appalachia as "a region apart," a land of geographical diversity and natural wealth that lagged behind the rest of the nation in measures of economic growth. Defining Appalachia broadly to include both the urban centers and the rural areas of ten contiguous states, the report made the case for a regional approach to common problems of distress and for a special national commitment to address those problems. While the most severe distress was concentrated in the rural, interior counties, even the urban-industrial centers of the region lagged behind their national counterparts. The realities of deprivation across Appalachia, the report noted, were reflected in measures of income, housing, education, and employment. The lack of urbanization and years of exploitation of natural resources without a return of wealth to local communities had left the region's development "retarded" and unable to support the kinds of "social overhead capital" necessary to succeed in a modern economy. Poor roads, poor schools, inadequate health care, dilapidated housing, insufficient community facilities, and weak institutions were the results of the failure of the normal process of development in Appalachia, what the report called "a record of insufficiency—a history of traditional acts not performed, of American patterns not fulfilled."[53]

To redress this legacy of neglect, PARC proposed that "a coordinated and adequately funded and sustained effort" be undertaken to restore the region's economic vitality. The commission recommended action on a regional investment strategy in four priority areas and proposed the creation of a permanent agency to implement the effort. Emphasizing the need for simultaneous investment in both human and economic resource development, PARC called for legislation to increase access to and within the region, establish programs to more fully utilize the region's natural resources, construct facilities to control and exploit the abundant rainfall of Appalachia, and create programs to provide immediate improvements in human resources. A comprehensive approach to the region's problems was necessary. "Only a balanced, coordinated series of programs," it emphasized, "can achieve the goals of this Commission and of the region."[54]

Included among the PARC proposals were recommendations for a major Appalachian development highway system, regional airports, flood control and sewage management facilities, programs for pasture improvement and cooperative timber marketing, recreational tourism development, research into coal utilization and power production, and funds for vocational schools, health centers, and housing. The report looked to pending antipoverty legislation to expand programs in job training, secondary education, adult literacy, medical care, nutrition, and other human services, but it requested additional funding for these special programs in Appalachia. To coordinate these efforts, PARC called for the creation of a new independent agency, the Appalachian Regional Commission (ARC), which would organize state, federal, and private efforts to develop the region, encourage multistate collaboration, and foster local community development and planning.

Experience had shown, the report concluded, that "the unique tangle of problems in Appalachia call for a uniquely tailored program and that neither the States alone nor the Federal Government alone are adequate to this challenge which involves them both so closely." Rather than recommending a single plan for Appalachia, therefore, the commission proposed immediate actions to "attack the central strands of the regional knot" and a mechanism for suggesting new actions and developing new programs in the future. "In the years ahead," the report observed, "the Appalachian program will be many programs, unified only by their singleness of focus: the introduction of Appalachia and its people into fully active membership in the American society."[55]

To assure continuity of effort between the submission of the report by PARC and congressional action to establish the new commission, PARC recommended that the organization of state and federal agency representatives created to draft the report itself continue. Prior to the establishment of a new unit, the PARC staff would sustain cooperation, further inventory the region's resources, and prepare detailed plans for the new development highway system, new water projects, training programs, and other public facilities. Consequently, Sweeney, Whisman, Harry Boswell of Maryland, Paul Crabtree of West Virginia, and other core staff continued to refine the program even while the proposed legislation was being debated on Capitol Hill.

Shortly after the release of the PARC report, President Johnson fulfilled President Kennedy's promise to visit Appalachia and to meet again with the Appalachian governors. On the afternoon of April 24, 1964, the president flew to Huntington, West Virginia, and greeted a delegation that included Governors Breathitt and Barron, Senators Jennings Randolph and Robert Byrd of West Virginia, Senator John

Sherman Cooper of Kentucky, U.S. Representative Carl Perkins of Kentucky, and U.S. Representative Ken Hechler of West Virginia. The trip was hastily arranged after Johnson suddenly decided to rally support for his War on Poverty by making two "poverty trips" to publicize the need for pending legislation. The first trip included stops in the Midwest, Pittsburgh, and central Appalachia and provided an opportunity to meet with the Appalachian governors who had been pressing him to follow up on the PARC report. Undertaken as a strategy to gain political ground for his own antipoverty program and to fulfill a promise by his predecessor, the trip to Appalachia changed Johnson's perspective on the region and energized his own commitment to passing an Appalachian bill.

From the Huntington airport, the First Family's entourage traveled by helicopter to eastern Kentucky, where the president and Mrs. Johnson saw mountain poverty firsthand. Near Inez, in Martin County, they sat on the porch of an unemployed sawmill worker with eight children who survived on an income of four hundred dollars a year. In Paintsville they toured a job training facility for unemployed miners. Along the highway they greeted hundreds of schoolchildren, many in neat but well-worn clothes. The sights of poverty—barren and stripped hillsides, dilapidated housing, and poor roads—moved the president, and he promised to help the people of the mountains to become part of the Great Society. "We are not going to be satisfied," he told a crowd on the courthouse steps in Paintsville, "until we have driven poverty underground, until we have found jobs for our people. We are not going to be satisfied until our people have decent housing, until our aged folks have medical care, until our people have equal rights."[56]

The next day Johnson concluded his visit by meeting with the Council of Appalachian Governors in Huntington. Governors Tawes of Maryland, Sanders of Georgia, Sanford of North Carolina, Clement of Tennessee, and Harrison of Virginia joined Governors Breathitt and Barron in pressing the president for the Appalachian program. Only Governors George Wallace of Alabama and William Scranton of Pennsylvania were absent, and Governor Scranton had privately spoken to Johnson in favor of the bill at a Washington function a few days before. The president had come to Huntington to gather the governors' support for his antipoverty legislation, but, according to John Sweeney, his attempts to talk about the War on Poverty were repeatedly shunted aside by the "unequivocal chirping" of the governors for the Appalachian program.[57] Finally, the president declared his support for the Appalachian bill, but he wanted to delay any formal announcement until after the House Education and Labor Committee reported favorably on the Economic Opportunity Act (EOA), the antipoverty legislation. "No one expects," Johnson told reporters as he left for Washington, "that this curse of centuries [poverty] can be wiped out in a few days or a few weeks or a few years. . . . But we intend to set the people of this region out on a bright highway of hope. . . . I hope to send a message to Congress in a few days to implement this program."[58]

The administration delivered the Appalachian Regional Development Act (ARDA) to the Hill three days later, on April 28, 1964, but in the ensuing months, the act continued to flounder in the shadows of the War on Poverty and election-year politics. Sweeney and the PARC staff began to prepare draft legislation soon after the release of the PARC report. On the plane back to Washington after his meeting with the Appalachian governors, Johnson instructed Sweeney to work with Charles Schultze from the Bureau of the Budget to prepare an acceptable bill. Schultze had been part of Walter Heller's original poverty discussion group and was concerned about both the scale and structure of the regional program. Sweeney assured the president that any legislation for Appalachia would concentrate, for the most part, on highways and infrastructure and would not interfere with any part of the poverty program currently before Congress.[59]

To avoid confusion with the EOA, the ARDA was submitted to the Senate and House public works committees rather than to the education and labor committees then considering the antipoverty legislation. The House began hearings on the bill in early May and the Senate in mid-June, but by July progress toward a vote had stalled. Both the House and the Senate were preoccupied in June and July with debates on the EOA and the Civil Rights Act and later with the political conventions and campaigns of the 1964 election. As the summer dragged on, supporters of the ARDA grew nervous that further delay would weaken the bill by opening the door to attacks from special interests.

The ARDA of 1964 contained most of the recommendations of the PARC report, and opponents of the bill quickly focused on familiar criticisms: the structure of the new commission gave the federal government too much power in state affairs; the commission duplicated other federal programs and competed with private interests; there was no provision for generating public power for regional development; the program discriminated against other regions with conditions similar to those of Appalachia; and it would benefit more prosperous urban areas of the mountains as well as impoverished rural populations. Sweeney and other administration spokespersons were able to counter most of the criticisms by pointing to the uniqueness of the Appalachian problem, the need for region-wide planning, and the collaborative-federalist nature of the new commission, but one challenge proved more difficult.

The PARC report had recommended the creation of a federally chartered, mixed-ownership corporation to provide access to private money for local development projects. Although the Johnson administration supported the recommendation, many in Congress opposed it because it would have created a semi-independent agency outside normal legislative review. Many Republicans, moreover, objected to this proposed Appalachian development fund on the grounds that it unconstitutionally required government to become a stockholder in a private corporation. Indeed, Governor Scranton of Pennsylvania, a Republican, while strongly supporting the other recommendations of the PARC report, refused to sign the letter of transmittal by the Council of Appalachian Governors at the beginning of the report and instead submitted his own letter of endorsement, opposing the mixed-ownership corporation.[60] Many in Congress also opposed this concept on the ground that "funds should be provided through legislative appropriation channels subject to congressional oversight" rather than through a permanent, independent corporation.[61] Eventually, the administration dropped the development corporation idea, leaving the subsequent agency perpetually dependent on congressional reauthorization for funding.

To boost congressional support for the bill, the Johnson administration expanded the region to be served by the ARDA, adding Ohio and South Carolina to the original nine states covered by the PARC report. Ohio governor James Rhodes originally opposed his state's participation in the program, preferring a heavy investment of state funds for highways and other improvements in the Ohio Appalachian counties to federal intervention. Encouraged to reconsider by fellow Republican Scranton and by growing pressure from Ohio's congressional delegation and from local officials in southeast Ohio, Rhodes acquiesced. South Carolina under Governor Ernest Hollings also had declined to participate in the Council of Appalachian Governors, but its new governor, Donald Russell, requested that the state be added to the ARDA in June, and the president eagerly agreed.

Despite bipartisan support, however, the ARDA languished in the House because of opposition from representatives from outside Appalachia who questioned the wisdom of favoring development in one geographic region over another. Congress eventually passed the EOA on August 7, 1964, launching the War on Poverty, and on September 25 the Senate passed its version of the ARDA, but the Eighty-eighth Congress adjourned sine die on October 3, without action on the Appalachian bill in the House. The fate of the ARDA now lay in the fall elections, with the hope for a more favorable environment for regional development legislation in the House. To sustain the work of the PARC staff until the next session of Congress, President Johnson issued an executive order in late October establishing the Federal Development Planning Committee for Appalachia. Following Johnson's landslide victory in November, this committee prepared revised legislation to submit early in the new year.

On January 6, 1965, the ARDA was reintroduced in the Eighty-ninth Congress as Senate bill 3. Now a top priority for the Johnson administration, the bill emerged from the Senate Environment and Public Works Committee by the end of the month, and it passed the full Senate on February 1 with only minor amendments. Bipartisan, widespread support eased the bill through the Senate. Jennings Randolph of West Virginia, the bill's chief sponsor, chaired the committee hearings and received strong support on the floor from Republican Hugh Scott of Pennsylvania and from Robert Kennedy, the late president's brother. As a result of Pennsylvania's interest in mine reclamation, $20 million in special funding was added to the bill for the restoration of abandoned coal lands, and Senator Kennedy attached a provision allowing fourteen contiguous counties in New York to join the new commission.

In the House, the new Democratic majority acted quickly to vote the act out of committee on February 17, and, despite an attempt by opponents to recommit, the ARDA passed the House on March 3 by a vote of 257–165. To reassure House and Senate supporters still concerned about providing preferential treatment for Appalachia, the administration promised to support the creation of similar regional development programs for other areas of the country that suffered from economic distress. Proponents also argued that the bill represented "a redress of basic past shortcomings of federal spending policies in the Appalachian region" and that the special expenditures in Appalachia would benefit the entire nation, not just the participating states themselves.[62] On March 9, 1965, less than a week after its passage in the House, President Johnson signed the ARDA into law.

The bill as enacted by the Eighty-ninth Congress included most of the recommendations of the PARC and was similar to the bill that had emerged from committee hearings in 1964, with a few important exceptions. Adding three states to the program resulted in the addition of five hundred miles to the local access roads program. The pasture improvement program, which had come under attack from midwestern members of Congress, was eliminated, as was the controversial Appalachian development corporation. The program for timber development was modified to limit planning and resource management services to nonprofit organizations so as not to compete with the existing timber industry. The secretary of the army was instructed to prepare a comprehensive plan for the development of water resources in the Appalachian region, and the secretary of agriculture was asked to convene an interagency federal task force for the purpose of recommending a long-range program for the reclamation and rehabilitation of strip- and surface-mined areas.

One small change was almost overlooked in the 1965 hearings, but it would have significant ramifications for the infant commission. Following the failure of the act to pass the House in October 1964, PARC director John Sweeney and Charles Schultze from the Bureau of the Budget added a sentence to the introductory paragraph of the 1965 ARDA declaring that "public investments made in the region under this Act shall be concentrated in areas where there is a significant potential for future growth, and where the expected return on public dollars invested will be the greatest." Federal representatives and some economists had discussed this "growth center" strategy during the initial meetings of the PARC, but state representatives and their governors who wanted greater flexibility in the distribution of development funds rejected the idea almost universally. Sweeney and Schultze, however, strongly believed that there would never be enough federal money to address the many problems of such a vast region and that political support in Congress would be stronger if resources were concentrated in less distressed areas of potential growth. An unpublished report commissioned by PARC from the Phantis Corporation also pointed to the difficulties of attracting industries to rural areas of Appalachia, which lacked basic infrastructure and human capital.[63] Although it was ignored in the rush to secure enactment, this addition to the ARDA would open a recurring debate among policy makers in the early years of the ARC and would prove to be one of the more divisive issues facing the regional partnership.

Concern about different strategies for development, however, was far from the minds of those who gathered in the Rose Garden on March 9 to witness the signing of the ARDA. For some in attendance—like John Whisman, Bert Combs, Harry Boswell, and Millard Tawes—the event was the culmination of five years of political negotiations at the state and federal levels. Conceived in the hopes and frustrations of a few Appalachian leaders, the idea for a regional commission was nurtured by intellectuals, planners, and state officials as a way to encourage cooperation and planning in a region long typified by government neglect and aimless growth. Others at the event were impressed by the unique ARC partnership, and they saw the commission as a prototype for a nationwide policy of strategic regional development, one that might link the greater resources of state and federal governments to the self-defined needs of local communities. Everyone hoped that the ARDA marked the dawn of a new era of national commitment to the problems of rural communities and distressed people.

As he signed the Appalachian bill, President Johnson observed that the objectives of the act were important, but its origins were equally significant. "Originated by the Governors of the Appalachian states, formed in close cooperation with the Federal Executive, approved and enacted by the Congress of all the people, this," he observed, "is the truest example of creative federalism in our times." Pointing to the low per capita incomes, high poverty rates, low education levels, and heavy dependence on public assistance that plagued many Appalachian communities, the president acknowledged the challenges facing the new commission. "The bill that I will now sign will work no miracles overnight. Whether it works at all depends not upon the Federal Government alone, but the states and local governments as well." Of all the legislative measures that he had received from Congress since becoming president, he concluded, "this measure today may well outlive others in its lasting contribution to the well being of our nation."[64]

Passing the ARDA and the EOA marked a watershed for Appalachia and set the stage for government-sponsored intervention in the mountains for decades to come. Both initiatives were part of Johnson's blueprint for a Great Society that would extend the benefits of modern life to all Americans. As such, they mirrored the best intentions of a generation confident of its accomplishments and ready to apply scientific knowledge to the problems of the disadvantaged. "In your time," Johnson told the graduates of the University of Michigan in May 1964, "we have the opportunity to move not only toward the rich society and the powerful society, but upward to the Great Society . . . a place where men are more concerned with the quality of their goals than the quantity of their goods."[65] A month earlier, the president had assured the people of Appalachia that the Great Society would not only bring jobs and higher incomes but the promise of dignity and opportunity as well.[66]

Conceived of idealism and compromise, the War on Poverty and the ARC were a mixture of popular ideas wrapped in the vagaries of the national politics and intellectual trends of their day. Both combined moral concern for the poor, practical expediency, and political self-interest to create a venue for change. Always a complex individual, Johnson himself reflected the multiple personalities that shaped the antipoverty agenda. The president clearly believed that he could use the power of his office to improve the lives of marginalized Americans. He was moved by the poverty he witnessed in Appalachia, but he also recognized the political value of hope and government largesse in an election year. Both of his "poverty trips" during the spring of 1964, undertaken to gather support for the EOA, were carefully orchestrated to maximize political benefits and to reassure local Democrats that fighting poverty would be good for them and for the economy.[67] Johnson was an ardent New Dealer, and his faith in the ability of economic growth to reduce the levels of poverty was matched only by his confidence in the capacity of government to produce growth. For postwar liberals there was nothing fundamentally wrong with the political and economic system that new roads, schools, and other public infrastructure could not correct.

Appalachia provided the ideal proving ground for this vision. Having played an important role in the rediscovery of poverty in America during the early 1960s, the region became the symbol of America's crusade to eliminate poverty after 1964. It was Homer Bigart's exposé of the plight of eastern Kentucky coal miners that moved John Kennedy to instruct his staff to prepare specific antipoverty legislation, and it was to central Appalachia that Lyndon Johnson came to dramatize that initiative. Certainly the roots of the War on Poverty were intertwined with the civil rights movement, urban decay, presidential politics, and the rising influence of social scientists in government, but Appalachia, with its contradictory images of American otherness, was at the center of that campaign. When asked whether the War on Poverty was designed specifically to help urban blacks, Adam Yarmolinsky, a key advisor to Kennedy and Johnson, commented that administration planners in 1963 paid less attention to the problems of the ghettoes than to Appalachia. "Color it Appalachian," he concluded, "if you are going to color it anything at all."[68]

As the antipoverty programs unfolded, moreover, Appalachia increasingly became the yardstick against which to measure government success in the War on Poverty. Not only was Appalachia on the front lines for the EOA, but it was also the only American region to receive a special program for infrastructure development. Consequently, media coverage of the region intensified between 1965 and 1968 as national correspondents flocked to the mountains to describe the battlefield and follow the poverty warriors up the hollows and into the fray. Broadcast journalists joined their print counterparts in utilizing Appalachia as a regular setting for commentary about the other America. Some decried the inadequate incomes of the region and criticized the new programs for not providing sufficient jobs. Others disparaged the government efforts for not attacking the "culture of mountain poverty."[69] Almost all saw the region as a burden on an otherwise progressive nation.

Such accounts transposed Appalachia into a marketable media commodity and helped to establish a pattern of critical but superficial commentary that would sustain the image of Appalachia as a problem area for years to come. Even after the War on Poverty collapsed in 1972, periodic investigations of conditions in the mountains continued as standard fare for television, newspaper, and magazine editors. The ARC survived, but it became the subject of regular criticism as a symbol of political boondoggling and the government's failure to drive poverty from its door.

The intellectual and political currents that came together in the EOA and the ARC helped to focus national attention on Appalachia, but media sketches and government programs rarely addressed many of the underlying problems of the region. Bothered by the idea of poverty in an affluent society and confident that planning and economic growth could overcome the lack of material goods and transform a backward culture, correspondents and policy makers seldom questioned the equity of politics and economic relationships within the region. Poverty in Appalachia, they believed, was simply out of step with the rest of America and could be conquered by government investments in public infrastructure to open up markets and by the extension of opportunities for the poor to join the cultural mainstream.

3

DEVELOPING THE POOR

It is difficult to separate the War on Poverty from the effusive confidence that permeated American society in the 1960s. Faith in the ability of economic expansion to produce abundance and a more equitable, just society seemed inherently logical. For a generation that had overcome the Depression, conquered fascism, and harnessed unprecedented technology, the future was brimming with opportunity. Lyndon Johnson hoped to tap this energy for change to extend the promise of American abundance to everyone, even those marginalized by race and class in urban ghettoes and by the accident of birth in rural places like Appalachia. Although much of Johnson's Great Society legislation was aimed at the educated middle class, with initiatives such as National Public Radio, endowments for the arts and humanities, land conservation, automobile safety, highway beautification, consumer protection, federal aid for education, and Medicare, it was the effort to eradicate poverty that reflected the era's highest goals and deepest failures.

Among the academics and policy makers who designed both the War on Poverty and the ARC, confidence in the ability of American society to build a more perfect world was deeply rooted in experience and faith. The triumph of wartime mobilization, the successful postwar reconstruction of Europe and Japan, and, above all, the unparalleled expansion of prosperity at home had convinced a generation of intellectuals that the American dream was not only possible but perhaps now widely attainable. The mass poverty of the Great Depression had been replaced by mass accumulation; Americans, in the words of postwar historian David Potter, had become a "people of plenty."[1] In the internationally competitive environment of the cold war, the nation's steady growth in personal income and consumption appeared to confirm the popular consensus that American capitalism had found the path to abundance.

Within this ideology of certainty, there was no place for poverty and little excuse for economic failure. Prosperity, it was widely believed, was now the promise, if not the norm, for the majority of Americans. Among a growing cadre of intellectuals, scarcity became an anomaly, a "paradox" of the marginalized few. The minority poor were a separate group from most Americans, a "self-contained, culturally deprived social group." Depressed areas of the country were now "poverty pockets" that rising affluence had left behind.[2] This "other America" lacked access to the opportunities (education, jobs, etc.) that had allowed the rest of the nation to prosper. Isolated in ghettoes and rural enclaves, poor people lacked the skills and motivation necessary to get ahead in modern society. Increasingly, poverty was viewed as a deviant condition, the result of the deficits of poor people and poor places themselves, rather than as the product of inequities fostered by society or economic modernization. That millions of unskilled workers had been displaced by the same mechanization that produced the affordable goods of the consumer age was seen not as a structural flaw in the market economy but as an unfortunate by-product of progress and growth.

Even the most liberal economists of the 1960s viewed poverty as a deviation from the norm, something that would eventually be eliminated by continuous growth   by the late 1950s had accepted the Ke growth. National wealth, th that lifted all boats. Indeed, J of American opulence, *The* panding private wealth in th Harvard economist was mo pursuit of growth had gene tion, pollution, deterioratii with inequality within the s public sector, he reasoned, but eventually eliminate p and other growth theory e nedy White House, where these ideas came to dominate the president's Council of Economic Advisors. Concerned that lingering poverty and unemployment were signs of a stagnating market, they believed that stimulating the economy rather than attacking poverty was the administration's number one problem.

It would fall to a new generation of social scientists to raise concern for economic inequality to the level of a national movement. Influenced by the same political, economic, and cultural changes that shaped postwar economic theory, social scientists in the two decades after World War II also came to view poverty as an anomaly, but rather than linking this abnormality to flaws in the American system, they found the roots of poverty in the culture and social psychology of the poor themselves. This new "poverty knowledge" was an outgrowth of the reorganization and expansion of the social sciences in the 1940s, especially the emergence of applied behavioral science theories that placed greater emphasis on individual performance and on the application of scientific knowledge to a wide range of human social problems. Postwar behavioral scientists professed to provide insights into human motivation that offered all-too-easy solutions for enlightened policy makers concerned with developing the "human capital" necessary for modern economic growth.[3] The behavioral sciences not only supplied a politically acceptable explanation for the "paradox" of poverty—the poor themselves were to blame—they also offered strategies for altering this destructive behavior without resorting to redistribution of wealth or to significant structural reform.

In the minds of cold war–era social scientists, moreover, the presence of poverty in the middle of affluent America was more than just a temporary consequence of economic stagnation. Persistent poverty challenged the optimistic assumptions that underlay the affluent society—the premise that the American path to affluence would eventually produce a unified, classless, and rich society. As Michael Harrington put it, the poor constituted a "separate culture, another nation, a way of life." With the poor unable to participate in the affluence, their numbers were not diminishing as the economy grew. "They are a different kind of people," he wrote. "They think differently; they look upon a different America than the one the rest of us look upon."[4] For activist intellectuals such as

Harrington, the presence of the other America was an embarrassment and a threat to the larger society itself. Bringing these forgotten Americans into the mainstream, they argued, was the preeminent challenge facing their generation, and this, they admonished, would require a broad-based government initiative to redeem the poor.

These two strains of postwar thought—economic growth theory and human capital theory—would come together in the design of the War on Poverty and provide a conceptual framework for government intervention strategies toward Appalachia. Although none of the major crafters of the War on Poverty were from the region or had any extensive knowledge of it, popular images of Appalachia rooted deep in the nation's consciousness predisposed Great Society policy makers to identify Appalachia as "deviant" and thus as a prime target in the antipoverty campaign. Though the region had long been perceived as an economic and cultural backwater, "a land where time stood still," its otherness could now be eliminated, they assumed, through development and assimilation into the mainstream.

Once defined as part of the "other America," Appalachia became a pawn in a great national experiment that sought to eradicate poverty without confronting the specific institutional and economic structures that abused the region in the first place. The catalyst for that experiment was the Office of Economic Opportunity (OEO), and although it was short lived and conceived to fight national perceptions of poverty and its causes, the OEO brought hope and empowerment to millions in Appalachia, fueling a nascent regional identity and stirring the waters of resistance in ways its designers did not envision.

When President Johnson announced the antipoverty initiative in his State of the Union address on January 8, 1964, the War on Poverty was a proclamation without a plan. The president's Council of Economic Advisors, under Walter Heller, had drafted a limited proposal for "widening participation in prosperity" through a series of demonstration projects in selected American cities, but Johnson had rejected the plan as being too timid for his vision. The new president wanted something that could define his presidency and make his mark before the approaching 1964 elections, something, he told Heller, that would be "big and bold and hit the nation with real impact."[5] He wasn't interested in demonstration programs; he wanted a poverty project in every community, and he wanted to make the initiative the centerpiece of his Great Society.

The task of designing a strategy for the poverty campaign fell to Kennedy brother-in-law and head of the Peace Corps Sargent Shriver. By tapping Shriver to head the initiative, Johnson not only tied the crusade to the memory of the slain president but gained the support of the Kennedy faithful and the northeastern intellectuals who had been calling for government action on behalf of the poor. Shriver had turned the Peace Corps into one of the most successful programs of the Kennedy era, and he had a longtime personal interest in volunteerism, youth, and juvenile delinquency, issues that the president initially saw as the core of the antipoverty program.[6] Like President Johnson, Shriver had an enthusiasm for challenges and an indefatigable commitment to work, and after his appointment on February 1, he immediately convened a task force to build on the recommendations already made by the Council of Economic Advisors. Working quickly, he organized a series of seminars and informal discussions that brought together a variety of idealistic young bureaucrats and leading academic experts on poverty. The task force completed its work within six weeks and sent the omnibus EOA to Congress on March 16, 1964.

The hastily designed proposal called for the annual expenditure of almost a billion dollars on a package of ten disparate and mostly untested programs. The initiative combined an assortment of strategies that reflected both the political heritage of the New Deal and the new social science theories of the postwar period. Much of the act focused government resources on workforce development and on helping poor youth to break the "cycle of poverty." Title I of the legislation, for example, established the Job Corps, modeled after the Depression-era Civilian Conservation Corps, which was designed to provide education and vocational training in rural conservation camps for disadvantaged urban youth. More than just a federal job program, however, the Job Corps, headed by university administrator Otis Singletary, was also an educational program aimed at teaching underprivileged youth the behaviors needed to get jobs in the new economy. The act also created the Neighborhood Youth Corps to offer community-based training and work experience for young people living at home and established a work-study program to help low-income college students remain in school. Similarly, the bill made funds available to the states to set up programs for unemployed fathers of needy children to gain work experience and job training. Favoring education over federal job creation, the EOA sought to change the behavior of the poor rather than to provide direct transfer payments that would leave them permanently dependent on the government for survival. It offered a "hand up" rather than a "hand out," as Johnson put it.

To develop the capacity of the poor to help themselves and to coordinate community services to combat poverty, the act called for the establishment of community action agencies (CAAs) run by local people, including the poor themselves. The idea of community action was at the core of the earlier Council of Economic Advisors' recommendations and consumed more than half of the new antipoverty budget. CAAs were intended to serve as the vehicles for quickly and directly channeling federal funds into local neighborhoods across the country. These nonprofit agencies would prioritize community needs and receive grants for a wide range of education and cultural enrichment projects, including adult literacy, health services, legal aid for the poor, and child development programs such as Head Start. To assist in organizing antipoverty projects and to provide direct training services, the act created a domestic volunteer service corps, Volunteers in Service to America (VISTA), patterned after Shriver's Peace Corps. Finally, the bill established the OEO to administer grants and to direct the effort.[7]

Although the EOA included a number of manpower development components long favored by liberal Democrats to retrain unemployed workers for jobs in a growing economy, the heart of the act lay in the process of community action. Not surprisingly, however, there was little agreement about what "community action" meant, and in the rush to formulate a plan, the idea came to represent different things to politicians, bureaucrats, and intellectuals. Almost everyone believed that the antipoverty campaign should be waged at the local level by local people rather than administered from Washington, but there was little understanding of how that strategy would work in practice. Johnson initially believed that the attack on poverty would concentrate on education and vocational training for inner-city and rural youths, and he saw community action as connecting parents, teachers, and other professionals in the task of educating children, after the pattern of FDR's National Youth Administration. Officials in the Bureau of the Budget and in other cabinet agencies thought of community action simply as an efficient mechanism to coordinate the delivery of antipoverty services, synchronizing a multitude of state and federal programs. Most academics saw the concept as an opportunity to reorganize the poor community around modern, middle-class values and structures.[8]

The idea of community action blended a number of theories of government planning and social engineering that had been evolving throughout the twentieth century, but it owed much to the intellectual changes taking place in the social sciences in the postwar era. The application of social science theories of community development to the problems of the inner cities, for example, provided a model for fighting poverty on a national scale (rather than case by case) that appealed to the drafters of the antipoverty program. Sociologists at the University of Chicago had long utilized their city as a microcosm of the larger society, and in the 1920s and 1930s they developed a theory of community disorganization to explain the persistence of poverty in the Chicago slums. The problems of the inner city, they argued, were environmental, the results of the dislocation of workers and weak community organizations that in turn produced alienation and hopelessness. Rather than concentrating eleemosynary resources on individual uplift, as had been the practice in traditional settlement house casework, the Chicago scholars urged social workers to focus their energies on building organizational connections that would improve the opportunities of the poor as a group. Low-income people, they suggested, lacked the organizational skills of the middle class to exert pressure on politicians, coordinate community services, and discipline themselves. The way to assimilate these poor, often immigrant populations into the mainstream was to assist them in developing the appropriate behaviors and institutions that made for successful communities.

Much of the field research of the Chicago school sociologists focused on the link between poverty and juvenile delinquency, since the latter seemed to represent a perfect example of the failure of community organizations to provide opportunities and discipline for young people. As national concern about urban crime and delinquency began to mount after World War II, social science research increasingly linked poverty and delinquency with community disorganization and urged public and private programs to expand community improvement efforts, aimed now at a new group of immigrants—Hispanics, southern blacks, and Appalachian migrants. In the late 1950s, the Ford Foundation launched an experimental project based on the Chicago model to revitalize slum areas and to increase employment opportunities for youth in four major cities and in rural areas of North Carolina. Under the leadership of Paul Ylvisaker, the Gray Areas Program helped to sponsor community development projects planned and implemented by local neighborhood organizations. Ylvisaker believed that these projects could demonstrate effective strategies of organizing poor people and poor communities to help themselves. Ford also sponsored a series of workshops, coordinated by the CSM, to educate law enforcement and social service agencies about the particular problems of Appalachian migrants in Chicago and other midwestern cities.

After the 1960 presidential election, many of the young activist intellectuals associated with the Gray Areas Program followed John Kennedy to Washington, and they carried the idea of community action with them to new positions in the federal government, especially on the staff of Attorney General Robert Kennedy. In 1961, at the request of the attorney general, John Kennedy created the President's Committee on Juvenile Delinquency and Youth Crime, headed by Robert Kennedy's college roommate David Hackett. Hackett and his staff quickly turned to the Ford Foundation for help in establishing demonstration projects to reduce delinquency. The committee launched a number of projects that applied the principles of the Gray Areas Program to the coordination of services for youth. At least two committee grants went to projects started by the Ford Foundation, in New York and New Haven, but the initiative suffered from limited funding, and Hackett was continuously frustrated by the absence of cooperation from other federal agencies. Several of these projects proved to be politically controversial because of their practice of "indigenous" participation, but Hackett believed that the idea of community action itself offered promise for attacking not only juvenile delinquency but also the larger problem of poverty itself. When Heller invited Hackett and other members of his team to participate in his antipoverty discussions in 1963, Justice Department staffers seized the opportunity to expand the lessons of community action onto a larger stage.

In the absence of any other comprehensive strategy to attack poverty and with the apparent endorsement of the new social science community, "Hackett's guerrillas," as the Justice staff came to be called, aggressively projected community action to the center of Heller's antipoverty proposal. Although few of the economists and bureaucrats on the poverty working group understood the implications of the strategy, the process of attacking poverty by coordinating local agencies and organizing local people appeared to be cost effective and politically sound. Most of Johnson's advisors, including the director of the Bureau of the Budget, Kermit Gordon—another former employee of the Ford Foundation—believed that community action would be administered through agencies of local government.[9] Even Shriver, who initially had reservations about the concept, saw the local CAAs as being "composed of distinguished people" who could "speak out on behalf of the poor" to elected officials.[10]

In reality, the concept of community action encompassed a range of strategies designed to assimilate the poor into the mainstream of American society. Some proponents saw the process as one of institutional change, helping to reorganize government services to open new opportunities for individuals to succeed within the existing system. Other, more radical strategists saw community action as a way to bypass conservative local governments and empower the poor to take charge of their own communities through political organizing. While some saw community action in terms of cultural rehabilitation, resident involvement, and top-down change, others advocated bottom-up strategies of resident control and empowerment. Most proponents of bottom-up change, especially those in the Justice Department, believed that CAAs controlled by the poor themselves were the only way to circumvent segregationist attempts in the South to set up all-white poverty programs.

One of the most ardent voices for empowering the poor was that of Richard Boone, who had worked for the Ford Foundation's Gray Areas Program before becoming an aide to Hackett's committee on juvenile delinquency and a member of Shriver's antipoverty task force.

Boone so persistently repeated the phrase "maximum feasible partici-pation" of the poor at task force meetings that it was eventually in-cluded in the language of the bill. A native of Louisville, Kentucky, Boone held degrees from the University of Chicago and had worked as a Cook County, Illinois, police officer before joining Paul Ylvisaker at Ford. Steeped in the Chicago school of community organizing, he was a protégé of Chicago social activist and labor advocate Saul Alinsky, who had been organizing stockyard workers on the South Side of Chi-cago since the 1930s. Unlike most of his university colleagues, who saw community organizing as a means of educating and assimilating the poor, Alinsky believed that the problems of the poor were essen-tially political and began organizing workers to pressure authorities for better municipal services. In the early 1960s, Alinsky took his grassroots style of political organizing into the black community of Woodlawn, where his model of resident participation challenged offi-cial control of welfare policies and programs to serve the poor.[11]

Boone shared the belief that people were poor because they lacked political power, and he insisted that the CAAs of the War on Poverty include the "maximum feasible participation of residents of the areas and members of the groups served" to assure grassroots control. Other poverty ideologues in the Justice Department shared Boone's fear of "establishment" control of CAAs, especially in the segregationist South, and they were encouraged when Shriver appointed Jack Con-way, a former Chicago labor organizer, as director of the Community Action division of the OEO. Conway had served as administrative as-sistant to United Auto Workers president Walter Reuther and shared Boone's commitment to organizing for political action. Boone subse-quently became director of policy and programming in the new Com-munity Action division.

Although empowering the poor became the mantra for a few key administrators within the OEO, most of the thinkers and planners who launched the War on Poverty initially saw community action as an organizational mechanism to improve service delivery and rehabili-tate the poor into mainstream culture. Most liberal reformers of the period assumed that the poor lacked only the skills and behaviors nec-essary to succeed in modern society. What the disadvantaged needed to lift themselves out of poverty, they believed, were education and opportunity, not political confrontation. The deficiencies of the poor could be addressed through behavior modification and job training programs rather than by the redistribution of wealth or political restructuring.

The assumption that poverty resulted from natural circumstances or the lack of personal motivation was deeply rooted in the American myth, but in the years following World War II, new behavioral science research added the proposition that poverty might be the product of certain cultural factors as well. Scholars had long recognized the cultural differences between "traditional" and "modern" societies and, in the early years of the century, had begun to document the folkways of American regions and minority groups. After the war some anthropologists developed the idea that certain group folkways, out of place in modern society, could also produce a "culture of poverty," passed from one generation to another, that kept entire populations of people in cycles of despair. For a postwar generation of intellectuals confident in the primacy of middle-class values and in the benefits of modernization, the culture of poverty theory offered a convenient explanation for government to act as an agent of acculturation.

Emerging from the work of anthropologist Oscar Lewis, the culture of poverty model became a widely accepted explanation in the 1960s for the "underdevelopment" of certain "third world" societies and, by extension, of impoverished populations within the United States. In two best-selling books, *The Children of Sanchez* (1961) and *La Vida* (1966), Lewis argued that people from "primitive" cultures were not inferior to modern people; they just lacked the skills, habits, and attitudes necessary to achieve success in the modern world. Their traditional cultures perpetuated apathy, divisiveness, and resignation and reproduced underdevelopment rather than integration into the modern, market economy. Lewis identified a long list of deviant psychological traits that were perpetuated by the family within these cultures and prevented children from breaking out of poverty. In addition to jobs and job training, he suggested, programs of cultural intervention were required if the children of poor families were to take full advantage of changing conditions and opportunities in their lifetimes.[12]

Although Lewis's research was based on fieldwork with families in Mexico and Puerto Rico, other scholars applied the culture of poverty theory universally to the poor, including to southern blacks who had migrated to northern ghettoes and pockets of hillbilly poverty in Appalachia and the Ozarks. In 1962 North Carolina sociologist Rupert Vance wrote that the physical isolation that had created a distinct culture in Appalachia now was in danger of producing "a permanent culture of poverty" in the mountains unless the government intervened to raise the "goals and aspirations of the people."[13] That same year Michael Harrington utilized the model in *The Other America* to suggest that the poor were like an "underdeveloped nation" within the United States.[14] This tendency to think about the poor as part of the third world not only allowed policy makers to see poverty as a universal condition that could be overcome by American-style "development" but also displaced responsibility for poverty onto the culture of the poor themselves. Later generations of scholars would reject the culture of poverty model as blaming the victim, but the theory played a powerful role in shaping many of the antipoverty programs of the late twentieth century.

Lewis, Harrington, and other leading advocates of the culture of poverty participated in the Shriver planning meetings to design the War on Poverty, and almost every program administered by the OEO reflected the theory. The Job Corps, for example, although it was one of the administration's few concessions to calls for a massive job training program, was essentially an education program whose primary goal was to teach young people how to apply for jobs. Senior Johnson administration officials referred to OEO employment programs like the Job Corps and state-sponsored efforts like Kentucky's "Happy Pappy" program for unemployed fathers as "our charm school" because they were based on assumptions "that people who didn't fit the established culture didn't get jobs."[15] Educational programs such as Head Start, after-school enrichment, VISTA, and homemaker skills training were designed to change the behavior of families, raise the expectations of youth, and prepare adults for jobs in the new economy. Even the participation of the poor in CAAs was deemed by many OEO administrators as just another tool to acculturate the poor into the value system and behaviors of the middle class, since most CAAs, they assumed, would be operated under the aegis of the local government.[16]

The culture of poverty model fit the popular idea of Appalachia flawlessly. Not only was mountain culture considered to be a remnant of the American past, but now the region's socioeconomic problems also could be attributed to that backward culture. After all, according to popular myth, the region was inhabited by old-stock Americans who, in the words of British historian Arnold Toynbee, had simply "acquired civilization and then lost it."[17] For many intellectuals and poverty warriors of the 1960s, Appalachia needed only to be redeemed from government neglect and geographic isolation. Once the mountaineers were returned to the cultural mainstream, the problem of poverty in the region would be alleviated without any significant restructuring of the political and economic system.

Indeed, one popular monograph distributed to poverty workers throughout Appalachia during the War on Poverty labeled Appalachians as "yesterday's people" and contrasted their anachronistic folk culture with that of modern, middle-class Americans. Written by Jack Weller, a New York–born Presbyterian minister who borrowed heavily from Oscar Lewis's ideas, the book found mountain people to be fatalistic, person oriented, present minded, and individualistic in a world given to reason, accumulation, community organizations, and faith in the future. The "personality" and "general tendencies of behavior in the mountaineer," Weller suggested, had ill prepared the mountain people for life in the modern world. "The greatest challenge of Appalachia, and the most difficult," he claimed, "is its people."[18]

Bolstered by an introduction from sociologist Rupert Vance and a foreword by Appalachian advocate Harry Caudill, the volume implied that "to change the mountains is to change the mountain personality," as Vance put it.[19] Weller himself did not consider the traditional mountain subculture to be wrong, only different, but it was an easy step for readers to conclude that cultural difference was the cause of mountain poverty. Endorsed, moreover, by the CSM and published by the University of Kentucky Press, the monograph linked the academic ideas of the culture of poverty with popular images of Appalachian otherness to provide an intellectual framework for regional uplift programs. Weller's book became a working manual for hundreds of antipoverty warriors and one of the most popular volumes on Appalachia in the 1960s.

As the OEO prepared to launch its assault on poverty in the mountains, it therefore did so from a position narrowed by politics, conflicting strategies, and misguided assumptions. Pressured by political expediency, antipoverty planners turned to untested theories and experimental urban programs to design a universal and practical strategy for change. Denied the option of direct income transfers of wealth to the poor, they relied on the latest academic theories of human capital development to provide a bridge for the assimilation of the poor into the cultural mainstream. Divided over the meanings of community action and local control, they initiated a process for change that pitted disparate forces and incompatible ideas against each other in a volatile environment and in unpredictable times. Initially an important symbol of the paradox of poverty in America, Appalachia became a critical testing ground for academic theories and popular ideas about government intervention on behalf of the poor. Already rent by decades of exploitation, corruption, and greed, the region also became a battleground for the political struggles and the alternative social visions that divided the Great Society itself.

The Eighty-eighth Congress passed the EOA on August 7, 1964, just three months before the presidential election. Staff of the new OEA scrambled to set up programs and channel funds into communities as quickly as possible to maximize the political benefits of the new program before the fall elections, but launching the War on Poverty proved to be a challenge. Early designers of the antipoverty program had proposed to fund a limited number of startup projects and to provide for a lengthier planning and evaluation period, but politics and the massive scale of the billion-dollar national effort demanded swift results. President Johnson had raised awareness of the initiative during his poverty trips the previous April, but planners at the OEO found that organizing the poor to design and submit applications for federal assistance was slow. The agency distributed hundreds of brochures describing the new federal programs and urging local officials to establish CAAs and submit proposals to Washington. When applications dribbled in slowly, the staff turned to conventional organizations and institutions to launch demonstration projects as models for local action.

In Appalachia there was no shortage of service organizations, government planning agencies, and educational institutions eager to take up Washington's challenge on behalf of the poor. For decades the region had drawn the attention of well-meaning missionaries, academics, social workers, philanthropists, and college students intent on understanding and/or resolving the otherness of the mountains. Many of these reformers were connected with each other through the CSM and other organizations that had been calling for government intervention in the region. Now, with the promise of federal funding, this network of people provided a ready vehicle for launching antipoverty initiatives in communities and institutions throughout the mountains. Although some programs of "national emphasis" filtered down from Washington and a few experimental, grassroots projects eventually bubbled up from the bottom, local and state governments, colleges and universities, and other institutions within Appalachia provided the organizational and communication structures for early poverty proposals.

Out of these institutions poured a generation with pent-up energy and idealism that transformed a medley of federal programs into a progressive, moral crusade. Interest in improving Appalachian life had grown among southern educators, church officials, planners, and social service providers since the early 1950s. Convinced of their ability to organize communities, overcome challenges, and uplift people, an army of social change agents swept up the hollows and coves after the passage of the EOA, bringing a flurry of public and private programs designed to address a host of community needs. Within a year, hundreds of CAAs, Head Start programs, job training centers, and other projects had been launched, serving almost every county of the region. Early projects established rural community centers, set up adult education programs, sponsored free health screenings, provided housing rehabilitation, and conducted summer reading programs in rural schools. Since most Appalachian counties qualified for 100 percent federal funding, initial grants were often utilized to hire professional staff whose job it was to manage the local, nonprofit CAA, organize constituencies, and develop new initiatives.

State and local governments across the region were eager to tap into the new source of federal dollars. Some states, like West Virginia, organized CAAs in almost every county to coordinate the delivery of expanded welfare services. Others converted existing economic development councils into nonprofit CAAs or created new, multicounty agencies to develop programs for large rural areas. OEO grants went to local school boards, state councils of churches, and colleges and universities, and the CSM received several grants for region-wide initiatives, including one of the first national demonstration grants for a student voluntary service program, the Appalachian Volunteers. One of the first CAAs funded in North Carolina was WAMY, a four-county antipoverty program in the Blue Ridge created earlier by the North Carolina Fund, an original partner in the Ford Foundation's Gray Areas Program.

Despite having a common source of funding and shared program guidelines from the OEO, this plethora of local programs and structures did not represent any regionally or nationally coordinated strategy to fight poverty in Appalachia. Sargent Shriver's report to the president outlining the War on Poverty had recognized that poverty in Harlan County, Kentucky, was not the same as poverty in Harlem, New York, but "the program's design did nothing to address Appalachian problems as different from those of Harlem."[20] Resembling more a conflagration of scattered assaults and experimental incursions than a well-orchestrated battle, the war to end poverty in the mountains was waged on multiple levels, utilizing different tactics in each community, and it produced a wide range of responses from indigenous people. What gave the campaign a collective momentum and unity of spirit was the moral sense of outrage, hope, and mission that the legislation itself unleashed. For Appalachia, the War on Poverty was as much an attitude, a moral crusade, as a set of programs. Eventually, among a core group of young poverty warriors, this commitment to social justice and reform would evolve into a regional social movement that reached far beyond the work of the OEO.

The idea of community action provided the only common theme that ran through the poverty program, but just as policy makers in Washington differed on the meaning of local control, the CAAs differed in how they administered federal funds in the mountains. Some were little more than transformed economic development commissions, controlled by local elites. Others evolved out of grassroots organizations and were designed to confront local bureaucracies and power structures in the interest of the poor. The majority of CAAs were more moderate, functioning primarily to deliver social services designed to modify the behavior of individual poor people. Where they included the participation of the poor, CAAs usually designated sympathetic county professionals to represent the poor or established local, community-based advisory boards.[21]

This was especially the case among many of the early CAAs launched in response to the initial call for applications to state and local officials, before the staff at the OEO began to insist on maximum feasible participation of the poor in the composition of CAA boards. The CAA in Rockcastle County, Kentucky, for example, was created out of the Rockcastle Development Association when the county became one of the first 182 counties eligible nationally for full OEO funding. The board of the new Rockcastle County Economic Opportunity Council included the county judge executive, the superintendent of schools, the county agricultural extension agent, the mayor of the largest town, and the chair of the county Democratic Party. With funds from its first OEO program development grant, the council hired a local schoolteacher as administrator and established an office in the school board administration building. Most of the agency's early programs involved expanding educational services to the poor, including establishing a Head Start program and hiring additional teachers and teachers' aides for summer enrichment programs.[22]

Service-oriented CAAs like the one in Rockcastle County burgeoned and became a common model for uplifting the poor throughout the region. Such programs focused federal resources on education and low-skill employment activities disguised as job training opportunities (such as clearing roadside brush and painting public buildings) rather than on more structural approaches to fighting poverty. In mountain counties, where local school superintendents often controlled county political machines, these strategies assured that poverty dollars would be channeled through local institutions, where power brokers could utilize the funds for patronage purposes. The public schools were usually the largest employers in rural counties, and jobs as recreational directors, trainers, teachers' aides, counselors, janitors, cooks, and bus drivers only increased the poor's dependency on the political status quo.

Even those CAAs that were more willing to listen to the poor themselves—often those whose directors had been hired from outside the area—opted for moderate programs of personal empowerment, establishing rural community centers, craft programs, sewing centers, and cooperative small businesses. In Kentucky, the Knox County Economic Opportunity Council, established at the same time as the Rockcastle County CAA, provided home economic aides, home improvement demonstrations, recreational activities, and early childhood programs in thirteen community centers located in discarded one-room schools in poor, rural districts. Representatives of these centers filled a third of the seats on the Knox County CAA board. Eventually the award-winning agency started a small furniture factory and handcraft shop for low-income workers. However, a study undertaken by University of Kentucky researchers three years into the program found that, despite these services, the agency had done little to alter the county's institutional structures or patterns of political alignments.[23] Such was the case in Mingo County, West Virginia, as well, where the local CAA's agency-based strategy, intended to improve existing service delivery programs, gradually evolved into a more confrontational strategy. Under the leadership of Mingo County native Huey Perry, the program eventually organized a political action league and a fair elections committee and established an independent grocery that threatened local political and business interests.[24]

At least at the outset of the War on Poverty, mountain power brokers welcomed the new federal programs and assumed that funding would be administered through state and local governments in the pattern established by the New Deal. Douglass Arnett, who studied the community action process in Clay County, Kentucky, pointed out that political leaders in the mountains "had no objections to giving more money or more services to poor people" as long as those "resources were channeled through existing institutions and organizations controlled by the local power structure."[25] Only when OEO administrators in Washington began to pressure CAAs to increase involvement of the poor on their boards and to directly fund demonstration projects by grassroots groups and nongovernmental organizations did the local political machines begin to question the intent of the national program. By that time, hundreds of outside VISTA volunteers, energetic college students, and idealistic community organizers fresh from the civil rights movement had arrived in the mountains. Increasingly they joined with poor people, labor organizers, and indigenous reformers to question the service delivery approach and to challenge the assumptions on which it was based.

From the beginning, a small but influential group of OEO administrators, led by Richard Boone and his associate Sanford Kravitz, believed that defeating poverty would require more than the expansion of existing social services programs. Convinced that the poor "need access to power as well as to resources," they advocated a bolder approach to community action and increasingly used their positions to encourage more radical change.[26] Deeply committed to the idea of maximum feasible participation of the poor, Boone pushed OEO staff to demand greater involvement of poor people on CAA boards, especially after some county governments in the South refused to allow black representation and some urban startup proposals in the North became dominated by representatives of the local city hall.

Although the principle of community action emphasized local decision making and the majority of funds flowed to CAAs organized under the aegis of local governments, the EOA reserved 15 percent of the community action budget for national emphasis programs and demonstration projects. As head of the OEO Policy and Planning division from 1964 to 1965, Boone utilized these funds to encourage more radical experimentation and to support demonstration grants to non-CAAs.[27] These grants often bypassed local power structures and extended support directly to grassroots organizations and academic institutions for programs designed more to empower the poor than just to assimilate them into mainstream culture. Many of these experimental projects drew heavily on the community organizing work of Chicago's Saul Alinsky and the youth-oriented efforts of the Gray Areas Program. They assumed that the needs of the poor would not be met until they were organized to voice their concerns on critical issues such as housing, jobs, health care, and welfare reform. Assisted by the growing number of VISTA volunteers and poverty consultants in the region, these programs nurtured a generation of young activists, both indigenous and nonnative, that increasingly rejected the service deliv-

ery model as ineffective if it failed to change the political and economic status quo. In Appalachia, as in northern cities, these special
demonstration projects proved to be both the most innovative and the
most controversial of the antipoverty programs.

Offering greater flexibility and freedom from local government oversight, demonstration grants tapped into new ideas and energies long
stifled by the traditional political culture in the mountains. Except in
labor unions, poor people had seldom been organized in Appalachia,
and formal middle-class institutions such as colleges and professional
organizations were sparse. The core of the region, from Morgantown,
West Virginia, to Knoxville, Tennessee, lacked a major university that
might have generated creativity and intellectual leadership, and the
scattering of small private colleges struggled, like castles in the wilderness, to uplift a talented few. The availability of federal funds offered
poor people and middle-class reformers the opportunity to mobilize for
change, and it unleashed the potential of academics and professionals
on the edges of the region who were eager to facilitate that change.

Whether funded by OEO demonstration grants or by the swell of
private foundation dollars that flowed into the region as a result of the
War on Poverty, nongovernmental initiatives burgeoned in Appalachia
in the 1960s and 1970s. Like the more service-oriented CAAs, the
nongovernmental antipoverty programs differed in their approaches to
mountain problems. Most recognized the weakness of Appalachian
civic institutions and advocated policies for social transformation, but
their tactics to accomplish reform varied according to class, conviction, and moment in time. Colleges, universities, and organizations
such as the CSM launched traditional programs of educational outreach, leadership training, and professional development designed to
enrich the learning environment of poor children or to provide technical assistance for community planning and economic growth. Many of
these efforts brought students, young professionals, and other outside
experts into the region. Grassroots organizations, on the other hand,
often led by poor people and their advocates, were more likely to challenge the local political and economic system by establishing cooperative businesses, creating community-based housing and health care
programs, and questioning the decisions of school boards and county

governments. Eventually even some of the more moderate, institutionally based projects clashed with regional power structures, and in time the progeny of the colleges and universities joined with the poor to organize dissent and resistance. Collectively, however, these nongovernmental efforts tended to question long established structures and relationships in the mountains and to test the resolve of national and local leaders to change them.

Colleges and universities played a pivotal role in the War on Poverty in Appalachia and in turn experienced major growth as a result of antipoverty research and demonstration contracts and other Great Society investments in higher education. Academics had long helped to shape the popular images and stereotypes of Appalachia, and social scientists at leading research universities on the perimeter of the region had contributed to the definition of Appalachia as a national problem area. Many of the initial planners and administrators at the OEO were scholars or at least well-trained intellectuals, and the experimental character of the War on Poverty reflected the academic model of testing hypotheses through selected demonstration projects. Although the limited demonstration model succumbed to the political demands of an all-out assault on poverty, the idea of applying knowledge to practice survived in both privately and publicly funded antipoverty efforts.

Since World War II, higher education had increasingly embraced the values of the private market, competing for an ever growing number of federal research grants and shaping the production of knowledge to meet political as well as administrative needs.[28] The rise of interest in "poverty knowledge" during the 1960s spurred the attention of academics and institutions serving Appalachia and resulted in the expansion of education and research initiatives that sought to apply new knowledge to the region's problems and that also contributed to the growth of the institutions. Especially at major research universities such as the University of Kentucky, West Virginia University, the University of North Carolina, and the University of Pittsburgh, social scientists were quick to focus their research agendas on the region and to propose intervention strategies. Faculty from these institutions contributed to the 1962 regional assessment *The Southern Appalachian Region: A Survey*, funded by the Ford Foundation, and served as consultants to the PARC. The University of North Carolina played a central role in the design of the North Carolina Fund, a state-level predecessor to the War on Poverty. George Esser, a UNC professor, became the North Carolina Fund's executive director.

In Kentucky, professors from the University of Kentucky, Berea College, and Morehead State University (all located on the periphery of the region) had been involved in raising awareness of mountain problems since the 1950s. Faculty contributed to the early regional development plan *Program 60* and prepared draft proposals in forest and water management, highway and agricultural development, and small-town revitalization, including the New Cities plan for community relocation. In 1961 the University of Kentucky College of Agriculture launched a major outreach initiative in eastern Kentucky, the Eastern Kentucky Resource Development Project, with a $754,000 grant from the W. K. Kellogg Foundation and a $1 million state appropriation. The seven-year project established a ten-member team of economic development experts at a new research and demonstration center in Breathitt County. The ironically named Quicksand Demonstration Center worked with local leaders on a variety of activities ranging from industrial planning to livestock production.[29] Such projects were designed to link the resources of the university with the needs of Appalachian communities in a pattern consistent with its land-grant mission. West Virginia University went so far as to reorganize its administrative structure to better coordinate outreach services to the Mountain State, creating the Center for Appalachian Studies and Development, the first of its kind, in 1964.[30]

Not only did university-based initiatives in Appalachia describe the problems of the mountains as developmental deficiencies that could be alleviated with the application of technology and knowledge, but, like land-grant universities elsewhere, they tended to focus their efforts on work with local elites. One of the extension community development specialists in the UK project described his job as helping mountain communities to "mature" by sponsoring county and multicounty public forums for regional leaders. "This 'developmental task' concept for communities," he wrote, "is derived from that discipline of educators, physiologists, sociologists, and anthropologists who believe that a child cannot crawl, walk, or run in a coordinated fashion, without first accomplishing certain developmental tasks (maturation)." He added, "Likewise, a community should not expect to have a large industry or outstanding commercial center until it has 'matured' sufficiently to support those aspects of community living which an industrial or commercial community must have for its people. The potential development of facilities and institutions of a community are almost entirely dependent upon the degree of mental, physical, and social development of the people involved."[31]

Along with other technical and education initiatives, the Eastern Kentucky Resource Development Project and the WVU Center for Appalachian Studies and Development helped to start county development associations and later to set up multicounty planning councils. Local leaders, however, often distrusted the outside experts, resented university paternalism, and were suspicious of political reform. When funding for the Kentucky project expired and the university was unable to sustain the initiative, the Kentucky area development councils squashed a grant proposal to the OEO to revive the program on the grounds that the university project contested with the councils "for the support of local officials and development organizations."[32] Mountain elites did not object to the placement of student interns on selected service projects in their communities, but they feared the loss of control over local development decisions that federal funding of university professionals might foster.

Colleges and universities, however, tended not to distinguish between student-centered projects assisting poor people in the field and the action-oriented intervention efforts of faculty and other professionals to facilitate community planning. Both were part of the educational mission of higher education in the 1960s. Even smaller, liberal arts colleges in the mountains encouraged students and faculty to apply their knowledge to society's problems, and many took advantage of new federal programs and foundation support to launch local outreach initiatives. For example, Mars Hill College, a small Baptist institution in western North Carolina, took the lead in organizing the antipoverty campaign in Madison County, one of the poorest counties in the state. Over the course of the next decade, the college doubled its enrollment, faculty, and operating budget and received national recognition for programs that placed student interns in a variety of new social service agencies in the county.[33]

Guided by a visionary, ex-Mennonite dean, Richard Hoffman, who had come south with the civil rights movement, the college organized the local CAA, the Madison County Opportunity Corporation, which wrote federal grants that established Head Start centers, family counseling and other mental health services, housing renovation projects, and job training workshops. Hoffman served for a time as executive director of the local agency, and the college president served on the board of directors along with prominent doctors and educators from the Mars Hill area. The chair of the Department of Sociology, Don Anderson, served as head of a new Madison County planning commission, the first such commission in the North Carolina mountains. Other faculty and administrators helped to create the award-winning Hot Springs Health Program, which provided health services to remote sections of the county. To better coordinate student participation in these outreach activities, Mars Hill College created the Community Development Institute, in which students worked part time as recreational directors, teaching assistants, secretaries, and staff aides in local poverty agencies. Between 1965 and 1970, the college established an Upward Bound program for local high school students and received funding from the OEO and the Southern Regional Education Board to train VISTA and other poverty workers. Many of the professional staff from these initiatives later became permanent faculty at the institution.

Other colleges in the mountains launched similar programs to involve students and staff in community service. A number of these institutions began as settlement schools earlier in the century and slowly evolved into two- and four-year colleges after World War II. Federal resources for Upward Bound, work-study, and other antipoverty programs helped these small colleges to extend their traditional mission of community-based service into more distant hollows while providing financial support for their students and enhancing institutional growth. One of the most successful programs was that undertaken by tiny Alice Lloyd College in eastern Kentucky. Created in 1916 as the Caney Creek Settlement School in Knott County, the college became a junior college after the death of its founder, Alice Lloyd, in 1962 and began receiving OEO grants in the mid-1960s to establish "outpost centers" in neighboring communities. By 1969, with assistance from the Bruner Foundation in New York, the program evolved into the Alice Lloyd

College Outreach Reserves (ALCOR), which placed live-in students in sixteen area communities to provide summer recreation and educational enrichment activities.[34]

Settlement schools had always taken an active role in providing health screening and nutritional education in mountain communities, and ALCOR developed a special emphasis on identifying family health problems, teaching dental hygiene and personal cleanliness, and linking poor families with public health services. Led by two Alice Lloyd graduates who would later establish their own health clinic in Knott County, Benny Ray Bailey and Grady Stumbo, the project brought in nurses and medical students from outside the region to work with the college volunteers and conduct health screenings. In 1971 the summer program was extended to three other eastern Kentucky colleges and renamed Appalachian Leadership and Community Outreach. The collaborative program involved more than 150 students deployed in seventy-seven locations in twenty-two counties.[35]

Student service-learning projects such as ALCOR blossomed in the mountains during the 1960s. Some programs placed indigenous Appalachian students in their own communities to sponsor educational enrichment activities, teach crafts, organize community cleanup campaigns, or link families with health and social service providers, but others tapped into a growing national trend for middle-class college students to volunteer their time in underdeveloped areas. The largest of these student volunteer efforts, the Appalachian Volunteers (AV), brought together native and nonnative young people into a multistate initiative that served most of central Appalachia. Not only did the organization provide fertile ground for a growing network of regional activists, but it eventually broke with its institutional founders to become one of the more radical reform groups in the region.

Formed in the winter of 1963–1964 as part of President Kennedy's emergency winter program for eastern Kentucky, the AV predated the passage of the EOA and reflected both the origins and the conflicting ideologies of the War on Poverty in the mountains. As early as the spring of 1963, the CSM had approached the Ford Foundation for money to form a volunteer organization of young people to provide education and social services to the people of Appalachia. The council eventually was awarded a small planning grant from the Edgar Stern Family Fund of New York, but the idea received a major boost in December 1963 when Richard Boone called Milton Ogle of the council and proposed to fund a pilot effort utilizing money from the president's special winterization fund. During the January 1964 winter break, more than three hundred area college students participated in the renovation of two rural schools in Harlan County, Kentucky, and, at a meeting of educators, council representatives, and government officials in February, the AV was formally established and extended to nineteen Kentucky colleges with the assistance of a fifty-thousand-dollar grant from the ARA. Later that year the council received the first of several OEO demonstration grants from Boone's office to expand AV services and hire a field staff to supervise student workers.[36]

Under Ogle's leadership, the AVs (as the volunteers were known) at first followed a traditional consensus and self-help approach to working with mountain people. Students ventured forth to refurbish one-room schools and winterize homes, utilizing materials donated by area businesses and working alongside resident volunteers. With the cooperation of local school superintendents, AVs provided enrichment programs in the schools, showing movies on hygiene, demonstrating traditional dances, constructing playground equipment, and leading group recreational activities. This strategy of working with local leaders to provide services to the poor was consistent with the CSM's philosophy of helping "any group working for the betterment of conditions in the mountains" and with the training that most early AV staff had received as students at Berea College.[37] As Ogle wrote in a letter soliciting materials from businesses, "Deprived people cannot be helped; they must help themselves."[38]

In the first year of the program, students fanned out into forty eastern Kentucky counties, hanging wallboard, repairing broken windows, replacing rotted floors, and painting woodwork on many of the more than one thousand one- and two-room schools that dotted the eastern Kentucky landscape. Weekend and summer volunteers restored twenty-one dilapidated houses in Slone Fork in Knott County, helped to organize a community center in Persimmon Fork in Leslie County, constructed a greenhouse at Mill Creek in Clay County, and directed summer recreational programs for children throughout the area.[39] A second OEO grant in 1965 added 150 VISTA volunteers to the program and funded additional staff to expand the AV into West Virginia, Virginia, and Tennessee. Two years after its founding, the AV was a showcase OEO program. The *Louisville Courier-Journal* praised the students as "young Samaritans" who "with little more than enthusiasm, hammers and saws" had made "a deep impression on the mountain people."[40]

The very success of the early AV, however, also dramatized the depth of the problems in the mountains and ultimately led to the decline of government support for the program. As hundreds of student volunteers poured into the region—many not native to the mountains—and as field staff established permanent residences and working relationships in rural communities, cultural and political conflicts began to strain the cooperative relationship between the young poverty warriors and local elites. Some student volunteers began to question whether the renovation projects did anything to end poverty or merely camouflaged the worst manifestations of a corrupt system. Returning volunteers found little change in the communities or in the status of the poor. Schools they had repaired a year earlier were soon run down again; windows were broken, and educational materials lost. "When you start fixing up a one-room school, you start wondering," one volunteer later recalled. "Why didn't the local school board fix this up a long time ago? Then you ask, why aren't there books?"[41]

The sudden growth of the AV in 1965 brought student volunteers from as far away as California and new staff from urban centers in the Midwest and East. Some were fresh from Harvard; others had worked with the Student Nonviolent Coordinating Committee in the South. A few came from class-conscious, union families in the Midwest, and one had been a community organizer in Chicago's Uptown.[42] The new arrivals brought a more assertive view of fighting poverty than was shared by the leadership of the CSM. Even many of the indigenous AVs increasingly questioned whether the service-oriented programs of the council were doing anything to empower the poor or to alter the structures that had generated the conditions in the first place. More and more the volunteers saw the county school superintendents and the judge executives with whom the council worked to gain entry to mountain communities as the problem, not the cure, and they strained at the institutional ties that kept them from engaging in political advocacy for the poor.

Throughout 1965 relationships between the volunteers and council leadership deteriorated as the young organizers pressed their more conservative elders to move beyond their service programs and into community action. The conflict of age and ideology came to a head in the spring of 1966 when Perley Ayer, director of the CSM, abruptly fired Ogle and the senior staff of the AV for insubordination. The remaining thirteen staff members summarily resigned and reorganized themselves the following day as a nonprofit organization, Appalachian Volunteers Inc. The newly independent organization moved its offices from Berea, Kentucky, to Bristol, Tennessee, and announced that it intended to become more assertive in organizing the poor. No longer constrained by the program-oriented consensus politics of the council, Ogle declared that the AV was "definitely an action agency."[43]

Within a few days, the OEO shifted its funding for the AV to the new organization, which immediately expanded its operations in the coalfields. By the summer of 1966, the AVs were supervising the training of almost five hundred VISTA volunteers and had established several outpost education centers intended as living spaces for volunteer workers in poor communities. Instead of painting schoolhouses and providing educational enrichment activities, AV field-workers now began assisting poor people's organizations and forming community groups around the issues of strip mining and welfare rights. Especially in eastern Kentucky and southern West Virginia, AVs became vocal critics not only of the coal industry and the local political establishment but of the more moderate CAAs as well.

In southeast Kentucky, for example, AV field-workers organized demonstrations against the eight-county Cumberland Valley CAA in the summer of 1966, resulting in the eventual dismantling of the agency and the reestablishment of one- and two-county CAAs that reflected greater participation by the poor. In West Virginia, AVs turned out hundreds of community people to challenge control of CAA boards by local elites and even seized control for a time of the Raleigh County agency.[44] By the end of 1967, AVs were directly challenging CAAs throughout central Appalachia to be more responsive to the needs of the poor and were helping local citizens' groups to demand greater voices in community health, education, and economic policies. No longer content with refurbishing schoolhouses and showing dental hygiene films to poor children, AVs became impatient advocates of change in a political atmosphere that feared structural change. For many state and local leaders, young AVs came to symbolize the veiled potential of the War on Poverty to upset the status quo in the mountains, a threat that increasingly concerned regional power brokers.

Although university professors, college students, social activists, and middle-class professionals differed in their approaches to fighting poverty in Appalachia, they shared a collective movement culture that bound them in a common crusade. Most professed a faith in the American dream, valued the poor, appreciated participatory processes, and expected social justice. Many approached their work with a strong moral conviction to serve the disadvantaged, and more than a few were ordained clergy, lay leaders, or students from church-affiliated colleges and organizations. Indeed, the organized church had long played an important role in popularizing and addressing the human problems of the mountains, and the War on Poverty offered an opportunity for national denominations and spiritually motivated individuals to refocus their energies on the region. Not surprisingly, the response of the church to the War on Poverty was as diverse in Appalachia as was that of secular institutions, ranging from individual self-help initiatives to community development and resistance.

Southern Appalachia had been the focus of home mission work by major Christian denominations since the late nineteenth century, and national religious leaders drew on their history of launching mission churches and settlement schools in the mountains when they responded to the campaign against poverty. A gulf had existed for years between the indigenous churches of the region and mainstream denominations. Rural churches in Appalachia were small, having evolved as extensions of local communities and specific family groups, and they were typically informal and independent of national affiliations. The few mainline denominations (generally Baptists, Methodists, and Presbyterians) were usually clustered in the county seats, reflecting both the social aspirations of the mountain middle class and their greater ties to the national economy. Even the larger coal camp churches, including Catholic missions, often owed their survival to the benevolence of the coal companies, and almost all avoided involvement in social conflict issues, preferring to concentrate on personal salvation rather than the social gospel.

Outside churches and nationally based religious organizations therefore took the lead in a second wave of home mission activities to the mountains after World War II. Like others before them, the latest missionaries blended the desire to provide humanitarian uplift in the form of education and health care with the hope of expanding their own denomination in the region. Denominational leaders had been active in the CSM since its founding in the 1920s, and after the war, participation in the council's spiritual life committee grew as many denominations established special managerial units to coordinate their revitalized mountain mission work. The Catholic Diocese of Covington, Kentucky, for instance, sent dozens of young priests into eastern Kentucky to establish new congregations, provide parochial education, and build rural hospitals. The Presbyterian Church (USA) created the West Virginia Mountain Project and sent seminary students to minister in poor and rural congregations during the summer. The Christian Church (Disciples of Christ) launched a special "church in town and country" unit to expand human and spiritual services to communities in the Cumberland Plateau.[45] Lutherans, American Baptists, Brethren, Episcopalians, Mennonites, and Quakers all organized special church divisions to coordinate charity and mission work in the mountains.

These denominational efforts provided a national network of urban congregations that supported evangelical work in the region, and under the leadership of Perley Ayer and Willis Weatherford, the CSM became the hub of efforts to expand the involvement of these congregations in mountain relief work as well. In some cases this meant raising monetary contributions for specific council projects or assisting mountain migrants in northern cities; in others it meant chaperoning suburban youngsters on weekend mission trips into mountain communities to remodel churches or restore dilapidated housing. With the rise of national concern about poverty in the 1960s, these programs established summer camps for needy children, book drives for schools and community centers, adult education and job training programs, and, of course, emergency relief efforts to distribute truck-loads of food and used clothing to help mountain families make it through the winter.

In 1963 this network of churches generated funds to rescue ten miners' hospitals that the UMWA planned to shut down in central Appalachia as a result of declining resources in the union's Health and Retirement Funds. Two years later, with the help of the National Council of Churches, eighteen denominations and religious organizations collaborated to form the Commission on Religion in Appalachia to coordinate ecumenical antipoverty programs in the region, provide continuing education for clergy, and "articulate the ethical considerations of business and industrial practices in Appalachia."[46] Church-sponsored antipoverty activities continued to reflect a wide range of philosophies and approaches, but by the end of the decade, church-supported organizers worked hand in hand with AVs, VISTA volunteers, and other poverty warriors. Some became more radicalized by their experiences and later played key roles in creating alternative, nonprofit community development corporations and in supporting citizen efforts to achieve land reform, economic justice, and environmental protection.

The broad diversity of religious responses to poverty in Appalachia was perhaps best reflected in the efforts of the Roman Catholic Church. Never a very large denomination in the mountains, the Catholic Church established a foothold in the region at the turn of the twentieth century in response to the arrival of European immigrants to the coalfields and other industrial areas. With the out-migration of many immigrant families during the Great Depression and the general abandonment of company support for churches and other coal camp institutions in the 1930s, the number of Catholics in the mountains declined until another generation of bishops undertook to grow new parishes in the region after World War II. Concentrating on small towns and county seats rather than coal camps, itinerant priests and nuns opened mission centers to serve the small Catholic population and to attract new congregants. Especially after the Second Vatican Council in the early 1960s, these village parishes began to reach out to surrounding rural communities to provide social and spiritual services to the poor no matter what their religious affiliations.

This was the path, for example, followed by Father Ralph Beiting, who came to eastern Kentucky in 1950 and stayed to found one of the largest private antipoverty agencies in the country. Assigned by his bishop to establish a new parish in Madison and surrounding counties, Beiting eventually ventured deeper into the coalfields as a street preacher and witnessed firsthand the poverty that plagued the region. By the late 1950s, he began to build on his spiritual message with a growing concern for the material needs of the primarily non-Catholic population, and, from his base near Berea, the young priest became active in the burgeoning regional efforts to draw state and national attention to Appalachia's problems. In 1958 he purchased a youth camp in Garrard County and established a used clothing warehouse in Berea for the poor. During the early 1960s, Beiting's Christian Appalachian Project (CAP) developed a small farm support program and opened a Christmas wreath factory in nearby Jackson County. Father Beiting supported his initial efforts to fight poverty by raising donations and attracting volunteers through speaking engagements in Catholic schools and churches across the country.

With the outbreak of the War on Poverty in 1964, Beiting incorporated the CAP as an independent nonprofit organization and expanded its service area to include eleven counties and a wide range of self-help programs. The CAP operated teen and child development centers, GED programs, workshops for handicapped adults, home repair programs, used clothing outlets, and family abuse shelters. Hundreds of weekend and summer volunteers were recruited from urban churches to work as counselors, advisors, and instructors in CAP youth camps and outreach centers. By the mid-1980s, the CAP was the largest nonprofit organization in the region, with 285 employees and an annual operating budget of more than $14 million. The organization managed eighty programs, touching an estimated ninety thousand people per year.[47]

Although the CAP was officially a nondenominational Christian organization, Father Beiting continued to serve as president and chair of the CAP board. To support his rapidly growing program, Beiting increased his speaking tours and developed a massive and effective direct-mail campaign that included a free copy of his book *God Can Move Mountains*. Beiting, his staff, and volunteers generally avoided involvement in local politics and in the issue-based organizing that the AVs came to represent, preferring to focus their energies on self-help opportunities for individuals. Few in the region or outside questioned the value of the CAP's humanitarian services, which reached thousands of the most desperately poor, but critics increasingly questioned administrative overhead expenses and challenged the ethics of Beiting's fund-raising strategies. Still, as late as 1987, more than 80 percent of the CAP's annual budget went to salaries and other administrative costs.[48]

Even more controversial among some poverty warriors, however, was the CAP's use of regional stereotypes in direct mail, television commercials, and other fund-raising efforts. Missionaries, educators, and writers had utilized emotional imagery and heartrending personal stories for years to dramatize the continuing need for donations to sustain their work, but Beiting's successful use of this strategy in direct-mail fund-raising produced questions about paternalism and the misrepresentation of the region within and outside the organization. Appeals for donations almost always included images of frail and destitute children and stories of personal hardship related by Father Beiting, who was often identified by the more popular "Reverend Beiting" in mass mailings. Letters and accompanying literature described the people of the mountains as descendants of "our early American pioneers" who were "some of the most creative, dynamic people ever to grace this continent" but who had fallen under the yoke of poverty and, with just a little help, could make a better life for themselves. With imagery reminiscent of early local color writers, Beiting's personal stories told of a region rent by violence, ignorance, and feuding, where outside volunteers struggled resolutely to bring help.

Perhaps the most controversial example of this appeal was the Bobbie Sue letter, which set records in the direct-mail industry for both income generated and continuous years of use.[49] Picturing a young girl standing on the porch of a ramshackle cabin and carrying her infant sibling on her hip, the letter introduced its readers to Bobbie Sue from Appalachia, who "through no fault of her own" had to "go to bed hungry many nights." Produced by a Washington DC–area fund-raising firm, the appeal reinforced universal stereotypes of Appalachian destitution while portraying the mountaineers as noble and long suffering, in need only of individual assistance and opportunity. "Through absolutely no fault of their own," the letter posited, "they have had to endure a fantastically high rate of unemployment, miserable living conditions, and empty promise after empty promise. Nowhere else in America will you find fewer educational opportunities, poorer housing, or less medical care covering such a large area."[50] Despite these conditions, the letter concluded, the people of Appalachia had not lost hope, in part because of the work of the CAP, whose continued success depended on donations from "concerned Americans across the country." The letter was "printed by Appalachian craftsmen" and signed by the Reverend Ralph Beiting.

The Bobbie Sue letter (and dozens like it from other organizations) reflected the compassion and concern that motivated the War on Poverty, but it also mirrored the national misunderstanding of Appalachia's history and problems. Like the service-oriented programs of most CAAs and the educational outreach programs of colleges and universities, the CAP avoided the larger structural problems of Appalachia's politics and economy and assumed that individuals could lift themselves out of poverty if given the opportunity and resources to change their behavior. Alleviating poverty, to many religious workers as well as to those in government and education, was a matter of individual and cultural change rather than societal transformation. Drawing on received images of Appalachian isolation and degeneracy to justify its programs, the CAP reinforced the popular idea of Appalachian otherness and limited its own ability to effect sustainable change. While meeting the critical and real needs of impoverished families, self-help organizations like the CAP failed to confront the realities of injustice and economic exploitation that continued to marginalize poor people.

Of course, some church-based poverty workers followed a different path. Like their secular counterparts in the AV, a few Catholic priests and nuns, especially after Vatican II, recognized the limitations of service-oriented strategies, and in time they adopted a more aggressive approach to community problems. Less burdened with the task of church building, individuals from religious orders such as the Glenmary Sisters were more likely to become enmeshed in rural community life and to utilize the community empowerment strategies of liberation theology that were beginning to sweep the Catholic world. Sent to the mountains in the mid-1960s to "help rural people survive and maintain rural values so they might reinvigorate the church," many of these workers left their religious orders to become permanent residents and activist leaders in communities across the region.[51]

Almost fifty Glenmary Sisters departed the order in 1967 to form their own experimental community in the mountains, and dozens of others left individually after reexamining their work in light of contemporary needs and issues. Freed from the restrictive, male-dominated rules of the church, these religious women became a powerful organizing force in communities throughout rural Appalachia, helping to set up health clinics, worker-owned businesses, homeless shelters, town water systems, arts programs, and scores of other community-based projects. Taking literally the call of Vatican II to be "in the world, acting on behalf of justice," the former Glenmary Sisters took up residences in rural communities, established friendships with neighbors, listened to concerns at community gatherings, and visited the poor. Unlike other poverty warriors, they did not bring prepackaged projects but shared their skills, ideas, energy, and networks of friends and resources. In time, they gained the confidence of the community.[52]

Listening to the concerns of the poor, the former Glenmary Sisters helped to organize community-based programs that provided alternatives to the institutionally based services that were often controlled by local elites. Building strong partnerships, especially among the women of these poor communities, they organized community-controlled health clinics and community centers, which in turn led to the creation of child development and tutoring programs. In east Tennessee, Marie Cirillo and others organized a coalition of local women into the Mountain Women's Exchange, which launched a craft cooperative and thrift shops and later established a satellite college program whose courses were offered by nearby colleges under a curriculum controlled by the community itself. In southwest Virginia, Anne Leibig and other former nuns helped to organize community arts programs, small business co-ops, and eventually the Appalachian Community Development Corporation, one of the first nonprofit, community-controlled economic planning and fund-raising organizations in the region.

Nor did the sisters shy away from advocacy and social action. Together with local citizens and with the assistance of students from Vanderbilt University, former Glenmary Sisters in Tennessee helped to form Save Our Cumberland Mountains, a 1,500-member environmental group that opposed strip mining and other land degradation. When they learned that many people in their poor counties were not receiving the social services to which they were legally entitled, the women began developing legal aid clinics and training local people to serve as legal advocates for the poor. In Wise County, Virginia, they helped to establish a legal support group, Concerned Citizens for Social and Economic Justice, and, through the Wise County Welfare Rights Organization, they worked with hundreds of people to get fair treatment from the local welfare department.[53]

Whereas efforts like those of the CAP and the CSM sought to supplement government programs that served the poor, the former nuns and their male and female counterparts from other denominations often bypassed government agencies to establish alternative businesses, clinics, schools, and other structures controlled by poor people themselves. Although they seldom engaged in political organizing in the manner that some young activists attempted to gain control of poverty agencies, school boards, and other county offices, these religious radicals challenged the values of a society that allowed corporate exploitation of land and natural resources to leave some mountain people impoverished and without basic human services. They acted to create community-based alternatives to existing structures and to confront those institutional structures on specific issues with community-based organizations and knowledge.

Like many of their secular counterparts among the AVs and VISTA volunteers, these more radical religious workers eventually rejected cultural explanations of poverty and became increasingly critical of the economic and political system that had produced the injustices they found in their communities. Living among the poor and listening to their concerns, they were convinced that the lack of a voice in local public policy decisions and dependence on local elites for jobs and services had left the poor powerless to control their own fate. Having rejected traditional, gendered structures in the church, religious workers questioned a corporate economic system that benefited the few at the expense of the common good. They increasingly found the problems of the mountains to lie less in the values of the people than in the actions of the corporations, institutions, and politicians that controlled the land and public resources of the region.

Nothing reflected the distance between Father Beiting's self-help approach of Christian charity and the participatory, community-based strategies of the former Glenmary Sisters quite like the publication of the pastoral letter of the Catholic Bishops of Appalachia in 1975. Written and produced by the Catholic Committee of Appalachia, a group composed of former Glenmary Sisters and other religious activists, the letter reflected the sense of unity that these Catholic workers felt with the people of their rural communities and challenged fellow Christians throughout Appalachia and the country to work for social and economic justice in the region. Poignantly titled *This Land Is Home to Me*, the report described the industrial and corporate exploitation of the mountains and condemned the culture of greed and "maximization of profit" that left the land ravaged and the people powerless and poor. A problem for all of America, Appalachia was a symbol of the failed promise of technological development and the "conspicuous consumption" that had become an idol in the larger society. With no plea for money, no images of undernourished mountain children, the bishops' statement laid the blame for poverty in the region on corporate profits, human greed, and wasteful economic development. "Powerlessness in Appalachia," the letter professed, could be overcome only through partnership with the poor, careful use of scientific resources, and community-based planning for future growth. The struggle for social justice in the mountains, the bishops concluded, was part of a larger struggle for justice in the world, and they encouraged Catholics in the region to investigate a wide range of issues, such as strip mining, land acquisition, the exploitation of cheap labor, occupational health and safety, union reform, taxation, cooperatives, education, tourism, and civic participation.[54]

Coming as it did at the end of the formal War on Poverty, the bishops' pastoral letter on Appalachia echoed the concerns and challenges that had emerged within mountain communities over the previous decade, and it revealed the great divide between the self-help efforts promoted by government and private programs and the calls for structural reform, alternative development, and social justice being made by a growing number of activists and community leaders. Proponents of this more radical perspective, however, remained in the minority during the height of the War on Poverty. Most antipoverty programs sought to extend social services to the poor and accepted the idea that if the poor could be trained to think and act like middle-class Americans, they would be successfully absorbed into the larger society.

As long as local elites believed that the goal of antipoverty programs was acculturation, they welcomed the new resources that boosted village economies and promised hope for the poor. Like other postwar Americans, the mountain middle class was confident that science, technology, and free markets would eventually bring affluence to everyone and that it was only isolation from these modernizing forces that had prevented the region from participating in the national prosperity. The new public and nongovernmental programs brought a spate of young professionals to the region—doctors, nurses, caseworkers, teachers, technicians, and administrators—and with them the demand for better housing, medical care, highways, education, and consumer goods. The promise of participation in the Great Society also raised the expectations of the poor, and therein lay the hidden danger for those who benefited from the status quo.

Despite its intellectual assumptions about poverty and about Appalachia, the War on Poverty (like the civil rights movement) revived a dialogue about basic American values that inspired poor people and their advocates to challenge existing institutions and structures. The idea of community action itself unleashed an energy that local power brokers could not control, and the partnerships among citizens, poverty warriors, educated professionals, and youth soon posed a threat to powerful economic interests inside and outside the region. As federal resources poured into the mountains and as activists increasingly confronted what they perceived as injustice, a cultural and political struggle ensued over the direction of development and the meaning of the good life.

Although state and local leaders eventually succeeded in controlling OEO funds, community organizing and grassroots resistance continued to grow in the mountains long after the agency's demise. Launched as an effort to reduce the cultural and economic distance between Appalachia and America, the crusade against poverty ultimately fueled a renaissance of Appalachian identity. It also fed a social movement within the region that voiced mounting concern about modernity, social justice, and the goals of the Great Society itself.

4

CONFRONTING
DEVELOPMENT

Controversy surrounded the War on Poverty from the beginning. In Appalachia, as in the nation's inner cities, the crusade kindled the flames of long smoldering dissent and eventually sparked a backlash of resistance from the old power brokers. Along with the civil rights movement and later the Vietnam War, the struggle to end poverty unmasked profound social divisions in America and in Appalachia.

Early popular enthusiasm for the campaign concealed a society of disparate values and competing conceptions of the American dream. Even the scholars and bureaucrats who designed the antipoverty program disagreed over the causes of poverty and the implementation of the EOA's most important provisions. Conservative politicians, always uneasy with the expansion of federal power, persistently challenged liberal assumptions about human engineering and the ability of government to solve social problems. Middle-class whites, proud of their own success in the drive for accumulation, resented the transfer of wealth to inner-city blacks and "shiftless" rural whites. State and local officials increasingly railed against a burgeoning Washington bureaucracy that threatened to bypass traditional leadership in favor of nonelected community organizers and academics. More and more young people questioned a political and economic system that resisted change and appeared to blame the poor for their own problems. Many of these misgivings about the Great Society would eventually erupt in the national turmoil over the Vietnam War, but the campaign to end poverty revealed just how deeply Americans differed in their visions of democracy and the good life.

Not long after the passage of the EOA, critics from the left and the right were attacking the antipoverty campaign as a muddled effort full of inefficiency and waste. The liberal *New Republic* described the early administration of the OEO as "organized bedlam" and accused Sargent Shriver's leadership team of not having a strategy for conquering poverty.[1] Much of the confusion in the first year centered on the control of urban CAAs, which some big-city mayors saw as patronage pipelines to grease their own political machines. Inner-city blacks, on the other hand, supported by labor organizers and civil rights activists fresh from battles with segregationists in the South, envisioned the programs as opportunities to gain independence from the white power structure, and they demanded that the OEO live up to the promises of self-help and community empowerment. Confrontations between city officials and community organizers in New York, Philadelphia, Chicago, Newark, Syracuse, and other cities damaged the public perception of the OEO even as the campaign against poverty was getting off the ground.

Within a year of its creation, the OEO was already an embattled organization, and even the president considered dismantling the agency and scattering its programs to other departments. Most of the criticism centered on the Community Action division. In May 1965 the National Conference of Mayors quietly pressured the White House to prevent CAAs from organizing low-income residents for political action and asked it to recognize the legal responsibilities of local officials over the programs. Charles Schultze, Johnson's budget director, agreed and wrote to the president demanding that the OEO stop encouraging the politicization of the poor.[2] Inner-city riots, violence in some Job Corps camps, and poor management decisions in a few OEO-sponsored organizations fueled public suspicions that the campaign was out of control. The weight of criticism from inside and outside the government pushed the OEO to pull back from its more aggressive, experimental initiatives and to concentrate on getting CAAs operating as coordinators of services for the poor. Within the OEO, advocates of maximum feasible involvement of the poor in the development and operation of local programs became increasingly frustrated. In August, six of Shriver's top aides left the agency to work in nongovernmental organizations that sought to empower low-income people. Among these were Richard Boone and Sanford Kravitz, who had played important roles in creating the AV.[3]

The OEO survived the assaults of 1965 and even emerged with a small increase in its budget, but the attacks began to take their toll. Administrative zeal for the War on Poverty waned, and the president's attention shifted to concerns about inflation and the escalation of the war in Southeast Asia. By the annual congressional budget debates of 1966, outraged Democratic mayors across the country were in open rebellion that Washington was subsidizing "wars of civic subversion" by organizing the poor against them, and Republicans were questioning the rising costs of domestic and defense expenditures.[4] With almost 200,000 combat troops in Vietnam, guns and butter were simply too much, conservatives claimed, and the nation would have to put wraps on the Great Society, especially the War on Poverty. Despite Shriver's efforts to point out the successes of OEO programs, pundits on the far left also condemned the campaign as "a bag of tricks" being played on the poor. Saul Alinsky, the Chicago organizer, labeled it "a prize piece of political pornography."[5]

With liberals increasingly complaining that antipoverty efforts were too feeble, and with Republicans openly determined to dismantle the agency, the OEO barely survived budget negotiations in 1966. The controversial Community Action division took the biggest cuts in funding, and the agency quietly agreed to allow urban mayors to veto program proposals in their communities. This policy was formalized in 1967 when the Green amendment, offered by U.S. Representative Edith Green of Oregon, required that all CAAs be state or local entities under the authority of elected officials. Three years after the passage of the EOA, the War on Poverty struggled for congressional support, its energy sapped by changing national priorities and fundamental disagreements over strategies and goals.

Doubts about the War on Poverty were slower to appear in Appalachia, in part because of the intensity of despair in the mountains and the hope generated by national attention. Mountain power brokers welcomed the early community action grants that funded service-oriented programs run by well-connected leaders and traditional institutions. By the time open apprehension about the antipoverty program emerged in the region, the OEO was already under fire at the national level, its budget limited and its future compromised by rising inflation and the Vietnam War. The seeds of change and resistance, however, had been planted, and even as government-sponsored funds for fighting poverty began to tighten, a wave of dissent washed across the mountains that would dramatize the depth of the region's problems and reframe the debate over regional disparity for years to come. The activism generated by the War on Poverty, moreover, stirred a renaissance of regional scholarship, culture, and identity that survived long after the poverty battles had calmed.

The confidence, idealism, and enthusiasm that accompanied the launching of the antipoverty campaign in Appalachia provided fertile ground for the emergence of a regional awareness and reform movement. An unlikely coalition of ages, classes, and cultural backgrounds came together in the poverty wars to challenge popular ideas about the region and confront economic and political injustice. Young people from inside and outside Appalachia eagerly transferred their classroom civics lessons into the "real world" of the community. Academics found a laboratory and resources with which to test larger theories of development and empowerment. Local citizens and poor people found allies who were economically independent and skilled in negotiating government bureaucracies. Labor leaders and civil rights activists found an abused landscape and a struggling people in need of their community organizing talents. They were strange bedfellows, but they came together in the trenches of the poverty program, sharing mutual frustrations and learning from each other. Their collective experiences would test the limits of the social services model and shift the focus of the antipoverty campaign from individual uplift and local action to regional collaboration and structural change.

Challenges to the prevailing ideas about poverty and Appalachian culture emerged from the contested terrain of the poverty program itself. The urgency and experimental quality of early community action initiatives encouraged creativity and the open exchange of ideas. Agency heads brought in experts on human behavior and community development to train the young poverty warriors. Some encouraged workers to serve as role models for personal improvement; others advocated more radical solutions to societal change. Student volunteers listened intently to the concerns of the poor with whom they worked and sometimes lived. They read widely about the region and quickly transferred knowledge from the civil rights movement, the women's movement, liberation theology, and later the antiwar movement to their work in rural Appalachia. For many, the task of fighting poverty in the mountains was indistinguishable from other social crusades of their time. College-age youth from across the country took up John Kennedy's call for public service, and young people from the mountains found new meaning in their own roots and new pride in their culture.

At first the ideas of individual opportunity and community action were vague enough to encompass a range of strategies. Assumptions about the culture of poverty in the mountains were widespread, and almost everyone believed that education and economic development would uplift the poor. Over time, however, the ideas about social change that were churning in the larger society mixed with experience and memory within the region to produce a whole new understanding of the Appalachian condition. This interactive process empowered activists across the region—natives and nonnatives, young and old, intellectuals and the working poor—to join in the common cause of a variety of political and economic concerns. In Appalachia, as in urban ghettoes, community action took on new meaning, and fighting poverty came to imply systemic reform.

This movement from individual uplift to community organizing strategies was evident in the transformation of the AV. Established in 1964 as an early student service organization, the AV initially recruited students from within the region but eventually included volunteers and staff from a variety of backgrounds and places. After receiving one of the first OEO grants, the organization evolved from repairing one-room schoolhouses and providing occasional enrichment programs for poor schools to placing permanent field-workers in rural communities and training hundreds of VISTA and other volunteers. As the number of poverty workers associated with the AV increased, the mission of the organization grew from human services to community development and eventually to issue organizing on a broader regional basis. In 1966 the AV split with the more moderate CSM and became a leading force for structural change in central Appalachia, helping to organize citizens around strip mining, welfare rights, health care, and other regional problems.

The radicalization of the AVs and other young people derived from both cultural and intellectual forces at work in American society in the 1960s. The same optimism and confidence that had fueled the consumerism of the post–World War II generation inspired their children to pursue transcendent goals of social justice and economic simplicity. For financially secure and better-educated youth of the mid-1960s, extending the American dream involved broadening the benefits of democracy, expanding civil rights, and challenging long established barriers to opportunity.

At first the cultural differences between some urban-raised volunteers and rural mountain residents created barriers to communication, but gradually the poverty warriors and local poor people found common ground. Many of the young volunteers rejected the consumer culture that was emerging in postwar America and questioned the benefits of unbridled corporate power. They found in Appalachia a welcoming culture that appeared to resist modernization and to appreciate interpersonal relationships and community. As one AV recalled, "It was an introduction to a culture, values, and a way of life that we didn't know anything about. The whole Appalachian culture and history was very fascinating. You felt very much welcomed and involved. There wasn't any of that outsider standoffish sort of stuff that you sometimes hear about."[6] Disenchanted with mass society, they longed for roots themselves and found a certain romantic simplicity and honesty in the lives of the rural poor.

Eventually these young outsiders learned to listen to the viewpoints of their mountain hosts, and they came to share many of their values and to appreciate their music and art. Among the Appalachian middle class, the volunteers remained little more than outside troublemakers, long-haired hippies who failed to understand traditional community mores. For many rural poor, however, the AVs were increasingly welcomed as well-meaning, although naive, young people who shared a common vision of a just world. Among many rural Appalachians, the love of children, inherent egalitarianism, and sense of fairness eased the way for acceptance and trust. On the battlefields of the antipoverty campaign, cultures merged, and ideas and perspectives that each brought to the struggle were transformed.

Among the first assumptions to dissolve in the wake of field experience for many volunteers was the belief that poverty resulted from inherent deficiencies in mountain culture. Whereas weekend recruits could more easily accept cultural and geographic explanations for economic conditions in the region, volunteers who lived and worked in mountain communities for any period of time had more difficulty attributing poverty to the values, culture, and isolation of a people they came to admire. Occasional volunteers could "pop in, pop off, and pop out," as local residents put it, but field-workers with their feet in communities understood the complexity of local circumstances and the political consequences of powerlessness. AVs and VISTA volunteers who lived in coal camps and other rural communities quickly rejected the culture of poverty theory and behavior adjustment strategies and searched for other explanations for poor housing, inadequate health care, deficient education, and joblessness among their neighbors. As they listened to local residents express "bitterness about their life experience, about the political structure and their relationship with the coal companies and other big industries," the volunteers adjusted their perception of powerlessness. "I felt like I was radicalized or politicized or whatever by the people who lived in the mountains themselves," remembered one AV.[7] Increasingly they came to understand the mountain experience in new ways, and they responded to alternative voices that defined the region's poverty less as the product of Appalachian culture than of economic and political self-interest.

One of the most important of these voices was that of Harry Caudill. Although Caudill's best-selling book *Night Comes to the Cumberlands* had little impact on the administrative design of the War on Poverty, his scathing exposé of the coal industry in the mountains was widely read by reporters and poverty warriors in Appalachia. Caudill himself was a tireless writer and lecturer, speaking frequently at VISTA, AV, and CAA training sessions and frequently guiding national journalists on discovery trips into the hollows. The eloquent Whitesburg, Kentucky, lawyer and environmental advocate reinforced what the young volunteers and journalists heard from community residents and connected local conditions to a pattern of regional exploitation.

More than anyone else in the 1960s, Caudill shaped an alternative image of Appalachia as an oppressed region and provided the intellectual framework for a generation of mountain activists.[8]

Caudill attributed the economic problems of central Appalachia to the years of government neglect and corporate greed that had turned the mountains into an industrial wasteland. Most Americans, he argued, had seen the face of Appalachian poverty—"the bleak hillsides, the gray mining camps, the littered roadsides, the rickety houses, and the tattered dispirited people"—but few were familiar with the other face of Appalachia, the affluence that remained discreetly out of view. "Absenteeism and anonymity," he pointed out to all who would listen, "curtain the vast domain of giant corporations which own the region's wealth." Coddled by state and local officials who were too often corrupt and self-serving, the absentee corporations drained the wealth of Appalachia just as surely as they stole the riches of Central America.[9]

Some of the nation's great steel and manufacturing corporations, Caudill explained, had turned Appalachia into "little more than an internal colonial appendage of the industrial North and Midwest." Exploited for its natural and human resources, Appalachia was a rich land inhabited by a poor people: "Its plight is worse than that of a banana republic receiving U.S. foreign aid. Its exploitative economy generates much wealth and much poverty. The wealth flows to distant cities; the poverty accumulates at home. Like Latin America, Appalachia can find no relief for its dilemma until there is far-reaching tax reform and an overhaul of the antiquated political structure."[10] There was a great need, he believed, for regional advocates "to impress upon the electorate the fact that they are living on a rich land whose inhabitants are poor because of mismanagement of the land base and the almost endless exploitation of the soil, minerals, and timber by both local residents and giant absentee corporations." It was their responsibility, he told AVs in 1966, "to inform the people of this fact, and to set in motion a revolutionary change of thought."[11]

Caudill's use of the image of Appalachia as an internal American colony fit well within the American liberal tradition of resistance to outside oppression, and it reinforced the frustration and anger that the AVs were hearing from local residents. Volunteers could see the trainloads of coal that flowed past unemployed miners' shacks to enrich distant investors, and they could envision their role as populists resisting corporate oppression and injustice. The colonial model, moreover, connected the Appalachian experience to universal theories of economic dependence stirring in the civil rights, labor, and antiwar movements. Whereas conventional service delivery strategies failed to confront structural inequalities within the system and cultural explanations simply blamed the poor as individuals, the colonial model provided a clear adversary—outside corporations and their local henchmen—around which to organize citizen resistance. For energetic but impatient young poverty warriors, it offered a framework for thinking about political and economic change in the region that linked local and regional problems with global human struggles.

The idea that Appalachia was an exploited resource colony not only provided an explanation for the paradox of poverty in a rich land but also pointed to intervention strategies more consistent with Saul Alinsky's formula for political organizing on Chicago's South Side than with Oscar Lewis's framework of cultural modernization. If Appalachia was to throw off the corporate domination that controlled its wealth, the poor people of the mountains must free themselves from the feudal system of local politics that protected the absentee interests. The challenge in Appalachia, activists soon argued, was to facilitate this change by organizing citizens locally around specific community concerns—political participation, health care, welfare rights, access to housing and education, and property rights—and to build a regional identity and regional alliances around shared regional issues.

This combination of community action and regionalism generated a movement culture that bound Appalachian activists, intellectuals, and local people to a common crusade that was larger than the War on Poverty and survived long after the OEO's demise. No longer a caricature of cultural deviance, Appalachia became a proving ground for the democratic process itself, a challenge to the fulfillment of professed American values. Shady politicians, self-indulgent corporations, elite institutions, and even corrupt unions became the focal points for confrontation; organizing the poor to take control of their lives and resources became the agenda for regional transformation. As Naomi Weintraub Cohen, a volunteer from New York, recalled, "By day you might say we were day-camp counselors and tutors of children. By evening we were out there organizing and getting people stirred up about issues. . . . We were trying to convince people that by community organizing they could change the West Virginia state law and make the law more responsive to the people and more protective of the property rights of the people instead of just the strip mine operators."[12] Inspired by postwar assumptions about what America symbolized to the world and motivated by what they saw and heard in mountain communities, the majority of poverty warriors sought justice from a system that they believed should work for everyone. Few anticipated the opposition that would emerge from those in the local power structure who had a different vision for the future.

By 1966 community action had become a larger battleground in Appalachia. The conflict now was not only over poverty but also over a political economy that had limited the region's potential and left its people dependent. OEO principles of self-help and maximum feasible participation for the poor reinforced existing Appalachian traditions of resistance and fueled a growing regional rebellion that took on momentum of its own. Confrontations were most intense in the heart of Appalachia, in the coalfields where industrialization had drawn the lines of power and powerlessness most intensely, but challenges to the old order erupted throughout the region as new community associations appeared in villages and rural districts alike to fight a plethora of local problems.

Mountain residents, especially in the unionized coalfields, already had a strong heritage of family loyalty and working-class solidarity, but the War on Poverty provided an unexpected catalyst for organizing community resistance. Among the thousands of poverty workers who descended on the region to help the poor were many who owed no allegiance to government programs or local social service agencies. Supported by VISTA, the Southern Conference Education Fund (SCEF), or any number of private or religious organizations, these independent volunteers were free to live and work among the poor and to determine for themselves how best to fight poverty. Eager and unencumbered by institutional guidelines and salary expectations, they tended to operate outside existing government structures. More willing to take risks than their agency-connected colleagues, these volunteer workers, some fresh from the civil rights movement, were more aggressive advocates of confrontation and civic action.

Although most early organizing efforts were localized, a regional network emerged among activists to share strategies and support grassroots efforts. After the AV separated from the CSM, it stationed field-workers throughout the coal counties to coordinate their work with that of other volunteers, to support citizen action groups, and to pressure CAAs to be more inclusive. Common training sessions, social activities, and planning retreats (often held on college campuses) provided opportunities for poverty warriors to share their experiences and to acquire a sense of camaraderie. The Highlander Research and Education Center, a labor and civil rights folk school in eastern Tennessee, quickly became a mecca for southern Appalachian activists, and local struggles soon developed into more broadly defined, region-wide campaigns.

Typical of the community organizations that evolved into issue-oriented networks of citizen-activists was the Highway 979 Community Action Council on Mud Creek in Floyd County, Kentucky. Formed in the winter of 1963 by residents of twelve poor communities along Highway 979, the group initially planned social and recreational activities for local children and adults. By 1966 the council was officially incorporated, and, with the assistance of VISTA and AV organizers, it launched initiatives to provide clean water and job training programs for the 1,300 homes in the area.[13] As an AV outpost demonstration project, the Highway 979 Community Action Council received OEO funds to establish its own printing company and began publishing a community newsletter called the *Hawkeye*, which became outspoken in its criticism of local officials, including the Floyd County school superintendent and the head of the Big Sandy Community Action Program.[14]

Outside organizers played an important role in facilitating the growth of the Highway 979 Community Action Council, but all of its leaders and the majority of its members were longtime residents of the community. Native activists such as George Tucker, Woodrow Rogers, and Eula Hall helped to organize a branch of a regional anti–strip mining group, a garbage disposal service, and the Eastern Kentucky Welfare Rights Organization. The latter was formed to assure that local schools complied with federal laws to provide free lunches and textbooks to low-income children and to guarantee that social workers and other public assistance employees treated welfare clients with respect. It also worked to provide legal and material assistance to poor families and transportation to the hospital, doctor's office, and other social service providers.[15]

For mountain women like Eula Hall, membership in organizations such as the Highway 979 Community Action Council and the Eastern Kentucky Welfare Rights Organization provided avenues not only to improve the lives of their children and neighbors but also to develop personal skills that would link them to networks outside their local communities. Hall became active in the national welfare rights movement, testifying before a congressional hearing in 1971, and she became a champion of coal mine health and safety legislation and surface mine regulation. Frustrated by the lack of health care in her community, she fought the local OEO comprehensive health program until she secured federal funds to build a primary care clinic on Mud Creek. Her struggles with politicians and bureaucrats gave her the toughness and knowledge to endure government cutbacks and even the loss of the building that housed the community action council and welfare rights organization in a mysterious fire. Hall and others like her continued to play leadership roles in the development of their communities for years to come, sustained by the confidence and skills acquired in these early antipoverty battles.[16]

Citizens' associations like the Highway 979 Community Action Council sprang up in communities across the region, initiated sometimes by the efforts of volunteer organizers and sometimes by the spontaneous responses of poor people themselves. Groups varied in size and mission. Some were created to defend the community from specific threats—the building of a dam, unsafe roads, school closings, or environmental degradation. Others were designed to gain benefits or services that were being denied by public officials—better education, improved housing, transportation, health care, even respect. More often than not, these objectives placed grassroots organizations in confrontation with local elites, who controlled the schools, county governments, and state agencies, including most of the OEO-funded antipoverty programs.

Indeed, the local CAA itself sometimes became the target of citizen action. Poor people had long been excluded from positions of power on school boards and other county offices, but the national rhetoric surrounding the War on Poverty raised hope that the federal government would support citizen efforts to participate as equals in their own development. The enthusiasm and organizing skills of the volunteer workers, moreover, encouraged low-income residents to challenge the administrative policies of elite-dominated CAAs and to demand a greater voice in determining how federal dollars were spent in their behalf. In some cases citizen groups advocated more and diverse job training programs or better access to health and child care services in their communities; in others they called for the elimination of politics in employment practices and greater representation on agency boards.

Among volunteers and community leaders, there were wide differences in approaches to grassroots organizing, and the tactics taken up by citizen associations varied from community to community. Some AVs, for example, preferred a bottom-up strategy of supporting community-initiated causes and local leadership; others favored a more directive approach, organizing busloads of poor people to turn out for CAA meetings and orchestrating confrontations more vigorously.[17] In areas where more militant volunteers were active, organized groups not only challenged the programmatic policies of the local CAAs but attempted to seize control of those agencies as well.

A case in point was the turnout of hundreds of protesters at community meetings in Knott County, Kentucky, that resulted in the dismantling of the eight-county Cumberland Valley CAA in 1967 and the creation of county-level CAAs that local organizers believed would be more responsive to the needs of the poor. The bitter fight over control of the program angered area officials, who accused volunteer organizers of being "communists" intent on "teaching class hatred" among peaceful citizens.[18] The controversy in Kentucky became a major example of conflict within the War on Poverty during congressional investigations of the OEO later that year.[19] It also led one AV organizer to launch a short-lived drive to mobilize the poor throughout Appalachia to "take the spending of anti-poverty money—our money—away from the political bosses and big shot businessmen."[20] The organization of united Appalachian communities failed, but it was a harbinger of many subsequent attempts to rally region-wide support for political and economic change.

Fights to take over CAAs were waged in West Virginia as well, where AV organizers helped local citizens to challenge courthouse control of poverty programs. In Raleigh County, AVs put together a coalition of citizens who elected one of their own as chair of the county CAA and replaced the director of the agency, a former school superintendent, with AV Gibbs Kinderman. Aggressive political organizing produced a similar outcome in Wyoming County, but AV-supported groups failed to seize control of CAAs in Mingo, Nicholas, Boone, and other southern West Virginia counties.[21]

Increasingly, antipoverty organizers in the Mountain State were convinced that if they were going to change the way the War on Poverty was being fought in Appalachia, they would have to challenge the deeply rooted power of local political machines that controlled not only the poverty agencies but every other government service. In the summer of 1967 more than four hundred antipoverty workers from ten southern West Virginia counties convened a "poor people's congress" at Concord College to discuss election fraud, unfair tax structures, backward schools, dishonesty in state agencies, and other barriers to social change. Out of that meeting, delegates from Mingo County established a fair elections committee to monitor voting and purge registration rolls in that historically corrupt county. Under the leadership of James Washington, a fifty-two-year-old African American former coal miner, the committee launched a fair elections campaign that involved hundreds of poor and middle-class citizens in the tiny coal county and, during the 1968 election, attracted bipartisan support from reform-minded politicians across the state.[22]

Mingo County represented one of the more infamous provinces in a region of autocratic little kingdoms. Long controlled by a coalition of political bosses, school administrators, and coal interests, Mingo had been the site of bitter class warfare earlier in the century, and little change had occurred in the ensuing years to alter the patterns of voting fraud and misgovernment that kept 60 percent of the population in poverty. The Mingo County machine maintained its grip on power through the intimidation of voters and manipulation of the ballot box. The 1960 federal census documented 19,879 residents twenty-one years old and over, but the county records listed 30,331 registered voters. In the 1964 election, 25 percent of the ballots were cast absentee, the majority filled out with the open assistance of party officials. Vote buying and voter hauling by state and local government employees were rampant.[23]

The fair elections committee resolved to overcome traditional fears of confronting the powerful courthouse gang by turning out hundreds of low-income citizens at community rallies and tapping "a small group of spunky housewives" to challenge the registration rolls. The fervor for fair elections was so intense that it attracted the support of statewide leaders, including former Republican governor Cecil Underwood and VISTA volunteer turned Democratic candidate for secretary of state Jay Rockefeller. In the face of heavy intimidation, committee members purged five thousand names from voter registration lists, and poor people's groups ran opposition candidates for a number of county offices. As one reporter noted, "To the machine, the bold challenge presented a clear and present danger to its rule." County officials lashed back with numerous illegal arrests of VISTA and AV organizers accused of being outside subversives bent on disturbing the peace of Mingo County. Despite the statewide notoriety, the old power structure carried the day. Fair elections committee poll watchers estimated that two-thirds of votes were bought in the disputed election.[24]

The modest results of the fair elections movement proved frustrating for those community organizers who advocated direct political action in Appalachian counties where powerful families and special interests controlled the social service agencies, the schools, and most other means of employment. Sympathetic politicians like Rockefeller tried to push through election reform legislation at the state level, but these bills failed to make it out of committee. In response, local machine leaders turned against the poverty programs, especially the AV and VISTA, and pressured the governors in West Virginia and Kentucky to remove the poverty volunteers from their counties. Although organized political action was confined to a few counties, elected officials everywhere in the mountains became wary of the links between the War on Poverty and efforts to mobilize the poor against them. Their concern proved to be warranted, but attempts to empower the poor through the ballot box were a difficult and at best long-term tactic.

After 1968 activists increasingly found other ways to battle the entrenched system. Citizen groups organized to establish health centers in remote communities and to oppose the construction of hydroelectric pump storage facilities and flood control dams that would inundate their neighborhoods. Residents of public housing projects in Asheville, North Carolina; Knoxville, Tennessee; Hazard, Kentucky; and Charleston, West Virginia, protested rent hikes and unsanitary conditions. Citizens of rural Letcher County, Kentucky, organized their own nonprofit housing corporation, the East Kentucky Housing Corporation, to build low-income homes in communities where more than 50 percent of the housing stock was dilapidated. Each of these efforts ran into resistance from local elites who controlled city, county, and area government.

Some of the most bitter and enduring struggles, however, challenged the power of the coal industry over the economy, health, and lives of coal country people and struck at the heart of systemic problems such as land use, taxation, and the hidden human costs of an extractive, single-industry economy. It was here that local fights against powerful special interests evolved into regional battles around issues that defined a larger Appalachian identity. Even those areas of Appalachia that had never experienced coal mining came to identify with the loss of independence, devastation of the land, and threat to cultural traditions dramatized by events in the coalfields.

Changes in the coal industry had been at the core of central Appalachia's economic distress since World War II. The introduction of new technologies had given rise to massive unemployment in the underground mines and to the emergence of surface mining practices that left the landscape scarred and degraded. Rural families could see the truckloads of coal that poured from expanding strip mine operations while their sons and daughters were forced to migrate out of state for jobs and while those who remained struggled to survive on charity and government handouts.

When the UMWA announced in the summer of 1962 that it could no longer honor the health cards of some eastern Kentucky miners and was closing ten UMWA hospitals in central Appalachia, roving bands of retired and unemployed miners attempted to shut down small mines that had refused to pay royalties into the union's Health and Retirement Funds. Spontaneous demonstrations blocked roads and shut down nonunion mines, and company tipples, bridges, and equipment were bombed in the middle of the night. After Governor Bert Combs intervened to quell the violence, leaders of the roving pickets organized the Appalachian Committee for Full Employment and in 1964 prepared to join the promised War on Poverty as a legitimate CAA. The unemployed miners' committee never received OEO money, which eventually flowed through the hands of local government officials, but the anger and determination to confront the industry survived in local families and reemerged in other battles over strip mine regulation, coal mine health and safety legislation, and union reform.

Indeed, out of the same communities that produced the roving pickets movement emerged one of the most famous grassroots organizations in the mountains, the Appalachian Group to Save the Land and People (AGSLP). Established after "Uncle" Dan Gibson faced down strip miners on Clear Creek in Knott County, Kentucky, in May 1965, the group came to exemplify the frustration and dissatisfaction that ran deep in the region. Gibson, an eighty-one-year-old Baptist preacher, was hauled off to the county jail after he used a squirrel rifle to stop bulldozer operators from stripping the land of his stepson, who was fighting in Vietnam. Armed neighbors rallied in the town of Hindman, where Gibson was incarcerated, and dozens of friends stood off the strip miners again the day after the elderly preacher was released. A few weeks later, more than 125 people assembled in Hindman to form the AGSLP, dedicated to stopping strip mining in eastern Kentucky.[25]

Opposition to strip mining in Kentucky had begun as early as the 1950s, but it was not until the TVA signed a contract in 1961 with two local men to provide the agency with cheap, surface-mined coal that grassroots opposition began to mobilize. The Kentucky General Assembly enacted a weak strip mine control act in 1954, but Governor Happy Chandler abolished the enforcement agency created by the act four years later. Governor Bert Combs reestablished the bureau, but its director, a former strip mine operator, was reluctant to enforce even minor controls. Harry Caudill introduced a bill to abolish strip mining in the 1960 legislature, but it failed for lack of support. By the mid-1960s, hundreds of eastern Kentucky residents had voiced their opposition to the new mining procedure that tore away the topsoil on the hillsides to get at the coal underneath and in the process rolled stones, trees, and mine waste onto the private lands and creeks below. Even the usually moderate CSM decried the practice.[26]

When Perry County coal operators Bill Sturgill and Richard Kelley began mining in the Clear Fork Valley utilizing large-scale surface mining equipment, including a seven-foot auger, area residents were shocked. They were appalled not only at the level of destruction to their fields and streams from mudslides and acid drainage but at the apparent disregard for private property rights by the companies that owned the mineral deposits below their land. Most strip miners utilized their legal privilege to access the minerals beneath the surface through turn-of-the-century broad form deeds that the Kentucky courts had validated over the rights of surface landowners. The movement of bulldozers onto small mountain farms threatened not only the land and environment but the little security that remained for hard-hit families. Leadership of the AGSLP therefore included middle-class environmentalists, several area politicians, and elderly men and women whose land was immediately threatened by development.

Within weeks of Gibson's arrest, a caravan of fifty cars from eastern Kentucky descended on Frankfort to pressure Governor Ned Breathitt to end surface mining in the commonwealth. After being presented with petitions bearing over three thousand signatures in support of abolition, the governor responded in a manner unusual for Kentucky leaders. He promised to tour the affected Appalachian counties and later announced that his administration would implement new policies to regulate auger and contour mining. Breathitt also proposed to intervene as a friend of the court on behalf of landowners in cases involving the broad form deed and to recommend permanent legislation to control surface mining in the 1966 General Assembly. Breathitt's position nonetheless favored regulating the industry over abolishing strip mining practices, a stand that was disappointing to landowners and environmental activists in the mountains.[27]

Before hearings could be held on the proposed legislation, however, another poignant confrontation on Clear Creek dramatized the resolve of strip mine opponents. Early in November 1965, several AGSLP members were arrested for violating an injunction issued by an area circuit judge that prohibited interference with the mining operations of Sturgill and Kelley's Caperton Coal Company in the Clear Creek Valley. Several local families had been gathering for weeks along a ridge in the Hardburly section of the valley to prevent the strip miners that had threatened Gibson's farm from crossing the mountain into their community. Among the group was sixty-one-year-old Ollie Combs, a recent widow who had joined the organization at Gibson's advice when mining equipment began to advance on Honey Gap, just above her home.[28]

Combs, who lived in a four-room, tarpaper-covered cabin with her five sons, feared not only that debris from the mining operations would ruin her twenty-acre homestead but that boulders loosed by the blasting on the steep hillsides might come crashing through her house, endangering the lives of her family. When the strip miners started through the gap on the morning of November 23, 1965, Combs climbed the ridge and sat down on a rock in front of the approaching bulldozer. She and two of her sons were arrested by the county sheriff and two highway patrol officers for violating the judge's injunction and hauled off to the county jail on the day before Thanksgiving. The spectacular image of Combs being carried off her own land by two law enforcement officers—a picture snapped by a *Louisville Courier-Journal* photographer, who was also arrested—appeared the next day in newspapers across the country.

Embarrassed by this and other photographs showing the elderly woman from Fisty, Kentucky, eating her Thanksgiving meal in jail, Governor Breathitt called on the coal industry to stop insisting on legal enforcement of the broad form deeds until the courts could rule on the matter. "I am on their side," the governor declared of Combs and her neighbors. He immediately implemented more stringent emergency strip mine regulations and ordered the state police not to enforce injunctions in cases involving the broad form deed. The following January, Combs testified before the Kentucky legislature, demanding that the body do something to stop the coal companies from destroying people's homes and land in the mountains. Harry Caudill and other advocates of the eradication of strip mining on mountainsides were unable to get an abolition bill introduced, however, and the governor's more lenient regulatory bill passed overwhelmingly. The new legislation required miners to restore hillsides to their approximate original contours, prescribed maximum slope angles for mining, and established a division of reclamation with the powers to levy fines and suspend mining permits. The law provided for only a handful of inspectors and a very limited enforcement budget.

In addition, the new strip mine regulations did nothing to ban the broad form deed and therefore failed to address one of the primary concerns of mountain activists, who feared a new round of invasions of family homesteads by the coal companies. Members of the AGSLP turned to the courts to challenge the right of strip miners to destroy the property of surface owners, but their case dragged on in the Kentucky courts through 1966 and 1967. In the meantime, they continued to monitor mining operations and to recruit new members. Among the hundreds of eastern Kentuckians who joined the group were more militant antipoverty activists, who were eager to carry the fight against the coal companies to other communities.

As the number of acres permitted for mining continued to grow, opposition to surface mining became a key organizing issue for citizens' groups throughout the coalfields. Chapters of the AGSLP sprang up in Perry, Harlan, Leslie, Floyd, and other eastern Kentucky counties, and AGSLP pamphlets, newsletters, and other materials on strip mining were printed by the AV and distributed widely to antipoverty groups in the region. One AV pamphlet listed the profits of the forty largest coal corporations and holding companies in central Appalachia, labeling the inventory "Appalachia's forty thieves."[29] Although AGSLP leaders continued to advocate peaceful resistance to strip mining while the legal challenge wound its way through the courts, some residents took more militant stands to stop the strippers. In the spring of 1967, saboteurs dynamited mining equipment in Knott and Perry counties, and gunfire was exchanged between protesters and miners in several communities. One "conservation group" formed a mountain gun club to assist surface landowners "who feared that a strip operation would move in on their land by leasing the surface for $1 and setting up a firing range."[30]

Among the AV organizers to join the AGSLP at this time was Joe Mulloy. The son of Louisville, Kentucky, working-class parents, Mulloy was determined to establish a chapter of the anti–strip mining group in Pike County, where he had come to work with VISTA and other poverty warriors at Poor Bottom on Marrowbone Creek, in the southern end of the county. Poor Bottom was one of the most depressed communities in eastern Kentucky. Mulloy soon met and befriended Alan and Margaret McSurely, two recently arrived volunteers with the SCEF, and together they began meeting with neighbors and holding community discussions concerning the volatile surface mining issue. Margaret had worked with the Student Nonviolent Coordinating Committee in the southern civil rights movement before coming to Kentucky, and Alan had been engaged in antipoverty work in northern Virginia. He was hired in the spring of 1967 as an organizer for the AV but lasted only four weeks with the organization before he was deemed too controversial and was fired. He stayed on in eastern Kentucky under the auspices of the SCEF's Southern Mountain Project.

The three organizers not only began to support the efforts of a group of local landowners opposed to strip mining on the creek but openly connected the destructive land practice to the systematic exploitation of the region by the coal industry. "It was obvious," argued Mulloy, "that in Appalachia the cause of poverty and unemployment was unequal distribution of the tremendous coal wealth and absentee ownership of 90 percent of the valuable mineral rights." The abolition of strip mining would be a giant step toward "controlling the entire multi-billion dollar industry that flourishes in the midst of some of America's cruelest poverty and hardship." Confronting the bulldozers on the mountain in Poor Bottom, he believed, could launch "a movement to reclaim the wealth of the region for the benefit of the people."[31]

Such assertions were by no means uncommon in the mountains in the late 1960s, but in Pike County they fueled the suspicions of reactionary local power brokers, who perceived the entire War on Poverty as a threat to their status and control. As in nearby Mingo County, West Virginia, a cadre of coal operators, merchants, bankers, police, and other public officials ran the Pike County government and most local institutions according to the command of King Coal. One local Republican politician, Thomas Ratliff, hoped to use the populous mountain county as a springboard for his statewide campaign for the office of lieutenant governor, and he saw the organizing efforts on Marrowbone Creek as mounting evidence of class insurrection, similar to the activities of civil rights activists and antiwar protestors in urban parts of the state. One of fifty millionaires in the town of Pikeville and a founder of the National Independent Coal Operators' Association, Ratliff then served as commonwealth attorney for Pike County. He believed that the AVs and VISTA volunteers were part of a larger effort by Communist sympathizers to undermine and destroy the status quo in the mountains.

In September, Ratliff and his associates seized the occasion of another well-publicized clash over strip mining to finally rid Pike County of the troublesome AVs. On June 29, 1967, elderly farmer Jink Ray and some of his neighbors, including Joe Mulloy and his wife Karen, blocked Puritan Coal Company bulldozers that were about to strip Ray's Island Creek farm. The company obtained a court injunction against the group, but the old man returned each morning to sit in front of the bulldozer to protect the land he had farmed for forty-six years. Finally the governor intervened and revoked the mining company's permit, but the incident was enough to cause Pike County coal and government officials to act against the young outsiders who they believed were responsible for stirring up local people. When subtle acts of intimidation failed to convince the outside organizers to move on, the courthouse crowd tried more direct methods.

Following a meeting on the evening of August 11, 1967, attended by Ratliff as well as the presidents of the local chamber of commerce and the coal operators' association and the director of the Big Sandy Community Action Program, the county sheriff and fifteen others raided the homes of the Mulloys and the McSurelys and arrested Joe Mulloy and Alan and Margaret McSurely on charges of sedition based on a 1920s state statute that had long since been declared illegal. This posse confiscated from the activists' homes books and other printed materials that Ratliff later labeled "a Communist library out of this world." The subversive texts included Karl Marx's *Das Kapital*, Barry Goldwater's *The Conscience of a Conservative*, the Holy Bible, *Quotations from Chairman Mao Tse-tung*, and Adam Smith's *The Wealth of Nations*.[32] The following day, Ratliff told reporters that county of-

150

ficials had decided to act on the McSurelys after "seeing a parade of strange looking visitors at their house, some coming in buses from places as far away as California." He indicated that he feared that poverty workers were organizing Chinese-like "Red Guards" in the mountains "to promote causes aimed at downgrading and maybe overthrowing the Government." The material taken during the raids, he concluded, was evidence of how the subversives planned "to take over Pike County from the power structure and put it in the hands of the poor."[33]

Joe Mulloy posted bail soon after his arrest, but the McSurelys spent the next week in the Pike County jail. Within days, Carl and Anne Braden, coordinators of the SCEF in Louisville, visited the McSurelys and were also arrested and charged with sedition. The Bradens had been charged with the same sedition law thirteen years earlier when they sold their Louisville home to an African American man in violation of local Jim Crow ordinances, and Ratliff believed that adding them as defendants would tie the Pike County arrests to a statewide conspiracy that targeted civil rights, antiwar, and antipoverty activists. A month later, a three-judge federal court dismissed the indictments by the Pike County grand jury on the grounds that the sedition statute was unconstitutional.

The court decision did not end matters for either the Mulloys or the McSurelys, however. The day after his arrest, Joe Mulloy received notice from the Louisville draft board that his 2-A deferment had been revoked and he had been denied conscientious objector status. When he decided to resist induction into the army, the leadership of the AV fired him, fearing that additional harm would come to the organization and its mission from further publicity regarding Mulloy's opposition to the Vietnam War and the draft. He temporarily left the mountains to work for the SCEF and to appeal his draft status, but he eventually returned to work in the mines in West Virginia and to fight for improved health benefits for miners.[34]

The McSurelys were caught up in a fifteen-year national battle with Senator John McClellan of Arkansas over the confiscation and use of their personal papers in McClellan's red-baiting campaign against liberals and civil rights activists. After their Pike County home was bombed in December 1968, threatening the life of their one-year-old son, the McSurelys left the mountains, never to return. The courts eventually ruled that the warrant used in the raid on their house and the seizure of their personal property in 1967 violated the Fourth Amendment. In 1982 a U.S. district court in Washington DC awarded them $1.6 million in damages from Thomas Ratliff and from the estate of Senator McClellan for violating their constitutional rights.[35]

Just before the McSurelys were driven from Pike County, perhaps the most bizarre spectacle of the eastern Kentucky poverty wars occurred when a committee of the Kentucky legislature held hearings to ferret out Communists and other subversives in the commonwealth. The Kentucky Un-American Activities Committee (KUAC) was established in the spring of 1968 at the request of newly elected Republican governor Louis Nunn "to investigate the activities of groups and organizations which have as their objectives . . . the overthrow or destruction of the Commonwealth of Kentucky by force, violence, or other unlawful means." Nunn had promised, if elected, to rid Kentucky of subversive groups such as the SCEF and the AV, and the hearings in Pikeville were designed to draw public attention to the threat posed by such groups. Most Kentuckians understood that the conservative, bipartisan bill that created KUAC was designed to intimidate civil rights advocates and rebellious youth. "This state has become a headquarters for subversion," cautioned one Republican legislator. "Communists are working all around us." Her Democratic colleague warned, "Hippies and beatniks and assorted reds and pinks are right in our midst."[36]

The three-day hearing also dramatized the social divisions that had split Pike and other mountain counties as a result of the War on Poverty. Nowhere were the contrasting visions of the rich and the poor, the powerful and the powerless, the old and the new more vivid than between Pikeville and Poor Bottom. Nowhere was the threat of community action taken more seriously than among the coal magnates of Pike County. Under fire from both Frankfort and Washington, the AV leadership chose not to testify before the KUAC "witch hunt," but local AV employee Edith Easterling scolded the committee for "conspiring against poor people." She related that she had been labeled a Communist in her own community because of her work with the poor;

her life had been threatened and her windows shot out. When asked whether she was in fact a Communist, she replied, "I am a Republican, and who ever seen a Communist Republican?" Reverend James Hamilton defended the AVs as "the nicest bunch of young people we ever had in the community," but a group of conservative college students at Pikeville College complained that the growing institution was becoming "too liberal" and that some of the new faculty were encouraging "opposition to the draft, the War in Vietnam, and the local established leadership."[37]

The most symbolic exchange, however, came from antagonists Alan McSurely and Thomas Ratliff. Speaking on a radio broadcast the night before one of the hearings, McSurely asserted that a "courthouse gang organized to work for a few coalmine operators" ran Pike County and that even though some persons in power "had the impression that it is illegal to work for peaceful change in government. . . . It is not wrong. It is not illegal." Ratliff countered the next day that if McSurely and his friends called "on Russian tanks to help them conquer Pike County, I intend to appeal to Mayor Daley of Chicago and [former Alabama] Governor George Wallace for help in defending Pike County."[38] The lines against change were drawn in Appalachia just as they were in the rest of the nation.

Little came of the KUAC hearings. By the time the committee finished its work in Pike County, the future of the AV and the War on Poverty in Appalachia was already determined. Under pressure to rein in the Community Action division of the OEO, Sargent Shriver terminated funding for the AV shortly after the arrest of Mulloy in 1967, and he cut back drastically on the number of VISTA volunteers sent to the region. U.S. Representative Carl Perkins of eastern Kentucky was able to salvage the OEO with the adoption of the Green amendment, requiring all community action funds to be administered through a local or state government agency, but the long-term survival of the agency was in doubt. Many AVs and VISTA volunteers drifted away from Appalachia, but a significant number remained in the mountains and assumed leadership roles in emerging regional battles with government and corporate interests. Some found jobs with nonprofit organizations; others settled into academia or arts programming; still others took jobs as teachers, miners, or social workers. For them, the struggle for the land and people continued without the hope of significant federal support.

Even before the KUAC hearings in October 1968, however, critics had begun to question whether the War on Poverty had accomplished anything in the mountains. A scathing evaluation of antipoverty programs published in the January 1968 issue of *Saturday Review* maintained that Appalachia was still the "forgotten land." Reporter Peter Schrag noted that, in the seven years since John F. Kennedy had drawn national attention to the region, "grand solutions have soured into new problems, the exploitation of land and people continues, and even the best and most hopeful efforts are jeopardized by a war 10,000 miles away and by ugly political machines all too close to home."[39] The following month, Senator Robert Kennedy toured eastern Kentucky for the Senate Subcommittee on Employment, Manpower, and Poverty and found conditions in the mountains that were, in his words, "intolerable, unacceptable, and unsatisfactory."[40]

Both Kennedy and Schrag complained of widespread disillusionment and dissatisfaction with current efforts to fight poverty. Kennedy heard witness after witness describe manpower programs that didn't provide enough work, welfare programs that didn't provide enough help, and food programs that didn't provide enough food. The editor of the *Whitesburg (Kentucky) Mountain Eagle* told Schrag that the "bare gut essentials are now being met," but the existing poverty programs served only to hide the real misery. The "limited and reluctant mandate" of the War on Poverty, Schrag concluded, had made poverty "bearable" and "invisible" in Appalachia, but it had failed to change the "vested interests" that dominated the region.[41]

In a prepared statement read before the Kennedy subcommittee, Harry Caudill recounted the history of exploitation in Appalachia that had produced some of America's most prosperous corporations and some of its poorest people. He described communities impoverished by low taxes, inadequate public services, backward schools, massive unemployment, and destructive mining practices, and he ridiculed the profits of absentee-owned mining companies who paid few local taxes but "cleared more than 61 percent of gross receipts" after the payment of operating expenses. The champion of mountain activists then called on the subcommittee to support federal legislation outlawing surface mining on steep slopes, establishing a national severance tax on minerals to be used for "human development" programs in coal counties, and creating federal job programs that would make the government the employer of last resort.[42]

At the end of Caudill's statement, David Zegeer, general manager of the local Beth-Elkhorn Corporation mine, asked to speak in rebuttal and provided another vivid example of how far the philosophical gap over the Great Society had widened in the mountains. While he agreed with Caudill that the area's main problem was a lack of good roads to attract industry, he found that much of the testimony seemed to indicate that industry was bad. "Bethlehem Steel [parent company of Beth-Elkhorn] coming here was one of the finest things that has happened in this area," he countered. It paid half a million dollars in taxes each year, provided employment for 850 people, and contributed almost a million dollars to the UMWA Health and Retirement Funds.[43] "I think this area should be very happy that corporations such as ours are here. They are good companies, honorable companies. If we are wrong in mining coal in eastern Kentucky, and if we are wrong in what is going on in Appalachia as far as industry is concerned, then I think this whole country is based on the wrong philosophy. To do it any other way, you are just talking about socialism. So if what we are doing is wrong, then this whole country is wrong."[44]

The Kennedy tour and the KUAC hearings the following fall marked a turning point in the War on Poverty in Appalachia. With the election of Republican Richard Nixon to the presidency, government focus shifted from fighting the causes of poverty, whatever they might be, to managing the growing welfare system. Under Donald Rumsfeld, Nixon's nominee to head the OEO, most of the operating programs of the agency (including Head Start, Job Corps, and neighborhood health centers) were spun off to other departments. Funds for the Community Action division were gutted, and the OEO itself was abolished in 1973. For Nixon and for subsequent presidents, the problem in Appalachia and other poor places was how to reduce the tax burden from growing transfer payments to the poor rather than how to reform the economic and social system that had produced the region's distress. From the government's perspective, the War on Poverty was dead.

The decline of community action grants and the suppression of outside poverty workers in Appalachia, however, did not end the battles over control of federal dollars or the confrontations over land use, politics, or human services in the region. Partisan groups continued to fight over the spoils of federal largesse, and social service providers, researchers, and administrators continued to vie for special funds designated to address the "Appalachian problem." If the War on Poverty did nothing else, it expanded the number of mountain professionals who provided health care, education, and legal services in county seats. Some of the new professionals used their skills on behalf of the poor families they served; others simply prospered on the growing buffet of government assistance programs. Rising federal transfer payments and construction projects also enriched the holdings of local banks and the commerce of small businesses, many of which were owned by politicians who benefited directly and indirectly from the federal funds. "For all their ignorance and isolation," chided Peter Schrag, "the economic and political interests of Appalachia have a highly developed knack for using outside help to perpetuate the existing structure and the condition of dependency."[45]

Even as federal expenditures for the War on Poverty were declining, elites fought over control of poverty dollars. Authority over public housing and economic development programs became as important as control of county roads and schools, and local political machines clashed with state and even federal authorities to maintain their influence. When Governor Nunn, for example, vetoed OEO funds for the Middle Kentucky River Area Development Council in 1969, he met stiff resistance from Democratic representative Carl Perkins and from the powerful Turner family that had run Breathitt County, Kentucky, politics for forty years. Turner patriarch Circuit Judge Ervine Turner had dominated Breathitt County since the days of the New Deal; his wife Marie was county superintendent of schools; their daughter Treva Turner Howell ran the area development council's poverty program; and their son-in-law Jeff Davis Howell was chair of the county Democratic Party. The Turner family owned one of the two largest banks in the county seat, Jackson, and their Republican opponents, the Smiths, owned the other. Despite efforts by Treva Turner Howell to attribute Governor Nunn's actions to a partisan appeal for Republican votes, reporters who covered the conflict recognized that the real feud was not over political patronage but over control of the economic benefits generated by federal expenditures in the county.[46] Not only had government programs enlarged the number of politically dependent jobs, but Medicare and Medicaid had proven to be a boon for local druggists and physicians. Grocers welcomed expanding food stamp programs, and checks for welfare, disability, and retirement flooded into county banks each month. Those who controlled access to the burgeoning transfer payments for the poor and to mushrooming federal grants for infrastructure development in distressed counties could influence the location and character of lucrative government "investments" in their communities. For some Appalachian elites, managing poverty was more acceptable than fighting it and sometimes more rewarding.

Yet the demise of the OEO failed to end citizen efforts to challenge the prevailing system. In fact, the War on Poverty generated a degree of independence and assertiveness that undermined old traditions of deference to authority and laid the groundwork for collective action on a variety of labor, health, and environmental issues. Low-income community leaders found common ground with their counterparts in neighboring counties on problems of welfare and social services; coal mining families from eastern Kentucky joined with others in West Virginia and Ohio to press for mine safety and union reform; young volunteer organizers from across the region established networks to oppose strip mining, outlaw the broad form deed, document absentee landownership, and lobby for fair taxation. Out of the crucible of community action came a variety of regional movements and a new spate of regional organizations.

Antipoverty activists, for example, played a critical role in support of the movement for black lung benefits that swept the region in the late 1960s. An occupational disease of coal mining that hardens the lungs and causes slow suffocation, black lung (pneumoconiosis) had disabled thousands of miners in the southern coalfields, but there were few laws to protect workers from the hazards of coal dust generated by the new mining machines. The medical community and workers' compensation boards in coal-dominated states refused to recognize the illness, referring to the symptoms simply as "miner's asthma." When the UMWA withdrew the health insurance cards of disabled miners and their dependents, desperate families in Raleigh County, West Virginia, formed the Association of Disabled Miners and Widows to fight for the restoration of health benefits, including those related to the debilitating lung disease.

While working as a volunteer on the construction of a community water line, Craig Robinson, a VISTA volunteer from New York, attended meetings of the Association of Disabled Miners and Widows and talked with dozens of miners afflicted with black lung. In 1966 he and another VISTA volunteer, Tennessee-born lawyer Richard Bank, helped to organize the Black Lung Association (BLA). With the assistance of two local physicians, Isadore E. Buff and Donald Rasmussen, the BLA began to lobby the West Virginia Legislature to recognize the disease for compensatory benefits and to regulate the accumulation of coal dust in active mines.[47] The BLA quickly developed chapters throughout southern West Virginia and neighboring Kentucky, gathering support from a variety of indigenous leaders. These included disabled union miner Arnold Miller, who would become president of the West Virginia BLA; welfare rights advocate Eula Hall; roving pickets member Granny Hager; strip mine abolitionist Joe Begley; and Bill Worthington, president of the Kentucky BLA.[48] This combination of leadership from indigenous mining families, together with the technical and research skills of outside VISTA volunteers and medical professionals, fueled a regional movement that cut across class, race, and culture and established a pattern of issue-based coalition building that would spread to other reform efforts.

The movement to pass mine health and safety legislation reached a crescendo in the winter of 1968–1969, following the tragic explosion of the number 9 mine of the Consolidation Coal Company at Farmington, West Virginia. Seventy-eight miners lost their lives as a result of the accumulation of coal dust and methane gas. The day after the disaster, UMWA president Tony Boyle expressed sympathy for the distraught families but attributed the cause of the explosion to the "inherent danger" of mining. He claimed that the company had a good safety record and a history of cooperation with the union. Infuriated at Boyle's dispassionate response and the union's apparent lack of concern for miner safety, dissident miners and members of the BLA denounced the UMWA and began a major drive to reform state workers' compensation and mine safety laws.

In February 1969, more than forty thousand miners in West Virginia, Ohio, and Pennsylvania launched an unauthorized three-week strike that shut down much of the coal industry. BLA members marched on the West Virginia capital, chanting, "No laws, no work." Former poverty warriors, college students, and health professionals joined the movement, garnering the critical support of nonnative political leaders such as former Marshall University professor Ken Hechler and former VISTA volunteer Jay Rockefeller. The strike ended only after the passage of state legislation that provided for black lung compensation and set new safety standards to control dust levels in underground mines.[49]

Later that fall, Appalachian black lung activists carried the battle to Washington DC, and, despite coal industry opposition, Congress passed the Federal Coal Mine Health and Safety Act of 1969, extending black lung benefits to all of the nation's coal miners. The new bill, however, left the management of benefits to the Social Security Administration, which promptly rejected more than sixty thousand applications in Appalachia alone. After two years of additional protests and the deaths of thirty-eight miners from a coal dust explosion in Hyden, Kentucky, Congress amended the act in 1972, easing the path for disabled miners and widows to receive disability benefits. The "black lung paycheck," as Harry Caudill labeled it, provided only a "tittle" of income to poor families in the mountains, but the administration of benefits and the enforcement of mine safety laws remained controversial for decades to come.[50]

Outrage over UMWA president Boyle's weak response to the Farmington disaster and the union's initial opposition to the inclusion of health benefits in the new mine safety act reinforced growing dissent among rank-and-file miners. Challenges to Boyle's control of the union began to emerge in the spring of 1969, and the success of the black lung movement fueled a grassroots rebellion to democratize the UMWA and purge its leadership of corruption. A one-time ally of Boyle, Pennsylvania district leader Joseph "Jock" Yablonski, challenged the powerful president for control of the union in the fall elections, but Boyle manipulated the vote and utilized union funds to defeat the dissidents. On New Year's Eve 1969, Yablonski and his wife and daughter were murdered in their Pennsylvania home. Boyle and seven others (including three eastern Kentucky men) would later be convicted of the crime.

For many southern Appalachian miners, the corruption of the union for personal gain, the loss of health benefits for retirees, and feeble progress on wage and safety conditions were evidence of the perverse power of the coal industry in their lives and communities. Regaining control of their union was the first step on the road to better health care, workplace safety, social independence, and economic security. Whereas dissident miners from the North and Midwest were determined to purge union leadership of authoritarianism and corruption, retired and disabled miners from southern West Virginia, eastern Kentucky, and southwest Virginia were equally concerned with pensions and health benefits. After the murder of the Yablonskis, members of the BLA, the Association of Disabled Miners and Widows, and dozens of other grassroots organizations joined with northern union insurgents determined to continue the crusade against the Boyle regime. Hundreds of activists, poverty warriors, and former AVs and VISTA volunteers rallied to support the insurgency as a vibrant example of a potential Appalachian "people's movement."[51]

Embodied in the group Miners for Democracy (MFD), the drive to reform the UMWA came to represent, for a time at least, the promise of collective action against the special interests and powerful bureaucracies that controlled mountain life. When the Department of Labor tossed out the results of the 1969 UMWA vote on evidence of fraud and intimidation, the MFD nominated Arnold Ray Miller, a retired miner who had led the West Virginia BLA, as its presidential candidate in the new election. Miller, who hailed from Cabin Creek, had only a ninth-grade education and suffered from black lung, but he represented the plight of thousands of retired and desperate miners in the southern coalfields who hoped that bringing democracy to the union would bring better economic conditions to coal communities.

Miller won the election in December 1972 and successfully returned democratic control to local union districts. He subsequently negotiated new contracts with the industry that improved wages and safety inspections, and he brought honesty to union management. For several years the soft-spoken Miller was a minor celebrity among social activists in the region, and the same spirit of resistance that inspired the MFD fueled a number of strikes in Kentucky and Virginia to organize UMWA mines, including a long and bitter strike at the Brookside Mine in Harlan County, Kentucky, from 1973 to 1974. By the end of the decade, however, Miller's popularity among the professional labor organizers within the union bureaucracy waned, and even the democratic structure that he had helped to bring to local districts proved to be divisive at the national level. He was forced to resign in 1979, as the union and the number of working miners both entered a long period of decline.[52]

If the movements for black lung compensation, mine safety, and union reform reflected a growing assertiveness among coal miners to fight for better health care and more responsive, democratic institutions, the drive to abolish strip mining engaged an even larger Appalachian community in the struggle for political and economic change. Nothing quite united Appalachian activists, small landowners, and mountain intellectuals across state borders in the late 1960s and 1970s like the anti–strip mining movement. Few causes touched on a broader range of social issues confronting the region: landownership, taxation, jobs, environmental quality, and even traditional values.

Rooted in the efforts of a few environmentalists to stop the destruction of hillsides and streams in the early 1960s, the movement matured during the War on Poverty as coalitions of elderly landowners and young activists developed grassroots organizations and took direct action to stop the encroachment of bulldozers onto family farms. By 1968 most Appalachian states had passed nominal legislation regulating the industry, but these laws were weak and poorly enforced. Surface mine control laws inevitably represented a political compromise between coal operators and citizens who wanted to abolish the practice entirely.[53] In fact, the amount of surface-mined land in Kentucky and West Virginia actually increased after the passage of state surface mine control acts, and the rising demand for coal during the energy crisis of the early 1970s spread the practice rapidly in neighboring states.

When lax enforcement failed to prevent destructive mudslides and the drainage of acid waste into local streams, angry activists developed new strategies to draw attention to the need for abolition. Early in 1971, for example, representatives from the Kentucky Conservation Council, the Lexington Garden Club, the CSM, the Sierra Club, and other environmental organizations formed the group Save Our Kentucky (SOK). With funding from an eastern Kentucky deep mine operator who opposed surface mining because it undercut the price of his deep-mined coal, SOK hired a staff and launched a public education campaign to end strip mining.[54] The group also proposed more equitable taxation of unmined mineral resources and began to pressure state lawmakers for the passage of a coal severance tax for the development of public infrastructure in coal-producing counties.

Other professionals from a variety of backgrounds also joined the movement. Young lawyers from the Appalachian Research and Defense Fund, established with OEO help during the 1960s to provide legal aid to the poor, offered legal assistance to landowners who were threatened by strip miners, and a few radical activists began to randomly picket strip mine sites to shut them down and garner public support for abolition. On one rainy morning in January 1972, a group of women from the Eastern Kentucky Welfare Rights Organization, the AGSLP, and SOK occupied a strip mine site in Knott County and stopped the bulldozers for fifteen hours, until violence and threats drove them from the mountain. Later that spring more than two hundred citizens of Floyd County shut down a strip operation after runoff from the mine damaged homes and gardens during a heavy rain.[55]

The political battles over abolition in West Virginia were intense as well. In 1971 a coalition of West Virginia citizen groups, unemployed miners, antipoverty activists, and environmental organizations attempted to secure legislation that would ban surface mining in the Mountain State, but as had happened earlier in Kentucky, the coal industry mounted strong resistance. Secretary of State Jay Rockefeller even joined the campaign, making abolition a central theme in his gubernatorial race and personally funding a citizens' action committee, Citizens Against Strip Mining. Thousands of West Virginians signed petitions, campaigned for abolitionist political candidates, and marched in the streets of Charleston in favor of eradication. Rockefeller, however, lost the election to incumbent Arch Moore, who gathered heavy support from the coal industry and the UMWA, and the legislature abandoned a proposal to phase out surface mining, passing instead a regulatory control bill.

Frustrated by their lack of success at the state level, anti–strip mining activists turned to regional collaboration to raise pressure on Congress for a national abolition bill. Leaders of anti–strip mining organizations from Kentucky, Ohio, West Virginia, and Virginia met in Huntington, West Virginia, and formed the Appalachian Coalition to coordinate a regional movement for a federal ban. Representative Ken Hechler introduced the first federal bill to abolish surface coal mining in February 1971, and Congress launched a long series of hearings on the proposal. The Appalachian Coalition rallied regional support for the legislation and coordinated the testimony of mountain residents before congressional subcommittees. The Appalachian group was joined by a number of national environmental groups organized as the National Coalition Against Strip Mining. Both the coal industry and the UMWA opposed the bill on the grounds that it would cripple the nation's energy supply and increase unemployment in already hard-hit areas, but they favored more limited legislation to strengthen state oversight of mining operations.

Support for a national ban on surface mining reached its height in 1972 following the collapse of a coal waste dam at the head of Buffalo Creek in Logan County, West Virginia. A series of dams had been constructed on the creek by the Buffalo Mining Company, a subsidiary of the Pittston Coal Company, the largest independent coal producer in the United States, but both state and federal mining authorities had ignored the loose "gob pile" dams, which by 1972 had turned the Middle Fork of Buffalo Creek into a series of black pools. On the morning of February 26, 1972, heavy rains caused one of the dams to collapse, sending a thirty-foot wave of water and rocks down the seventeen-mile length of the creek, killing 125 people in a matter of minutes and leaving over 4,000 homeless. Despite its history of poor safety practices and the fact that the Federal Coal Mine Health and Safety Act of 1969 had outlawed coal impoundments like the ones on Buffalo Creek, Pittston assumed no responsibility for the tragedy. A spokesperson for the company claimed that the flood was simply "an act of God."[56]

The Buffalo Creek disaster briefly focused national attention on the consequences of uncontrolled strip mining, but the loss of life and the destruction of fifteen communities in southern West Virginia had little impact on the congressional debate. Four months after the Buffalo Creek massacre, as it would become known in the mountains, nine hundred activists gathered at the National Conference on Strip Mining in Middlesboro, Kentucky, called to draft a statement on surface mining to be presented to the Democratic and Republican conventions that year. The conference, which brought together grassroots activists and environmental leaders from across the nation, adopted a resolution demanding the prohibition of strip mining in the United States. Although the Democratic National Committee later endorsed a general statement opposing strip mining, neither party was willing to accept abolition, and by the end of the summer even the National Coalition Against Strip Mining moved to a position accepting regulation instead of prohibition.[57]

Congress deliberated for more than six years before finally passing the Surface Mining Control and Reclamation Act of 1977. As was the case at the state level, industry and union opposition, combined with the energy crisis of the early 1970s, doomed efforts to abolish surface mining at the national level. Even after national conservation groups abandoned prohibition in favor of federal supervision of mining and reclamation practices, President Gerald Ford vetoed two regulatory measures before President Jimmy Carter signed a weaker bill in the summer of 1977. While Carter favored stronger legislation, he acknowledged that the "watered down bill" would enhance "much needed production of coal" while protecting the "beautiful areas" where coal was produced.[58] Appalachian groups, led by the Appalachian Coalition, expressed their opposition to the bill on the grounds that it set up federal guidelines but left enforcement to the states, failed to protect private property and compensate landowners, and allowed mountaintop removal as an approved mining procedure. The legislation did outlaw highwalls, require slopes to be restored to their approximate original contours, and establish the federal Office of Surface Mining to regulate the industry, but it failed to end surface mining itself. The struggle over the environmental and human costs of surface mining would continue in Appalachia for years to come.

The fight for a national abolition bill dramatized the gap between middle-class conservationists who saw surface mining essentially as an aesthetic and moral assault against the environment and Appalachian activists who perceived the practice as part of a larger system of regional exploitation. Conservationists were more willing to compromise in favor of government regulation, but the former poverty warriors and poor people who led the mountain resistance organizations distrusted the ability of institutions to protect their lives and homesteads. At a people's hearing on strip mining held in Wise, Virginia, on December 4, 1971, more than two hundred activists gathered to hear mountain residents deplore the courts, legislatures, and other "institutionalized channels" that refused to respond to the plight of local people. Joe Begley from Letcher County, Kentucky; Rufus Brooks from Logan County, West Virginia; John Tiller from Brammel, Virginia; Bessie Smith from Knott County, Kentucky; and dozens of other speakers echoed the words of the Reverend Warren Wright, a Letcher County, Kentucky, farmer and anti–strip mining activist, who urged the crowd to rise up in democratic protest against the "industrial and political conspiracy" that was ruining the mountains and mountain life. The "question of strip mining," chided Begley, was "more than a question of beauty and trees." It was also a matter of "the destruction of farms and homes."[59]

Regional activists used the struggle against strip mining to expand their networks, to organize new citizen-based organizations, and to foster what they believed was a "regional democratic movement."[60] Regional strategy meetings like those held in Middlesboro, Huntington, and Wise brought together local opponents of surface mining, but they also provided venues for sharing information and ideas on a variety of other issues. New organizations such as Save Our Cumberland Mountains in east Tennessee sprang up to oppose strip mining and to work for landowner rights in their areas. Led by young radicals like

Michael Clark of the Church of the Brethren Appalachian Caucus and the Reverend B. Lloyd of the Anglican Appalachian People's Service Organization, a number of religious organizations, including the Knoxville-based Commission on Religion in Appalachia, joined the crusade. Leaders of SOK, especially its director, James Branscome, and writers Harry Caudill and Jack Weller, spoke widely at college and university rallies throughout the mountains, spreading the idea that Appalachia was an exploited colony within modern America and that surface mining was only one manifestation of a corrupt political and economic system.

Many of the new organizations published newsletters that reached thousands of readers inside and outside Appalachia, but no organization played a larger role in providing a network for regional activism than the CSM. Traditionally a rather moderate voice for reform, the council was taken over in 1969 by young activists who redirected the old organization's mission toward more radical causes and restructured its many commissions to reflect the interests of youth, community organizers, and the poor. The council no longer represented "professional persons, settlement school, religious, health, and education workers, and businessmen and philanthropists" interested in Appalachia but instead became a communication vehicle for the bottom-up democratic movement that activists hoped would sweep the region.[61]

Under the leadership of Warren Wright, the council established a number of new commissions to reflect a wide range of constituents and issues: aging, black Appalachians, community action, education, natural resources, poor people's self-help, regional development, youth, urban affairs, and welfare reform. Throughout the 1970s, the council's annual meetings and periodic commission forums brought together a mixture of community activists from across Appalachia. More important, the council magazine, *Mountain Life and Work*, was a widely distributed source of information and opinions about movement struggles and regional events. As executive director for 1970–1971, Wright reoriented the council toward "a different kind of war on poverty," one that would increase the "political awareness" of mountain people. "They have to learn," he told a reporter soon after taking office, "that the people own the system and that the system doesn't own them. I want them to know the extent to which they've been defrauded."[62]

The new CSM reflected the revolutionary change of thought and strategies that had swept Appalachia since the announcement of the War on Poverty. Mountain advocates no longer saw the culture or geography of the region as a primary barrier to development; instead they challenged the very assumptions and institutions on which the rhetoric of growth and opportunity was built. As council member Sally Maggard told the readers of *Mountain Life and Work* in 1972, the essence of the controversy over strip mining in Appalachia was "not wildflowers" but the definition of "progress" itself.

> In Appalachia, exploitation goes hidden under the rhetoric of economic development. People are forced out of their homes and from their farms because it is more profitable to let mud slide into living rooms and across cornfields than it is to mine coal with care. Little thought is given to farmlands which would have fed families for generations to come. People find that there are not jobs in the mountains because a cheap and ruthless method of mining requires few laborers. People are forced to take mining jobs which destroy their homes and the entire economic base of the region, or else move away to migrant cities like Dayton, Cincinnati, Baltimore, or Chicago. Miners are injured and die because it is more profitable to mine coal in unsafe conditions than it is to run safe mines.[63]

The challenge facing the mountains, Maggard and other activists concluded, was to confront those "powerful individuals" who controlled the region's resources (including human resources). Abolition of strip mining alone was not the answer. To carry the struggle to the political and economic power brokers outside the region, in 1972 the new council opened an office in Washington DC, staffed by Alan McSurely, to assist the lobbying efforts of Appalachian groups.[64]

The growing network of regional activists and organizations that confronted issues such as strip mining and black lung disease created a fertile environment for the growth of citizens' groups that confronted a variety of other concerns throughout the mountains. Residents of rural North Carolina communities fought the expansion of a national park visitors' center near the Blue Ridge Parkway. Others in Kentucky and West Virginia organized to resist the construction of dams that would flood family farms. Citizens in southwest Virginia, eastern Kentucky, and West Virginia established local chapters of the regional group Citizens for Social and Economic Justice that helped parents negotiate with school boards for better lunch programs and free textbooks and provided paralegal services for low-income people.

Some of the organizations that sprang up in the 1970s were designed to coordinate the efforts of diverse local groups on a larger regional basis. In eastern Kentucky, community-based groups formed the Human/Economic Appalachian Development Corporation to better assist craft and agricultural cooperatives, low-income housing programs, and other alternative economic development efforts. At a meeting in May 1977 in Williamson, West Virginia, 150 representatives of fifty mountain organizations created the Appalachian Alliance to synchronize region-wide "direct action" in support of individuals and communities that were "working to gain democratic control over their lives, workplaces, and natural resources." The alliance hoped to provide "a unified voice for Appalachian people," serve as a forum for communication among regional organizations, and change public policy through research on issues ranging from landownership to strip mining and health delivery.[65]

The most notable product of the Appalachian Alliance was the publication of a study of landownership patterns in eighty Appalachian counties, financed by the ARC in 1978 and undertaken by the alliance's Appalachian Land Ownership Task Force. Staffed primarily by young activists and college students, the task force identified the large corporations and land companies that controlled up to 90 percent of the surface land and 100 percent of the mineral resources in some Appalachian counties. These wealthy landowners paid only a small fraction of the taxes for schools, roads, and other public facilities in impoverished communities. Absentee ownership, the report concluded, limited job opportunities and economic development alternatives, restricted the local tax base, and shifted the burden for public services to local residents.[66]

Disparity in taxation had long been an issue for Appalachian activists, and in the 1970s pressure mounted to institute a severance tax on coal and other minerals and to equalize assessments on surface and subsurface property. Throughout most of the industrial history of Appalachia, the natural wealth of the region had been mined by large corporations and shipped out of the mountains untaxed, leaving local schools and other community services starved for public support. The coal industry's powerful grip on state and local governments kept property taxes low and taxes on unmined minerals even lower. Most Appalachian states depended on regressive sales taxes to support state government expenditures, and even after the passage of meager severance taxes on coal in the early 1970s, the revenue from extractive taxes flowed to the state general fund for distribution statewide (in Kentucky) or into the repair of coal haul roads (in West Virginia and Virginia). In 1976 a "mountain caucus" of eastern Kentucky legislators succeeded in returning 4 percent of severance tax funds in the commonwealth to coal-producing counties for capital projects that promoted economic development, but most coal communities and nearby rural counties where coal production had diminished received few benefits from the funds.[67]

Nor did the mining industry contribute its fair share to county property taxes. Studies of landownership and taxation in Appalachia found a direct correlation between the poverty of a county and the percentage of property owned by mineral companies. In Claiborne County, Tennessee, for example, one British company owned 17 percent of the county's land but paid only 3 percent of the county's property taxes (an average of twenty-five dollars per assessed acre for forty-four thousand acres). Seventy-five percent of the county's revenue came from state and federal sources. In fourteen West Virginia counties, twenty-five companies owned 44 percent of the surface land, yet they were assessed for only 20 percent of the area taxes. On the whole, in central Appalachian counties, only 48 percent of total revenue came from local sources, compared with 65 percent nationally.[68] The disparity in taxation of unmined mineral assets beneath the surface was even greater. In eastern Kentucky counties, the tax on unmined coal was set at such a low rate that it was considered uncollectable, despite the coal's potential value to its corporate owners.[69]

Inequities in the tax structure led activists from the Appalachian

Alliance and local concerned citizens to form a coalition to challenge Kentucky's tax system, including property tax rates and the distribution of severance tax revenues. In 1981 they formed the Kentucky Fair Tax Coalition (KFTC), which unsuccessfully lobbied the Kentucky legislature to raise unmined mineral taxes but eventually won a state supreme court decision that unmined minerals should be taxed no differently than other real property. The following year, the coalition became a citizen-based membership organization and changed its name to Kentuckians for the Commonwealth. In time, KFTC would become one of the largest grassroots organizations in Appalachia and would expand the fight for fair taxation to include challenges to the broad form deed, which many activists saw as the worst example of coalfield injustice. After the statewide Save Our Homeplace campaign in 1988, the citizens of Kentucky finally passed a constitutional amendment effectively limiting the power of coal companies to mine without the consent of the landowner and requiring companies to pay for damages caused by mining.[70]

The revolution within the CSM and the emergence of regional organizations such as the Appalachian Alliance, the Human/Economic Appalachian Development Corporation, and KFTC reflected the metamorphosis of the War on Poverty in Appalachia by the early 1970s. What had begun as a nationally initiated and locally fought campaign to bring poor people into the mainstream of modern American life had stirred a collective response in Appalachia that not only redefined regional identity but cast the social and economic troubles of the mountains in a broader context. For the remainder of the twentieth century, Appalachia would endure not only as a socioeconomic problem area—a persistent reminder of the failure of the national War on Poverty—but as a battleground for American values. Conflicts over environmental quality, welfare reform, public decision making, and economic development would continue to divide mountain communities as they did the rest of the nation, but a new regional consciousness would make those battles especially intense in the mountains and increasingly portentous for the rest of America.

Nurtured by growing networks of indigenous people, former poverty warriors, and young professionals, a new regional consciousness emerged in the mountains that challenged prevailing assumptions about the otherness of Appalachia and about the process of development as well. The Appalachian movement, of course, reflected a mosaic of contributions and political philosophies. Even the mountain middle class, which had initially rejected the word "Appalachia" because of its connection with poverty, increasingly accepted the label as a useful marketing strategy for countercultural products and applied it to businesses, organizations, and even furniture styles. University scholars, especially in the social sciences, gained long denied recognition for their study of mountain life and culture, and academic presses vied for manuscripts on regional topics. The demand for Appalachian artists and musicians mushroomed, and regional colleges introduced courses in Appalachian studies to accompany those in African American studies, women's studies, and other innovative fields.

But the heart of the Appalachian studies movement lay in the young activists who remained in the mountains after the collapse of the antipoverty crusade and continued to fight for social justice and change. Not only did these college students and former poverty warriors discard cultural stereotypes in favor of structural explanations of mountain poverty, but many also rejected the idea of progress implicit in American models of development in the post–World War II period. Like the counterculture movement that swept the rest of the country, the new Appalachian regionalism evolved from both the cultural and the political radicalism of the Vietnam War era and reflected as much a desire to change the course of the nation as it did a determination to escape assimilation.

In many ways the burgeoning Appalachian movement was antimodern, defending traditional lifestyles and romanticizing Appalachian culture. Some of the former poverty warriors openly abandoned the emerging consumer society and sought to return to the land on individual homesteads or communes. These "back to the landers" cherished simplicity and found meaning in the old-time ballads and handcrafts. Some formed lasting friendships with neighboring poor families who, out of economic necessity, preserved the old ways. Thousands of native Appalachians rediscovered their own heritage and gained new pride in place and family ties. In an era of rapid social change and rising ethnic consciousness, Appalachians old and new discovered their roots and came together to defend their people from assault.

At its core, however, the regional movement represented a thoroughly modern effort to protect human rights and to spread the promises of security and freedom from want to a larger community of people. While they feared that public institutions and government were easily co-opted by private interests, mountain radicals and reformers shared a common faith in the democratic traditions of fairness, self-determination, and justice. They opposed the concentration of wealth and political power in the hands of the few and accused business leaders of putting profits before the common wealth of the community. They favored government intervention to regulate the abuses of corporations and looked to expand government services, but they also sought to preserve private property rights when family farms were threatened by corporate greed or public development. They believed that "good government" could conserve the land and sustain the people through civic engagement and community-based economic enterprise. The problem in Appalachia, they came to agree, was not poverty or strip mining or health care alone; it was a pattern of corruption that had tainted the whole system.

Many of the strongest advocates of the new regionalism were students or young intellectuals associated with colleges and universities serving Appalachia, and they were quick to link the injustices of the mountains to global struggles against racism, imperialism, and corporate capitalism. The War on Poverty always had an important academic component. The theories of human behavior and economic development that drove government programs in the region came out of institutions of higher education, as did many of the volunteers in the antipoverty crusade. Training sessions for AVs, VISTA volunteers, and other poverty workers were frequently held on university campuses, and in many mountain communities the local college provided the only public space for community forums and workshops.

The expansion of higher education in the region during the 1960s and 1970s brought growing numbers of working-class students into the classroom and provided young people with critical access to new ideas and broader social movements. Most of the mountain activists, for example, were steadfast opponents of the Vietnam War, and they connected their fight for regional justice with larger concerns about American actions throughout the third world. "The same values and national priorities which allow this country to inflict massive destruction upon the Vietnamese," declared one Appalachian movement publication in 1971, "are responsible for poverty, cultural imperialism, and the attacks upon the land and people of Appalachia."[71]

During the 1970s several Appalachian colleges established centers for Appalachian studies and developed curricula to support growing faculty and student interest in the region. Most of these programs offered coursework in Appalachian history, literature, and culture, preferring to study the region and its problems and avoid active engagement in controversial and politically divisive issues. Activists, however, gathered around a number of institutions and used them to support regional organizing initiatives. Clusters of Appalachian advocates developed around West Virginia University, Marshall University, the University of Kentucky, the labor and civil rights school at the Highlander Research and Education Center in Tennessee, and Don West's Appalachian South Folklife Center in southern West Virginia. Near Morgantown, West Virginia, for example, activists organized the People's Appalachian Research Collective to develop an Appalachian "action-study center" at WVU and to work with researchers at the university's Institute for Policy Studies.

Several former AVs settled into graduate study at the University of Kentucky and helped to establish the Appalachian Center in 1976. Appalachian centers were also created at Berea College (where there was an active group called Students for Appalachia), Mars Hill College, Pikeville College, and Appalachian State University, and regional studies programs were launched at Ohio University, Emory and Henry College, Lees College, Union College, Alice Lloyd College, and other institutions. Marshall University activists created the Appalachian Movement Press to promote the development of regional consciousness and, for a time, ran a cooperative labor school with Antioch College. In 1971 almost a dozen colleges and federal agencies in North Carolina, Tennessee, and Virginia organized the Appalachian Consortium to encourage a better understanding of the region's history and culture.

Faculty on a number of campuses had begun teaching courses on

Appalachia in the 1960s, and following an initial Appalachian studies conference at Virginia's Clinch Valley College in 1970, research and teaching on Appalachia expanded on college campuses throughout the mountains. Academic interest culminated in a major gathering of regional advocates at the Cratis Williams Symposium at Appalachian State University in 1976, which led to the creation of the annual Appalachian Studies Conference in 1978. Relationships between institutionally based scholars and more radical community activists were cordial but tense from the first of these meetings. Reflecting their basic distrust of institutions and cultural (rather than political) definitions of the region, activists at the Clinch Valley College conference shouted to the more conservative academic participants, "You are the enemy." Some radical intellectuals later warned unsuccessfully against the creation of an institutionalized Appalachian studies association.[72]

For Appalachian movement activists, the emergence of a regional studies industry threatened to use Appalachian people for personal and institutional gain in the same way that the region's labor and natural resources had been exploited for decades to benefit elite and predominantly external interests. They feared that the new regional consciousness would turn Appalachian culture into a commodity to be studied, bought, and sold in the consumer marketplace rather than an expression of fundamental conflicts within American politics and life. While they welcomed a more positive regional identity, their concerns lay in the challenges facing communities, the expansion of democratic processes, and the protection of individual rights. "For those of us who believe that the struggle is for the soul of man in a technological society," wrote native activist James Branscome, "the resistance of Appalachian culture against assimilation into Middle America demands earnest, indeed prayerful, attention."[73] Veterans of the War on Poverty, many of whom would become college professors, lawyers, and journalists in the new Appalachia, would make every effort to see that the budding regionalism sustained that commitment.

The tension between more moderate regionalists and those who saw their role as agents of social change reflected the fundamental dilemma of the Great Society. Could the nation bring the benefits of postwar prosperity to minorities and disadvantaged populations without confronting the uneven ground on which that prosperity was built?

The history of the War on Poverty in the mountains suggested that mainstreaming the poor instead of altering the political and economic inequalities that caused dependence was a lesson in mutual frustration. Indeed, the antipoverty campaign designed to eliminate regional distinctiveness only generated a renaissance of regional identity that professed a vision for the good life different from that emerging in the rest of the "consumer republic." Appalachia was at once the other America and the conscience of America.

"I used to think that what was needed was to bring mountain people into the economic mainstream," wrote Michael Smathers in the closing years of the War on Poverty. "I thought it would be possible to do this and still preserve some of the positive, humanizing qualities of mountain cultures. I no longer think this is either possible or desirable. Our challenge is not to join mainstream America. It is to recreate a renewed and authentic form of what the mountains have always been. From the time that the first white settlers deliberately cut their ties with the coastal culture of colonial America to start a new life in this wilderness, the mountains have offered an alternative to mainstream America." This alternative society, Smathers added, was nearer to being absorbed than it had ever been. The task before his generation was to renew this alternative and restore it to the nation. Americans might all need to learn a lesson from the mountains, he concluded:

> While I was home last summer, I attended a celebration of historic Old Rugby in Morgan County, Tennessee. For a while that afternoon I sat in a yard listening to some musicians and speakers. Two flatland women were sitting on chairs in front of me, and one of them was being bothered by a long stem growing out of a plant behind her. There was nothing pretty about this stem. It was sort of ugly. It bore neither flowers nor leaves. But on the upper end it held two immature seedpods, and to me it represented life. The one woman complained to her friend about the nuisance of the stem, whereupon her friend leaned over and with some effort broke the stem.
>
> That action seemed to me a typical response of technological society. If a flower bothers you, break it. If the environment restricts you, change it. If people get in your way, manipulate

them. I believe that the more typical mountain response in this situation would have been to move your chair—to adapt yourself rather than to manipulate your environment. It is a practice we all need to learn—to move our chairs before we use up the world and bury ourselves in our own waste.[74]

ountain Farm (Warren Brunner)

Coal Loader Blaine Sergent on His Way Home, 1946 (Russell Lee Photographic Collection, Special Collections Library, University of Kentucky, Lexington)

Father and Son Miners, 1946 (Russell Lee Photographic Collection, Special Collections Library, University of Kentucky, Lexington)

Miners Buying Groceries at the Company Store (UMWA Photographic File, Collection on Appalachia, Special Collections Library, University of Kentucky, Lexington)

Miners' ID Tags, Clay County, Kentucky, 1964 (Warren Brunner)

Miner on His Last Day of Work (William Strode)

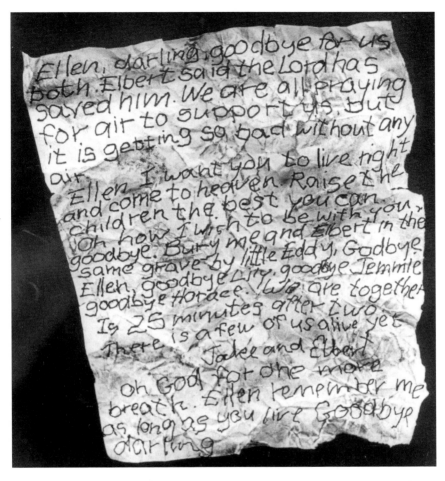

Letter from a Trapped Tennessee Coal Miner (UMWA Photographic File, Collection on Appalachia, Special Collections Library, University of Kentucky, Lexington)

Harry Caudill at a Small Truck Mine, 1962 (Anne and Harry Caudill Papers, Special Collections Library, University of Kentucky, Lexington)

Dog Hole Mine, 1964 (Warren Brunner)

Working a Low Coal Seam, 1966 (Warren Brunner)

Hillside Farm, 1964 (Warren Brunner)

Flooded Mountain Communities, 1963 (William Strode)

Lynch, Harlan County, Kentucky (William Strode)

Dying Coal Town, 1964 (William Strode)

Log Cabin Farm, ca. 1964 (Warren Brunner)

John D. Whisman (John D. Whisman Papers, Special Collections Library, University of Kentucky, Lexington)

President John F. Kennedy and the Appalachian Governors, 1963 (John D. Whisman Papers, Special Collections Library, University of Kentucky, Lexington)

President Lyndon B. Johnson and Lady Bird Johnson in Martin County, Kentucky, 1964 (John D. Whisman Papers, Special Collections Library, University of Kentucky, Lexington)

Appalachian Volunteer, 1965 (Appalachian Volunteers Records,
Special Collections and Archives, Hutchins Library, Berea
College, Berea, Kentucky)

One-Room School, 1965 (Appalachian Volunteers Records, Special Collections and Archives, Hutchins Library, Berea College, Berea, Kentucky)

The Widow Ollie Combs Resists Strip Mining of Her Property, November 23, 1965 (William Strode)

Widow Combs Eats Thanksgiving Dinner in the Knott County Jail
(William Strode)

Retired Miners Rally for Black Lung Benefits, 1975 (Highlander Series, Collection on Appalachia, University of Kentucky Libraries, Special Collections)

Senator Robert Kennedy Tours a Coal Camp, 1968 (Appalachian Volunteers Records, Special Collections and Archives, Hutchins Library, Berea College, Berea, Kentucky)

Appalachian South Folklife Center, Summers County, West Virginia, 1968 (John D. Whisman Papers, Special Collections Library, University of Kentucky, Lexington)

Picketers at the Brookside Mine, 1974 (UMWA Photographic File, Collection on Appalachia, Special Collections Library, University of Kentucky, Lexington)

Roses Creek, Tennessee, 1972 (Warren Brunner)

Surface Mine, 1985 (Warren Brunner)

Drag Line at a Mountain Surface Mine, 1985 (Warren Brunner)

Grundy, Virginia, 2007 (Richard Copeland III)

The New Appalachia, 2007 (Richard Copeland III)

Fines Creek Valley, Haywood County, North Carolina, 2007 (Ronald D Eller)

5

GROWTH AND DEVELOPMENT

The modern American faith in technology and growth was nowhere more evident than in the programs of the ARC. Just as the OEO attempted to alleviate Appalachian otherness by modernizing mountain culture, the ARC sought to bring the promise of a modern economy to the mountains. Confidence in American capitalism and faith in science, technology, and public planning convinced most postwar policy makers that growth produced prosperity and that economic expansion could be managed to create better communities. For the designers of the legislation that created the ARC, the construction of "developmental" highways, vocational schools, health facilities, and other public infrastructure would help to link the mountains more directly to national markets, a process that would in turn promote growth and prosperity in the lagging region. As much as any other Great Society program, the ARC played a vital role in the modernization of Appalachia during the decades after the waning of the antipoverty crusade.

Unique among Great Society programs, the ARC was designed as a partnership between state and federal governments, and thus it represented an experiment at two levels. The commission's shared decision-making process distributed power among thirteen governors and the White House, anticipating the new federalism that would characterize government programs in the 1970s. Administered by a cadre of confident young bureaucrats and professional planners, the ARC was also a model for the new science of planned regional development. As such, it was the first agency to apply economic growth theory to public investments in underdeveloped areas within the United States. A domestic version of the Marshall Plan, the ARC was both an expression of American political culture in the postwar years and a sign of popular confidence in the ability of science and technology to produce the good life.

Like the OEO, the ARC owed its intellectual origins to theories of human and economic development that emerged in the social sciences following World War II. Whereas the framers of the War on Poverty utilized behavioral theory to design a strategy for assimilating mountain culture into mainstream culture, the ARC tapped the ideas of economists and planners to bring the region's lagging economy into line with national markets and expanding consumer services. Not surprisingly, American economists disagreed on the way to manage the postwar economy. Some believed that government should intervene in a limited way to maintain balance, stability, and security in a mature economy. Others were strong advocates of aggressive government action to promote steady growth through policies that maximized production, consumption, and full employment. Growth theory was ratified in the Employment Act of 1946, which made the pursuit of full employment and maximum production official government policy, and it was institutionalized in the creation that year of the president's Council of Economic Advisors.

The emphasis on growth rather than on economic stability reflected the tremendous outburst of national optimism after World War II and was fueled by the emergence of the consumer culture in the 1950s. In contrast to the economy of scarcity of the Depression era, the postwar economy of abundance appeared to promise a better life for everyone, without the political problems of redistributing limited wealth. Advocates of growth theory believed that government should work aggressively to increase the nation's productivity and that rising productivity, rather than structural reform, would reduce conflict over issues of social equity. As economic historian Robert Collins has observed, policy makers turned to the social sciences "to move issues of social strife out of the political arena and into the court of scientific analysis." They assumed that rising demand for new consumer products would stimulate further growth, and the cycle of demand and consumption would benefit everyone. In this way "economic growthmanship" expressed the ascendant values of the modern consumer culture and appealed to business, labor, and middle-class voters alike.[1]

In 1960 growth became one of the central mantras of John F. Kennedy's New Frontier. Under the leadership of Walter Heller, Kermit Gordon, and other growth theory economists, the Council of Economic Advisors emerged as the leading proponent within the administration of utilizing government resources to promote economic expansion. Even the War on Poverty was based on the promise of economic growth. As Walter Lippmann observed in March 1964, "A generation ago it would have been taken for granted that a war on poverty meant taxing money away from the haves and . . . turning it over to the have nots. . . . But in this generation . . . a revolutionary idea has taken hold. The size of the pie can be increased by invention, organization, capital investment, and fiscal policy, and then a whole society, not just one part of it, will grow richer."[2] For Heller and other economists, the goal of the OEO and the ARC in Appalachia was not only to increase the per capita income of the region but to change the region's culture and economy so that it could contribute to, and benefit from, national growth.

Expansion of the region's economy was always the primary goal of the Appalachian Regional Development Act. The Appalachian governors who initiated the legislation distinguished between temporary aid for relief from unemployment and permanent investments for development. Appalachia, they argued, was underdeveloped and needed the infrastructure—including highways, factories, schools, and water systems—to sustain a modern economy and lifestyle. Determining how best to promote development, however, involved a contentious and highly politicized debate. As defined by Congress, Appalachia was a diverse region, and the political needs of thirteen governors militated against any single strategy or regional plan. Consequently, the early policy struggles within the ARC focused on investment strategies to achieve regionally measurable growth rather than on issues of social equity or on the cultural and environmental consequences of development itself.

At the center of the ARC debate about regional growth was a single sentence added to the second ARDA before its passage in 1965. To placate key economic advisors on the White House staff, PARC executive director John Sweeney attached language mandating that public investments made in the region under the act concentrate in areas where there was significant potential for future growth. Added because of budgetary fears that it would waste limited federal resources to attempt to address the problems of every small community in such a vast region, the sentence also reflected the prevailing philosophy of most national economists that growth started at growth poles (urban areas) and filtered outward to peripheral rural communities along developmental axes (highways) that connected rural people to urban services. This concept of growth center development took on special significance within the ARC process after strong advocates of growth theory were appointed to head the commission. Sweeney, formerly an economist with the Department of Commerce, became the ARC's first federal cochair; Ralph Widner, a Pennsylvania urban and regional planner, became executive director; and Monroe Newman, an economist out of Penn State University, became chief economist.

Introduced to American economists and regional planners in 1963 and 1964 just as the PARC staff was drafting the Appalachian legislation, growth pole theory heavily influenced the drafting of the ARC management code and subsequent development strategies.[3] Building on the work of French economist François Perroux, American planners suggested that the most efficient policy for public investment aimed at spurring national economic growth was the concentration of resources in the few expanding metropolitan centers that demonstrated the greatest potential for growth. These centers would be linked with each other and with smaller "urban growth complexes" by a modern transportation network that would provide access to jobs and public services to the surrounding rural "hinterland." Furthermore, the identification and support of a few "leading regions" (based on their comparative potential for growth) would allow these areas to reach a "critical size" that would sustain development and knit the entire nation into "a single, unified economy, culture, and urban system."[4]

When applied to Appalachia, this national development strategy had significant policy implications. As Widner recalled, "One of the major arguments used to oppose a special regional development program for Appalachia . . . was the fact that the region is filled with thousands of tiny, dying mining camps and rural communities. A program for the region would be doomed to fail . . . if the regional effort was intended to resuscitate all of them through haphazard distribution of Federal largesse."[5] The solution, Sweeney told *U.S. News and World Report* shortly after the passage of the ARDA, was to "concentrate all of the [ARC] spending for economic development in places where the growth potential is greatest. . . . Ignore the pockets of poverty and unemployment scattered in inaccessible hollows all over the area . . . and build a network of roads so that the poor and unemployed can get out of their inaccessible hollows and commute to new jobs in or near the cities."[6]

Traditional models of development had assumed that growth would occur simultaneously in both core (urban) and peripheral (rural) areas, but growth pole theory required that infrastructure and social overhead investments concentrate in dominant population centers to maximize growth, rather than being dispersed to a larger geographic region. In Appalachia there were few growth centers (defined initially as areas with populations of 250,000 or more) except in the larger valleys and along the periphery of the region. Large areas, such as eastern Kentucky, had no major urban centers within the boundaries of the ARC.

Politicians in rural Appalachia therefore feared that this growth center strategy would divert critical resources for their depressed communities into cities on the edge of the region, and they were quick to rebuff the idea. In the first year of operation, the states rejected a proposal, prepared under contract with a California-based consulting firm, to concentrate ARC resources on industrial recruitment projects in major cities such as Birmingham, Knoxville, Charleston, and Pittsburgh rather than on the region's rural heartland. John Whisman from Kentucky, who was appointed as states cochair of the ARC in 1966, engaged in open dispute with Sweeney over the intent of the legislation: "The people in Washington take a look at Eastern Kentucky and then they go right across the whole business before they see anything that arouses their attention . . . a place that in their opinion has the capacity for growth. . . . There is a general feeling in this country that this is going to be a great urban nation and that everybody is going to live in the cities and that all the investments to make more jobs ought to be put in the cities and then you can move and go to the cities."[7] If national growth pole theory were applied to Appalachia, Whisman argued, large areas of the region would be excluded from the benefits of ARC funding, especially hard-hit areas of central Appalachia. Despite these protests, significant nonhighway investments during the first four years of the ARC program flowed to major metropolitan centers, including more than $10 million each for Pittsburgh and Huntsville, Alabama, and more than $4 million each to Scranton, Pennsylvania; Cumberland, Maryland; Gadsden, Alabama; and Greenville, South Carolina.[8]

Under pressure from the governors, Whisman, Sweeney, and the commission staff eventually worked out a compromise that retained the essential elements of the growth center strategy but provided political flexibility for state ARC offices to invest in nonmetropolitan areas. Conceding that Perroux's central argument about the relationship between growth poles and hinterlands focused on the "fields of economic forces" of development rather than on a discrete point in geographic space, the planners devised a three-tiered model that permitted agency funds to flow to midsize cities and towns that lay along the developmental axes between metropolitan centers and rural hinterlands. This policy allowed the states to determine their own growth areas as defined by existing public services and labor market commuting patterns. In central Appalachia, these growth areas included clusters of smaller cities organized with surrounding rural counties into sixty local or area development districts. When connected to larger urban centers by good highways and transportation facilities, these second-tier cities could provide employment and services for remote hinterland populations within a fifty-mile radius, thus creating an integrated regional development plan within a larger national development system.[9]

As a result of this compromise between the technicians and the politicians, county seats and clusters of communities with populations over seven thousand became the focus of ARC development efforts. In addition to regional metropolitan centers, smaller municipalities such as Pikeville, Prestonsburg, Hazard, Asheville, Beckley, Johnson City, Parkersburg, and Bristol were now eligible to receive funding for water and sewer lines, industrial site access roads, and other infrastructure development projects. Categorical grants for education and health would be given priority to improve the labor pool in these communities and to expand their role as regional service centers. Although the states were encouraged to concentrate their "human capital" investments in these high potential growth areas, the ARC code also permitted investments in health and vocational education infrastructure in more remote areas to enable the rural population to take advantage of the services and job opportunities to be developed in the growth centers. In fact, between 1965 and 1969, the commission allocated about 40 percent of its nonhighway funds to health and education projects in the rural hinterlands and concentrated the remainder in designated growth areas.[10]

The compromise over growth center policy allowed governors greater discretion in distributing ARC funds within their states, and it preserved the theory of growth pole development important to Washington bureaucrats. On one hand, the policy fulfilled the congressional mandate to invest in areas of greatest potential for growth and maintained the core-periphery concept of development between urban and rural places within Appalachia. On the other hand, by concentrating ARC resources in the smaller cities and expanding "big road" communities (while channeling limited assistance to severely distressed rural areas), the strategy also met the political needs of the governors, who benefited more from public expenditures in the voter-rich and politically powerful county seats than in remote rural communities.

Implicit in the ARC growth center strategy, of course, was the assumption that urban life represented the ultimate goal of regional development. For Widner and other senior professionals at the commission, economic growth was directly related to urbanization. As he explained at an ARC committee meeting in New York in 1967, "The progress of an area's economy depends to a very large extent upon the ability to provide the necessary range of services and concentration of labor force required by modern enterprise. In general, as an area's economy grows, it does so slowly until it reaches a critical mass of services, training, labor force, and public and private capital, all of which is vital to support most modern enterprise in an area." At some stage, when such concentrations have built up, he added, "the costs of congestion also builds up, and development pushes outward into the surrounding hinterlands."[11]

"The brutal truth," Widner told *Harper's* in 1968, "is that America now has only two choices: either (a) urbanization or (b) urbanization." This meant that those working to improve the quality of life in Appalachia must give up "the old American dream . . . that [we] might return somehow to the pastoral life in country villages and small farms." It also meant that little, dying towns in the mountains must "be encouraged to die faster" and that millions of rural mountaineers would "have to move away from their creek bottom corn patches and played-out mineheads."[12] They could migrate either to already over-crowded metropolitan areas, a prospect the ARC hoped to minimize, or to carefully planned, medium-size cities within or near the region.

Widner believed that, if the mountains were to keep pace with the rest of the country, the goal of development in Appalachia must be to "induce some degree of urbanization" in a region "substantially un-der-urbanized." As late as 1970, a staff report to the commission suggested that the Appalachian program could achieve this objective by strengthening selectively those "urban centers, either existing or to be created, which on the basis of performance, location, and potential are the most likely ones to grow in urban service employment."[13] For northern Appalachia and extreme southern Appalachia, this meant the encouragement of growth and development of ARC counties near existing metropolitan centers, but for the Blue Ridge and central Appalachia, it meant the depopulation of rural communities and the movement of populations into selected growth areas that served as extensions of distant urban centers.

These two less urbanized parts of Appalachia would be developed to play alternative roles in a modern economy. The Blue Ridge and the Great Smoky Mountains, located between the large cities of the East Coast and the Midwest, would become "the playground of the future for metropolitan millions who live on either side," and the Cumberland Plateau would be given over to natural resource development, its surplus labor force encouraged to move to "new towns" constructed along the Appalachian corridor highways or to commute to branch manufacturing plants in the smaller towns and villages. Extremely rural and remote counties would receive few ARC funds. In adopting this modified growth center strategy for the development of Appalachia, the commission staff assumed that the automobile and other technology had drastically changed the conditions under which rural people lived in the modern world and that rural parts of Appalachia had to adjust to this change. In the future, fewer people would be employed in agriculture and mining and more in manufacturing and service trades. In addition, thanks to the automobile and to the proposed Appalachian corridor highway system, people would be able to "reach jobs and services each day 20 miles or so away."[14]

ARC investments in the most rural parts of Appalachia were therefore designed to prepare mountain people for life in the modern consumer world, if not to encourage them to migrate to distant cities or nearby growth areas. Despite that in central Appalachia fewer than one in six people lived in communities of more than 2,500, the objective of ARC development in the mountain heartland was to "accelerate urbanization" through improvements in transportation, health, and education.[15] By investing public resources in health care, technical training, and higher education facilities, the commission hoped to build a skilled labor force that might attract new industries to the region, but it recognized that such investments might also "equip young people to leave the region for other parts of the country where economic opportunities were more attractive."[16] By constructing a modern transportation network and upgrading the Appalachian labor force, the ARC hoped to integrate the mountains and mountain people more directly into an emerging urban society.

Like the War on Poverty, the ARC was an experiment in social and economic change, rooted in prevailing assumptions about the modernization process itself. Highways and urban development were assumed to be the catalysts for prosperity, and science and technology provided the formula for success. Commission staff members were quick to apply the latest systems theory to the analysis of regional problems and to the adoption of intervention strategies. "Appalachia," Ralph Widner admitted to a group of Washington DC engineers, "is something of a laboratory in which a new set of political, social, and economic principles is being tested pragmatically, but within the framework of our constitutional political system."[17]

Although both the professional planners and the politicians agreed that the motivation for the experiment was growth, they frequently disagreed on how best to attain it. As ARC administrators acknowledged, Appalachia's problems were more than technological. Achieving consensus in the political sphere would become a recurring challenge, and by the early 1970s, even the technicians conceded that "modernization of state and local governments in the region had to be encouraged."[18] The commission would have less success, however, in altering tax policies, encouraging democratic leadership, reforming public institutions, and confronting corruption than in bringing the facade of a modern economy to the mountains.

At its core, of course, the ARC was a political organization, and as such it responded to the vagaries of personality, partisanship, and power. Congress had rejected the model of a public corporation for the Appalachian program in favor of establishing a state-federal cooperative agency. Unlike the TVA, which possessed autonomous power to manage physical resources in the Tennessee River watershed, the ARC was designed as a comprehensive development organization responsible to the president, to thirteen governors, and ultimately to Congress. At every level of the ARC policy-making and planning processes, differences in values, philosophy, and self-interest intersected to influence programs and administrative strategies.

Theoretically, projects were to be proposed at the local level by area development districts, passed along to the state's governor's office for approval, and endorsed by the other governors and by the federal cochair, who represented the president. A jointly funded staff led by an executive director would then administer grants from funds appropriated by Congress. The ARC structure was more democratic than that of other federal agencies, although critics pointed out that the local development districts that initiated projects were not broadly representative or participatory and that Congress restricted funding to categorical grants in specific areas and occasionally attached allocations for special projects in the districts of powerful legislators.

During the early years of the program, funding levels and enthusiasm for the initiative minimized policy disputes within the organization. Following the compromise over growth center strategies, the states, the federal cochair's office, and the Washington-based staff worked together aggressively to implement the annual billion-dollar regional development strategy. By 1970 the commission had authorized the construction of almost 2,500 miles of the Appalachian Development Highway System and over 500 miles of access roads for airports, industrial sites, and schools. Although 80 percent of total ARC appropriations were designated for highway construction, between $200 million and $300 million annually was set aside during this period for nonhighway projects. In addition to funding water and sewer, mine reclamation (primarily in Pennsylvania), and solid waste projects, the commission provided supplemental funding to help construct 269 health facilities, 174 community colleges, and almost 300 vocational schools.[19]

In its first four years of operation, the ARC gained a reputation in Washington for getting things done quickly by cutting through established bureaucratic procedures and making resources available to initiate funding from other agencies. The commission's seventy-person staff of planners, direct access to the governors, and system of local development districts composed of elected officials provided a structure for coordinating multiagency responses to crises and complex projects. This was especially evident after the tragic collapse of the Silver Bridge across the Ohio River in 1967. By rapidly bringing together the personnel of transportation and public works committees from the states involved (Ohio and West Virginia) and pressuring the Army Corp of Engineers, the ARC staff was able to begin the reconstruction of the bridge within three weeks. Normal bureaucratic procedures would have taken up to six years.[20]

The best example of ARC capacity, energy, and goals during these early years, however, was the Pikeville cut-through project in Pike County, Kentucky. Pikeville was one of the designated growth centers in eastern Kentucky. Although it was the hub of central Appalachian banking and coal interests, it was plagued by almost annual flooding of the downtown business district from the waters of the Levisa Fork of the Big Sandy River. Pikeville was located on a narrow neck of land formed by a loop in the river, and the main line of the Chesapeake and Ohio Railroad ran right through the middle of the town. Beginning in 1969, the ARC coordinated an effort involving fourteen government agencies to reroute the river through a massive cut in the mountainside to get the waterway, the railroad, and the highway out of the downtown area and open the recovered land to urban redevelopment. The commission initiated the early planning and engineering studies and facilitated the efforts of state and local officials—led by Pikeville mayor William Hambley—to garner federal construction funds. In 1970 the City of Pikeville received the first of more than $21 million of federal grants for the cut-through project, which rivaled the building of the Panama Canal in the amount of earth that had to be removed. The railroad tunnel under the mountain opened in 1978, the river relocation was completed in 1980, and the new highway was opened in 1987.[21] By the turn of the century, as a result in part of the efforts of the ARC, Pikeville had grown into a modern, comprehensive service center.

The role of the ARC as a catalyst for planning and interagency cooperation increasingly engaged the agency in program expansion. As challenges to the War on Poverty began to undercut the OEO and led to its eventual demise, the ARC placed greater emphasis on human capacity development as part of its comprehensive mission. In 1968 Congress authorized the commission to provide technical assistance to local governments and nonprofit organizations that wished to apply for federal housing grants, and the agency launched a major initiative to improve early childhood development and nutrition programs. With the election of Richard Nixon to the presidency, the commission responded to the new emphasis on revenue sharing by facilitating gubernatorial interest in preschool education, occupational rehabilitation, and job training. The 1969 and 1971 acts reauthorizing the ARC extended its flexibility even more by allowing demonstration grants for program operations in work-related areas of health care and education.[22]

The Nixon administration at first expressed little interest in the ARC, giving rise to fears that it might be abolished along with other Kennedy-Johnson initiatives, but after meeting with the Appalachian governors in Louisville on his way to the baseball All-Star Game in St. Louis, the president endorsed the agency as an example of his new federalism. Adopting a strategy that would save the commission from several subsequent efforts to kill it, the governors convinced Nixon that the ARC was a model of state-federal cooperation, a unique agency that received bipartisan support in both the region and Congress. The elimination of specific funding categories for nonhighway allocations in the 1971 reauthorization act, moreover, provided the governors with more flexible funding in the form of block grants, free from the controls of state legislatures. The Appalachian highway program relieved pressure on state transportation funds to build expensive mountain highways, increasing the resources available for other parts of the state, and the governors wielded almost unlimited power to distribute ARC nonhighway funds allocated for their states.

In 1971 President Nixon appointed Donald W. Whitehead as the federal cochair of the ARC. Whitehead was a Massachusetts lawyer and had been northeast field director for Nixon's 1968 campaign. He had come to the commission in 1970 as general counsel with little knowledge of the region or of the ARC. A forceful and assertive leader, Whitehead became a strong advocate for the agency in an administration consumed first by the Vietnam War and later by Watergate. During his six years at the ARC, he pressed the governors to commit to a single regional development plan rather than to thirteen state plans, and he oversaw a major reorganization of the commission itself. However, his self-confident style and his tendency to see the ARC as just another Washington line agency rather than a federal-state collaborative stirred tension within the commission, especially among some of the senior staff.

Since 1965 the ARC had evolved as a bureaucracy, complete with competing personalities and loyalties. The staff of young professionals, mostly from the Washington area, had grown in confidence and ability to manage projects in the ever changing political environment of the states. By the early 1970s, the governors' enthusiasm for fighting poverty in Appalachia had waned, and the frequent turnover of their ARC alternates and representatives hindered continuity in programming and reduced the level of long-range planning for development. The Washington-based ARC staff provided the only region-wide and systemic perspective to the commission process. John Whisman embodied the institutional memory of the agency and, with the decline of involvement of the governors, acquired increasing power as the states' representative on the ARC executive committee.

With the appointment of Whitehead, a struggle for control over the ARC ensued within the triumvirate at the head of the commission. Whisman and Whitehead clashed, leaving the executive director and the staff in the middle of a struggle between the states' representative and the federal cochair's office. Whitehead hoped to revitalize the direct involvement of the governors in the decisions of the ARC and objected strenuously to Whisman's casting a single vote for all of the governors in the executive committee when there was no statutory authority for him to do so. As the father of the ARC and a major contributor to the PARC report, Whisman believed that the commission was straying from its original intent, especially on the matter of growth center development.[23] The conflict was resolved when Whisman was forced to resign because of publicity surrounding minor violations of travel reimbursement procedures, but the dispute blackened the image of the commission and resulted in the reorganization of the agency in 1975.[24]

Under pressure from West Virginia senator Jennings Randolph, ARC's chief sponsor in the Senate, the 1975 ARDA reauthorization diminished the role of the states' Washington representative, required a quorum of the governors to be present to approve the annual budget, and obligated state alternates to be members of the governor's cabinet or personal staff. The reorganization eliminated the power struggle within the Washington offices of the commission, but it failed in the long run to engage the governors personally in the work of the ARC, and in subsequent years gubernatorial interest continued to decline along with federal allocations. The 1975 act did reapportion the division of ARC funds within the region to channel more resources to central Appalachia, but it continued to base the allocation primarily on population. Overall, a decade after the passage of the ARDA, 37 percent of ARC funds still flowed to northern Appalachia, 40 percent to southern Appalachia, and only 23 percent to central Appalachia.[25]

The reorganization of the commission and the adjustment of the allocation formula dramatized the challenge facing the ARC as it entered the post–Great Society era. Although conditions in the central part of Appalachia had generated national support for the creation of the commission, political necessity had extended the boundaries of the ARC far beyond the Appalachian heartland, and both politics and economic theory had concentrated most of its resources in the population centers of the northern and southern subregions. Critics in the media and in Congress increasingly pointed out the irrationality of a formula that allocated the fewest ARC dollars to the counties with the worst economic conditions, but few within the commission were willing to confront the problem. Alvin Arnett, who replaced Widner as executive director in 1971, recalled, "As long as you kept Senators Eastland or Stennis of Mississippi happy with their little sewage treatment projects and Senator Robert Kennedy happy with his New York thruways, you just don't ask the other questions."[26] Even the minor reapportionment of funds in 1975 came after heated debate within the commission, since the northern and southern governors vigorously resisted shifting any part of their funds to the central region.

More and more, however, critics outside the ARC did ask the "other questions." Detractors within the region had challenged the structure and goals of the Appalachian program from its inception. Harry Caudill called the ARDA "a grim hoax" that had little chance of restoring Appalachia to health because it failed to address the real economic and political problems of the region.[27] Kentuckian Harriette Arnow, author of *The Dollmaker*, labeled the act a "tragedy" that had given "false hope to many who needed help the most."[28] Many anti-poverty activists saw the Appalachian program as "chiefly a boon for the rich and for entrenched political interests." Five years after the ARC's creation, *New York Times* reporter Ben Franklin, writing for the *Louisville Courier-Journal*, found that low-income people in the sixty poorest counties in central Appalachia remained "almost untouched" by the commission's programs.[29]

By the early 1970s, the ARC had become a favored target of journalists and activists frustrated with the demise of the War on Poverty. The *Louisville Courier-Journal*, for example, ran a weeklong series on the commission in April 1973, concluding that it was a "boondoggle" that had become "just another pork dispenser, calloused to the human needs of the region it was created to serve." Reporter Bill Peterson found that the ARC had "little measurable impact on the economy of Eastern Kentucky or the rest of central Appalachia" and that, despite the claims of its promoters, it had done "little to coordinate the efforts of other federal agencies in the region." He noted that the thirteen states of the commission were more interested in their own individual improvement projects than in region-wide planning; the agency had ignored major regional problems like black lung disease, mine safety, and strip mining.[30]

The *Whitesburg (Kentucky) Mountain Eagle* accused the Wash-

191

ington-based ARC staff of being out of touch with the real conditions in Appalachia. The outspoken paper claimed that commission leaders were planning the wholesale depopulation of large portions of the coalfields, including the resettlement of mining families into distant "new towns."[31] Even the ARC partnership was a facade, wrote Howard Bray, executive director of the Fund for Investigative Journalism in Washington DC, since the governors themselves "have had little to do with guiding the program." The real source of ARC decision-making power, Bray suggested to readers of the *Progressive* magazine, was to be found in Congress, which was focused primarily on "bricks and mortar" projects that resounded to the benefit of individual members of Congress. "The Commission," he determined, had "failed to come to grips with the true causes of much of the . . . distress that has plagued Appalachia for decades."[32]

A group of young researchers came to similar conclusions when they issued *A Citizens' Handbook on the ARC* in 1974. Calling themselves the ARC Accountability Project, the authors endeavored to inform mountain residents of the failures of the agency in preparation for reauthorization hearings that the ARC was holding throughout the region—the first public forums in the commission's nine-year history. The investigators found the government program deficient in a number of areas: accountability, access, assumptions, and achievements. "The ARC was never structured to meet the needs of poor and working people," they concluded. "Nor was it meant to benefit a truly representative base of Appalachia's citizenry. In virtually every one of its programs, the direct beneficiaries of ARC's development strategies are the already entrenched power structures."[33]

Widely distributed among activists and academics, *A Citizens' Handbook on the ARC* summarized most of the criticisms of the ARC leveled by Caudill and others. The local and area development districts were dominated by nonrepresentative boards that comprised small-town mayors, county officials, and their appointed cronies. Easily controlled by area political machines, the development districts utilized the ARC funding process to enhance the political interests of local power brokers, and they provided "no mechanism for public access, redress, or accountability." The commission's growth center strategy, furthermore, exacerbated the poverty and depopulation of rural areas and facilitated the continued drain of wealth from the region by absentee industries. Education and health programs were designed to encourage out-migration from rural areas rather than to improve public services where people lived, and the ARC had failed to justify the expenditure of almost 80 percent of its budget on an uncompleted highway system. "The time has come to turn the authority of the Appalachian Regional Commission around or demand that it cease to exist," recommended the researchers. "It is time for a different vision of regional resource development. It's time for a whole new set of goals which encourage a different sense of how to use resources to create job security, provide social services or otherwise contribute to a qualitatively different way of living."[34]

An alternative vision for Appalachia, however, eluded the ARC. The Nixon administration continued to pursue a national policy of economic growth while shifting administrative control and revenues back to the states. The ARC approach to project management was consistent with White House goals, and the nonhighway budget of the agency survived unscathed, averaging around $300 million annually throughout the decade. Despite the demise of the War on Poverty, federal spending for entitlement programs (food stamps, Medicaid, and Social Security) increased 76 percent in the 1970s as the nation shifted its attention from eradicating poverty to managing the welfare system. The portion of the total ARC allocation dedicated to nonhighway projects increased by 20 percent as well.[35]

Growth in federal transfer payments and infrastructure expenditures contributed to a resurgence of economic activity in the mountains between 1965 and 1975, providing at least statistical evidence that progress was being made in alleviating mountain poverty. Per capita income in the region increased from 78 percent of the national average in 1965 to almost 83 percent in 1974. Unemployment and poverty rates declined, and housing stock, educational attainment, and infant mortality rates improved. Central Appalachia continued to lag far behind the rest of the country in most socioeconomic measures, but even there, personal income grew from 52 percent of the national average to 65 percent in the decade after the passage of the ARDA. The migration of people out of the region slowed and even reversed in some counties.[36]

Part of this economic activity was attributable to the recovery of the coal industry. Coal production had begun to rise in the late 1960s, but demand for Appalachian coal skyrocketed after the Organization of Petroleum Exporting Countries (OPEC) raised the price of oil by 400 percent in protest of American support for Israel after the 1973 Yom Kippur War. While inflation soared throughout the rest of the country, spurring a business recession in 1975, the coalfields boomed again as they had done periodically since the turn of the century. Coal exports more than doubled by the end of the decade, bringing new jobs, in-migration, and small-business growth. The boom would collapse with the restoration of world oil production levels in the early 1980s, but the energy crisis temporarily restored faith in natural resource development as a private sector cure for Appalachia's problems.

At the same time that rising government expenditures and the recovery of the coal industry diverted attention from the persistent inequities and weaknesses of the mountain economy, other forces, deeply rooted in the environmental movement and in the War on Poverty of the 1960s, combined to challenge the prevailing devotion to "more" and to question the ARC approach to development. By the mid-1970s, substantial numbers of Americans had become disenchanted with the moral direction of a government that had produced the Vietnam War and the Watergate scandal and with an economic system that seemed to reward greed and unrestrained consumption. Building on a movement that began in Britain, intellectuals and scholars within the United States increasingly questioned the limits of growth and the environmental and social costs of technology. Adding their voices to the work of British scholars like Peter Laslett (*The World We Have Lost*) and E. F. Schumacher (*Small Is Beautiful*), American critics such as Wendell Berry (*The Unsettling of America*), Rachel Carson (*Silent Spring*), Robert Bellah (*Habits of the Heart*), and others rejected the idea of growth-based development and led an ever widening reaction to consumerism.

In Appalachia, as in the rest of the country, the new movement represented a shift in values that revealed a different way of thinking about land, quality of life, and the meaning of progress. Regional activists, fresh from the political wars against poverty and racial injustice, turned their attention in the 1970s to the abolition of strip mining, the improvement of health and working conditions for miners and textile workers, the protection of mountain forests from clear-cutting, and the defense of family farms from the construction of hydroelectric facilities and the expansion of national parks. Likewise regional scholars rejected the notion of Appalachian exceptionalism and recast the region's recent history and culture as the consequence of the same modernization and unbridled development that had shaped the rest of the nation. What Appalachia needed in the future, they argued, was not more growth but a different kind of development.

Although traditional mountain lifestyles offered alternatives to the postwar culture of consumption, the rejection of growth-based strategies for progress in Appalachia reflected more than romantic nostalgia for a simpler past. In contrast to the self-absorption and escapism of much of the hippie culture, much of the counterculture movement in the mountains was grounded in conventional American values of economic and social justice, cooperation, tolerance, respect for family and community, and a spiritual sense of land as place rather than commodity. The same organizations that opposed unregulated second-home development in western North Carolina supported striking miners in eastern Kentucky and farm families fighting federal land condemnation in southwest Virginia. Groups like the new CSM and the Appalachian Alliance rallied members in opposition to strip mining, gender discrimination in coal employment, brown lung disease among textile workers, and the concentration of absentee landownership in the coalfields and the Blue Ridge.

As a result of these contrasting visions for the good life, much of the public discourse about the future of Appalachia in the late 1970s focused on achieving a balance between economic growth and environmental quality. On the one hand, Appalachia needed jobs and economic expansion to lift its people out of poverty. The region needed to increase the production of its mines and mills, encourage tourism and second-home development, and attract branch manufacturing plants that could increase the local tax base and provide revenue for schools and roads. On the other hand, economic development should not destroy the landscape, exploit the people, or threaten traditional values.

Growth should be limited and development sustainable to protect the natural and human assets of the region.

With the election of Jimmy Carter to the presidency in 1976, balanced growth became the national objective of an administration elected to restore moral direction to a nation struggling with inflation, unemployment, and energy challenges. Appalachian leaders assumed major roles in the national effort to find a middle path between economic growth and environmental protection, between consumption and conservation. Responding, for example, to the national energy crisis and to growing pressure to end surface mining in the mountains, the Senate Environment and Public Works committee, chaired by West Virginia's Jennings Randolph, called in 1976 for a national conference on balanced growth. Two years later, President Carter's secretary of commerce, Juanita Kreps, a native of western North Carolina, organized the White House Conference on Balanced National Growth and Economic Development. Chaired by West Virginia governor Jay Rockefeller, the gathering brought more than five hundred delegates to Washington DC and spawned several smaller, regional conferences, including one in Charleston, West Virginia, sponsored by the ARC.

The White House conferences on balanced growth, however, failed to resolve the inherent tensions over the goals of development. Although organizers hoped to achieve some compromise between unbounded growth and no growth, reaching agreement on the definition of "balance" proved to be impossible in an atmosphere where the real issues were wealth, power, and conflicting visions of the good life. Especially in Appalachia, the call for balanced growth opened old conflicts over landownership, land use, taxation, government regulation, and environmental quality. National priorities, as well, sometimes fueled bitter regional clashes, as when the demand for energy alternatives sparked a rise in coal production and inspired proposals to increase federal funding for research in coal technology.

Appalachian opponents of strip mining were angered further when national environmental groups compromised on the abolition of surface mining in the passage of the Surface Mining Control and Reclamation Act of 1977. They saw strategies to build a new national energy policy around coal as furthering the destruction of the mountains. Proposals that reduced American dependence on foreign oil by increasing the production of coal, they argued, only shifted the real costs of energy consumption onto the people of the coalfields. Given the rising percentage of coal being produced by surface mining, they feared that Appalachia would become a "national sacrifice area."[37]

Other coal country leaders, however, saw the adoption of a coal-based national energy policy as a boon for the region. Named to chair the President's Commission on Coal as well as the White House Conference on Balanced National Growth and Economic Development in 1978, Governor Rockefeller acknowledged that there were "environmental tradeoffs" to the increased consumption of coal but insisted that these costs had to be balanced against the goal of national energy independence. Appalachian coal mines, he suggested, were prepared to increase production by 100 million tons a year, and this prospect would help not only to reduce the national dependence on foreign oil but also to alleviate the unemployment of thousands of miners in his state. With current environmental regulations and new clean coal technologies, he added, coal could be burned responsibly and without dirty smokestack emissions.[38] None of the conferences and commissions on balanced growth produced much consensus, but they did illuminate what Rockefeller described as "the incredible array of tensions involved with growth."[39] These conflicts intensified with the skyrocketing inflation and subsequent recession that followed yet another OPEC oil crisis in 1979–1981.

Despite these failures, the efforts by the Carter administration to achieve harmony on national economic policy opened a dialogue within the country about the limits of economic expansion. The president appeared to encourage, even welcome, debate. In Appalachia, community forums, academic conferences, and regional publications explored the prospects for more balanced development, and even the ARC appeared more flexible and open to alternative voices. Under Robert W. Scott, the former North Carolina governor whom Carter appointed as federal cochair of the ARC in 1977, the commission launched an early childhood basic skills education initiative, reached out to groups representing the elderly and women, and approved $4 million in aid to ease the financial problems of former UMWA hospitals in the coalfields. Scott's successor, Al Smith of Kentucky, supported a $100,000 grant to the Appalachian Alliance to study landownership patterns in six Appalachian states and extended a research fellowship to longtime ARC critic Harry Caudill.[40]

Increased support for human development programs and greater flexibility in funding nontraditional organizations reflected a shift in national politics since the 1960s and a maturing of the ARC. Many of the commission's more creative programs came at the initiative of the federal cochair's office rather than at the request of the states, and the bulk of agency expenditures continued to be dedicated to the construction of highways and other infrastructure. The new policy initiatives, however, represented a limited retreat from the postwar confidence in growth and technology and a greater concern for diversity and inclusion. Despite the objections of South Carolina governor James Edwards, for example, who feared that an ARC bailout of health care institutions in the coalfields would inadvertently support a recent coal miners' strike, the central Appalachian ARC governors agreed, in an unprecedented vote, to provide aid for the operation of regional hospitals "used by everyone, including miners."[41] The commission also launched an initiative to speed up the processing of black lung disease claims and extended funding to help launch the Council of Appalachian Women.

The War on Poverty had expanded opportunities for the education and employment of women in the mountains, both at the entry level and in professional positions. The North Carolina–based Council of Appalachian Women promised to work on a wide variety of projects to meet the needs of mountain women, including research to determine how women could participate more fully in ARC programs, conferences and workshops to strengthen the Appalachian family, efforts to eliminate job discrimination in education and job training, initiatives to improve health and child care services, and the creation of a group insurance program and a credit union.[42] The short-lived council was composed primarily of professional women, but it reflected shifting gender roles in the region, as did its sister organization in West Virginia, the Coal Employment Project. The latter assisted women in breaking down gender barriers to work in the mines, a historically male-dominated industry. With the help of the Coal Employment Project and other organizations, the number of women employed in Appalachian coal mines grew from none in 1973 to more than 2,500 in 1979. Women miners continued to face harassment and discrimination in wages and work assignments, but the efforts of the Coal Employment Project represented the growing movement of women into the public workforce in Appalachia as in the rest of the country.[43]

Likewise, ARC support for research on landownership patterns in Appalachia echoed changing attitudes toward natural resource management and control. Recognition that absentee ownership had shaped much of Appalachia's tragic history of dependence was well known in the 1960s, but acknowledging the consequences of this "colonial" relationship was dangerous in government circles and could easily result in one's being labeled a radical or a Communist. A decade later, in a world where distant governments and energy cartels held America hostage, ownership and control of local resources were as genuine concerns for the long-term future of the region as were increased coal production and employment. Although the ARC failed to act on any of the recommendations that resulted from its pioneering study of landownership trends (a pattern common to almost all of the research funded by the agency), that the commission would underwrite such controversial research speaks to the comparative openness of the organization during the Carter years.

Undertaken by a coalition of regional activists and academicians, the landownership study exposed the depth of absentee control of Appalachia's natural resources and linked that control to almost every problem in the region—inadequate taxation, mine safety, black lung disease, strip mining, the decline of farming, deforestation, floods, substandard housing, welfare, and more. Detailed analysis of over 20 million acres in the heart of the region revealed not only that ownership of land and minerals in Appalachia was concentrated in the hands of a few giant corporations but that these corporations were increasingly the subsidiaries of multinational energy conglomerates. More than 40 percent of the land surveyed—some 8 million acres—was held by only fifty private owners and the federal government. Large corporations controlled almost 40 percent of the land and 70 percent of the mineral rights in the survey, and the vast majority of those resources were owned by entities outside the county in which the property was located. The survey found that more than 75 percent of the mineral owners paid annual taxes on their properties of less than twenty-five cents per acre.[44]

As a result of this concentrated pattern of landownership, the researchers concluded, options for alternative economic development were limited, taxes were inadequate, and public services were starved. Nor was this a problem restricted to the coalfields, since government ownership of land and tourism development constrained the economic choices of noncoal counties as well. An estimated one-third of the farmland in the survey was lost to agricultural production in the 1970s, and about half of the region's farmers quit farming. "No one who has lived for any time in Appalachia," admitted John Gaventa, one of the coordinators of the study, "can be surprised to hear that a handful of absentee corporations control huge portions of the region's land and minerals and pay a pittance in local taxes. But the documentation of landownership and taxation in county after county establishes for the first time the pervasive pattern of inequity, and this factual information should provide the basis for long-needed changes."[45]

Gaventa was too optimistic, for in many ways the landownership study represented a turning point itself in the debate over the region's future. Released in 1981, the report could not have come at a worse time for the ARC. Controversial even when the commission decided to fund it, the study drew little attention at an agency suddenly threatened with extinction by the inauguration of Ronald Reagan. Determined to cut federal budgets and eliminate regional commissions, the new Republican president failed to include the ARC in his executive budget requests, and agency leaders abandoned the politically sensitive study to rally support for their own organization's survival. With its very existence in jeopardy, the ARC ignored the recommendations of the 1,800-page report. Although widely recognized by this time as a growing regional problem, absentee landownership slipped once more from the political agenda.

The alliance between activists and academics dissipated as well in the years following the publication of the groundbreaking study. Conceived after the disastrous floods that swept southern West Virginia and eastern Kentucky in 1977 and organized at the first Appalachian Studies Conference the following year, the landownership study brought together more than a hundred former antipoverty warriors, graduate students, and college professors in one of the largest and most detailed explorations of rural landownership in American history. Co-ordinated by the Highlander Research and Education Center in east Tennessee, the grassroots project combined meticulous research in county courthouse records, statistical analysis, and a lengthy discussion of policy implications. After the publication of a summary volume in 1983, however, the task force disbanded, and coalitions of citizen-activists and academics became increasingly rare in the region. The Appalachian Alliance eventually faded, and the Appalachian studies movement, growing with institutional acceptance, shifted its energies to matters of teaching, learning, and theoretical research.

The collaborative landownership study also revealed a watershed in the evolving structure of the Appalachian economy. The recovery of the coal industry spurred the globalization of the mountain economy just as the energy crisis exposed the dependence of American consumers on foreign oil. By the end of the 1970s, a few multinational energy conglomerates dominated Appalachian coal production, and the giant firms managed their mineral resources, mining methods, and environmental impacts at even greater distances from the communities in which they operated than had the great domestic corporations of an earlier day. To feed the rapidly growing energy demands of the nation and to meet rising air quality standards, more and more low-sulfur coal from Appalachian strip mines poured into the furnaces of American power plants. Older, metallurgical coal mines, mostly underground mines, closed down as steel production shifted abroad, and coal employment in the mountains began a final, precipitous decline.

Elsewhere in the region, the globalization of markets was evident in the daily lives of residents. The construction of Appalachian corridor highways and burgeoning government transfer payments began to instill new life into the larger mountain towns. Chain stores and nationally franchised restaurants opened in new commercial centers at the edges of many towns, and small housing developments and trailer parks replaced old farms on city peripheries. Mountain residents soon had access to the same mass-produced clothing, food, and entertainment as other Americans, and some found employment in the small shoe factories, food processing businesses, and sewing plants that set up operations in local industrial parks.

The rush to create jobs motivated many southern mountain leaders to join scores of other public officials in the great "buffalo hunt" to bag runaway manufacturing plants from the North with promises of government-funded building sites, low taxes, and cheap labor. Rural communities throughout the region organized economic development commissions, established industrial parks, and constructed speculation buildings at public expense with the hope of luring northern branch plants that pledged to provide one hundred to two hundred low-wage, low-skilled jobs each. Funds from the ARC became a prime source of revenue for the access roads, water lines, and job training programs necessary to compete for companies' attention. The majority of the industrial sites, some built on abandoned strip mines, went unoccupied, but a few attracted small assembly plants, metal fabrication facilities, and clothing manufacturers.

Communities located along the southern interstate and ARC corridor highways benefited most from industrial recruitment strategies. By 1980 more than 1,700 miles of the Appalachian Development Highway System and almost 4,000 miles of interstate highways were completed in the region. These modern roads connected larger towns in the mountains and the foothills with external markets, increased access to the mountains for tourists, and facilitated the transportation of coal to electric power plants outside the region. The new highways reduced the travel time for rural residents to reach stores, health care, education, and employment opportunities in the designated growth centers, but they furthered the decline of community-based businesses and services in the outlying districts.

The use of special federal funds to construct the Appalachian Development Highway System was intended to free up state resources to improve secondary roads, connecting more remote communities to the regional transportation network, but the improvement of state and county roads failed to keep pace with the new Appalachian corridor system. Small towns farther removed from the four-lane highways languished as local residents turned to the cities for jobs, entertainment, and the latest consumer goods advertised on television. Consequently, the social and economic distance between urban and rural Appalachia increased as the uneven access to better transportation drained human and financial resources into the growth centers.

Even local entrepreneurs were drawn to the amenities of the transportation corridors and tended to relocate their investments in the burgeoning corridor towns rather than nearby rural communities. For example, not long after the local developers of a data processing company opened a facility in distressed Harlan County, Kentucky, they moved the plant to London, Kentucky, along Interstate 75, at the western edge of the mountains. A decade later, Appalachian Computer Systems employed more than four hundred low-wage data entry workers there, and the London area (home to Harland Sanders, founder of Kentucky Fried Chicken) became one of the fastest-growing places in the commonwealth.[46] Harlan County, meanwhile, continued to suffer population decline. This pattern was followed throughout the region. Of the more than 400,000 new manufacturing jobs attracted to Appalachia between 1965 and 1980, 60 percent were located within thirty miles of one of these major highways.[47]

Communities situated at the intersections of ARC corridors and interstates often experienced rapid growth as regional employment, retail trade, and public service centers. The population of Raleigh County, West Virginia, for instance, expanded from seventy thousand in 1970 to almost eighty-seven thousand in 1980, after the completion of ARC's Corridor L between Beckley and Morgantown. Beckley, located at the intersection of Interstates 77 (on the West Virginia Turnpike) and 64, became a regional medical services center for the southern West Virginia coalfields, and, after the opening of the New River Bridge in 1977 (for which ARC contributed $29 million of the $42 million cost of construction), the town became a major center for tourism development as well. In little more than a decade, Beckley grew from the tenth-largest city in West Virginia to the third.[48]

The growth of towns such as London and Beckley reflected even more fundamental changes in the Appalachian labor force. Despite the expansion of manufacturing facilities in the 1970s, industrial employment accounted for less than one-tenth of the new jobs created in the region during the decade. Along with the rest of America, Appalachia gained the bulk of its 1.5 million new jobs in the service sector of the economy, especially in retail trade, health services, and education. As the nation moved from an industrial-based economy to a service-oriented economy, Appalachia was drawn more tightly into the consumer society, and its workforce increasingly mirrored that of a postindustrial world. Industries that had once provided the majority of nonfarm jobs in the mountains—coal, textiles, and furniture—reduced their labor needs through mechanization or shifted their production offshore, leaving thousands of low-skilled and undereducated workers to compete for jobs as waiters, sales clerks, receptionists, and other entry-level service positions.[49]

Some areas of the country, including many northern Appalachian communities, were better equipped to make the transition to a service- and information-based economy. Superior adult education levels, greater research and higher education infrastructure, and stronger civic capacity eased the adjustment from heavy industry to high-tech production and corporate services in the old steel towns of the North and Midwest. A long history of educational neglect in central Appalachia, however, hampered the jump to the new economy in the most economically distressed parts of the region. Despite significant improvements in education and job training since 1965, Appalachian workers still lagged far behind the rest of the nation in technical skills and education levels. The proportion of Appalachian people over twenty-five years old with a high school education had increased from 57 percent to 83 percent of the national average, but almost one in three Appalachian adults remained functionally illiterate, compared with 20 percent of all Americans. Among the unemployed in the mountains in 1980, 46 percent were functionally illiterate. Only one in nine Appalachians had attained a college degree, compared with one in six in the rest of the nation.[50]

The new service economy was also more female than the older industrial economy. The numbers of Appalachian women with jobs outside the home increased significantly after 1970 as rural mountain women found employment in low-wage manufacturing jobs and entry-level service positions. Retail chain stores such as Kmart and Wal-Mart and fast-food restaurants like Hardee's and McDonald's provided disproportionate employment for women, as did the motels, resorts, and gift shops associated with the tourism industry. Women also found jobs as bank tellers, real estate brokers, office managers, and other semi-professional positions. Most of the new jobs in the mountains were in the low-wage sector of service employment. They seldom offered health or other benefits or provided job security or opportunities for advancement. Increasingly the Appalachian household looked much like that of the rest of the nation, with both spouses employed outside the home, though in the mountains this trend was driven as much by economic necessity as by gender parity.

Encouraged by changes in the mountain labor force, improvements in transportation and other infrastructure, rising education levels, and advancing per capita incomes, ARC planners were convinced that progress was being made in Appalachia. *Appalachia: Journal of the Appalachian Regional Commission* reported in the spring of 1979 that "at last, at long last" the region was "on the way" toward "vigorous, self-sustaining growth." Progress would take time, the journal acknowledged—time for residents of Appalachia to learn how to work with the ARC partnership, time to complete the infrastructure for development, and time to find the "balances between the nation's need for energy and the region's fragile environment." Problems remained, admitted the publication, but after fifteen years of effort, the ARC had laid "a new economic, social, and psychological foundation" for development.[51]

ARC optimism, however, turned to frustration with the election of Ronald Reagan in 1980. Neither claims regarding the success of its programs nor arguments based on the persisting needs of the region or on the organization's unique structure would alter the new president's opposition to regional commissions. Reagan's single-minded determination to reduce both taxes and the size of the federal bureaucracy left the Appalachian program and other Great Society initiatives vulnerable to budget cuts and elimination. Shortly after the inauguration, White House officials informed the Appalachian governors that the ARC would be closed, all noncommitted funds would be rescinded, and the highway program would be transferred to the Department of Transportation. In his subsequent executive budget proposal, and annually throughout the remainder of his presidency, Reagan included no funds for the Appalachian program.

The president's decision to abolish the ARC had little to do with his views about Appalachia or his opinions regarding the economic goals of the commission. Indeed, his knowledge of the region was extremely limited, and he shared the agency's commitment to economic growth as the solution to most of society's problems. Unlike many liberals during the Carter years who had begun to question the limits of growth, Reagan exuded the optimism and faith in economic expansion that characterized most of the World War II generation. He had campaigned on a promise to revitalize the nation's stagnating economy by reducing taxes and government regulation. "Our aim," he told the nation in his first address on the economy, "is to increase our national wealth so all will have more, not just redistribute what we already have which is just a sharing of scarcity."[52]

Reagan's economic strategy for the country was based on the assumption that increasing investment and productivity by reducing personal and corporate taxes would generate business expansion and create jobs. This supply-side economics rejected the Keynesian intervention in the economy that produced the welfare state and called for a halt to the growth of government programs and budgets that had mushroomed since the New Deal. Great Society programs such as the War on Poverty, the president believed, had inhibited growth by proliferating business regulations and increasing government debt. Regional development agencies like the ARC only added another unnecessary layer of bureaucracy to big government and should be abolished.

Appalachian leaders had attempted to head off the demise of the ARC even before the inauguration. Soon after the election, a group of Appalachian governors sent a letter to the president-elect, petitioning for the continuation of the commission, but received no response. After the White House announced its intention to close the agency, the governors issued a resolution calling on the president and Congress to delay the action and to work with the commission to design an orderly phase-out program. While some advocates of the Appalachian program argued that there was still much to be done in the region, others accepted the president's position but favored a more gradual reduction of the commission's role in regional development. Led by ARC federal cochair Al Smith and Kentucky governor John Y. Brown, who served as states cochair, ARC supporters turned to Congress to save the agency, which had long been a favorite of powerful members on both sides of the aisle.

Following a bipartisan appeal, the House Appropriations Committee requested that the commission prepare a "finish-up" plan that would allow the ARC to complete its work over a three- to five-year period. The commission submitted the finish-up proposal in late 1981, providing a rationale for the continuation of the program on a year-to-year basis through 1987. The House Appropriations Committee subsequently funded the commission at less than half of its previous levels and continued that level of annual funding through the 1990s. The Senate narrowly complied. Although its appropriations were reduced significantly, the ARC survived the Reagan revolution and continued to provide limited public resources for Appalachia when federal spending cuts limited the resources otherwise available for housing, health care, and other community infrastructure. With Congress determined to continue to appropriate funds, President Reagan finally replaced Democrat Al Smith in 1982 as federal cochair of the ARC and appointed Winifred Pizzano, a Republican health services administrator from Illinois, to head the agency.

Its future uncertain and its appropriations slashed, the ARC limped into the 1980s, struggling between the politics of survival and the task of addressing persistent problems in the mountains. Much of the energy of the Washington-based staff was channeled into the fight to defend the agency and to sustain annual appropriations from Congress. Two southern representatives, Jamie Whitten of Mississippi and Tom Bevill of Alabama, emerged as unlikely champions of the ARC in the 1980s, interceding on behalf of the commission in subcommittee budget negotiations and reaping an abundance of special ARC projects for their districts. The annual struggle for appropriations left the agency even more vulnerable to accusations of pork-barrel politics.

The finish-up program proposed by the Appalachian governors in response to the funding crisis placed priority on the completion of the Appalachian Development Highway System, drastically cut support for nonhighway programs, and reduced research and regional planning operations. Highways had always been one of the most popular parts of the Appalachian program with planners and policy makers, and roads received high priority in the scaled-back agenda for development. The new strategy pledged to complete 630 miles of the remaining 1,300 unfinished miles of the Appalachian corridor system by 1990. The plan would emphasize the completion of roads that had the highest traffic volume, were most needed to transport coal, and completed critical state-line crossings.[53]

Acknowledging that economic growth in the region had been uneven and that many Appalachians still did not have the education and job skills necessary to compete in the modern, postindustrial economy, the commission reorganized nonhighway projects into an area development finish-up program and concentrated its efforts in three areas: job creation, health care, and assistance to persistently distressed counties. At a major conference in Atlanta in the spring of 1983, the ARC launched a five-year job training and private investment initiative designed to improve the basic skills of the Appalachian workforce and to encourage private capital investment. In addition to supporting the efforts of state governments to recruit more high-tech industries to the mountains, the agency hoped to spur local entrepreneurship and small-business development, especially in the service sector. The commission also undertook new initiatives to reduce the high school dropout rate and to revitalize vocational training programs at both the secondary and postsecondary levels.

In the area of health, the ARC committed itself to a three-year plan to bring modern health care to the sixty-five counties not yet reached by basic health services and to further reduce the region's chronically high infant mortality rate. Since 1965, the commission's health program had evolved from an emphasis on hardware and hospital facilities to the promotion of comprehensive regional health planning with the goal of providing primary care within a thirty-minute drive of every mountain family. Indeed, the health program was one of its most successful initiatives. Working with state and local health professionals, the agency fashioned a demonstration model for primary health care in the 1970s—with a focus on preventive, basic, family-oriented services—that provided a blueprint for the creation of the National Rural Health Initiative. The ARC closeout program aimed to extend primary care services to every Appalachian resident by 1985, including those in the most remote parts of central Appalachia, and to increase the number of health professionals throughout the region. The latter goal would be achieved by tapping into the National Health

Services Corps, which recruited physicians, including special-visa foreign-born physicians, to "health shortage areas."[54]

The most challenging part of the ARC finish-up program, however, was the distressed counties program, established to address the problems of the most persistently poor counties in the region. The program was created in part as a response to media and congressional criticism that the agency had done little to ameliorate the poverty of the most severely distressed counties in Appalachia and in part out of a concern of ARC staff that, having improved conditions in the urban and peripheral counties, the commission should focus its final resources on the hard-core poverty areas. These counties were located primarily in eastern Kentucky and southern West Virginia and in rural areas scattered throughout the ARC-defined region. Since the 1960s, they had exhibited less improvement in per capita income, poverty, and unemployment rates than other counties and continued to reflect the greatest need. The program urged the states to concentrate their area development funds in these sixty or so counties and set aside special regional funds for safe drinking water and waste-disposal projects for these communities.

Although the area development finish-up program reflected growing attention to human development and basic community services at the ARC, smaller, nonhighway allocations diminished the political importance of the commission to Appalachian governors and almost eliminated the strategic planning role of the ARC on the state and regional levels. Compared with other state budgeted programs for development, the ARC allocation was becoming less significant, especially when new agency regulations limited commission contributions to 50 percent of total project costs. The loss of major, direct ARC funding for the local development districts, moreover, pushed the multicounty districts to become even more dependent on local government support for their operating budgets. More and more they functioned as program delivery centers for local government services (especially in job training and care for the elderly), and their role in community development and area-wide planning diminished.

A final recommendation of the finish-up strategy included the creation of an Appalachian development foundation, which would raise endowment funds from individuals and corporations and invest them in regional development projects to replace the threatened federal funds. Pointing to the history of exploitation of the region's natural resources by absentee developers, the Appalachian governors hoped to raise a permanent endowment to sustain the work of the commission based on donations by coal, timber, and other businesses that had acquired their wealth from the region. "In recent years," the ARC governors told Congress in 1981, "some corporations have shown an increased commitment to the communities in which they do business. We believe many corporations and individuals have an interest in remedying some of the past neglect in Appalachia and a stake in fostering a strong diversified economy."[55] After establishing an office in Washington and hiring a director, however, the Appalachian Development Foundation eventually failed, closing its doors in 1987 without—to paraphrase Harry Caudill—raising a tittle of corporate responsibility.

The failure of corporate interests to accept accountability for Appalachian development in the face of diminishing government involvement was not surprising. After the expansive years of the coal boom in the 1970s, energy prices plummeted in the early 1980s, and the subsequent glut of oil sent the world economy into decline. Appalachia was slower to recover from the recession of 1981–1982, and the region's economy remained sluggish throughout the remainder of the decade. Coal exports from the mountains rose from 49 million tons in 1973 to 104 million tons in 1981 but plummeted to 73 million tons by 1983.[56] Although mechanization would increase productivity in the late 1980s, it provided employment for fewer miners. The number of operating mines declined once again, and many out-migrants who had come back to the region to work in the mines in the 1970s now found themselves unemployed and unable to return to their factory jobs in the Midwest because of the flight of American steel and manufacturing companies offshore. At the end of the decade, the number of working miners in Appalachia reached an all-time low. The most recently hired workers, often women miners, were the first to lose their jobs.

The economic decline of the 1980s reduced the ability of state governments to respond to the needs of mountain communities as well. The loss of federal social programs and the reduction of ARC budgets during the Reagan years increased the burden on state and local governments to meet basic program needs in health, education, and community development when most states were suffering from a loss of tax revenues as a result of the recession. Appalachian states especially were pressed to maintain basic services, let alone initiate new social and economic programs. West Virginia, for example, suffered an unemployment rate of 21 percent in 1983, the highest rate recorded for any state since 1940, and Standard and Poor's reduced the general obligation bond rating for the Mountain State from AA+ to AA–.[57] Similarly, Kentucky experienced a budget shortfall of $186 million, resulting in major reductions in nearly every department and agency of state government. Governor John Y. Brown took the entire $265 million of coal severance tax revenues to meet the budget deficit in the state general fund, returning none of the levy to the coal-producing counties to repair coal roads or encourage economic diversification.[58]

Retrenchment in government programs and in the economy as a whole did not return Appalachia to the pre–Great Society conditions that had brought national attention to the region, but it did slow the pace of improvement, and some of the most severely distressed rural counties of the mountain heartland lost significant ground. Overall the region's per capita personal income compared to the rest of the nation dropped from 82.7 percent to 80.8 percent between 1979 and 1989, but that figure obscured fundamental differences within the ARC region. Northern Appalachia suffered from the continuing deterioration of its old manufacturing base as it transitioned to a postindustrial economy. Southern Appalachia saw personal income increase by 3.2 percent and population rise by almost 9 percent as a result of the growth of military expenditures and the expansion of metropolitan centers such as Atlanta, Winston-Salem, and Huntsville. Central Appalachia witnessed the worst decline, with a drop of 7.3 percent in personal income and a 5 percent rate of population loss over the decade, as its economy, based on coal, apparel, and timber, collapsed because of mechanization and globalization.[59]

Rising poverty rates also reflected a growing polarization within the region. The socioeconomic gap between central Appalachia and peripheral parts of the ARC region increased along with the gap between the mountain heartland and the rest of the United States. Whereas Appalachia outpaced the nation in the 1970s in reducing poverty, that trend reversed in the 1980s as the percentage of the region's population below the poverty level increased from 13.7 percent in 1980 to almost 15 percent in 1990. Poverty in central Appalachia declined from 34 percent in 1970 to 22 percent in 1980 but jumped to more than 25 percent in 1990. In some counties of eastern Kentucky and southern West Virginia, poverty rates were three times the national average. Women and children bore the heaviest burden of rising poverty. The number of female-headed Appalachian families increased by 36 percent during the decade, while median family incomes declined by 4.5 percent regionally and by 13.5 percent in central Appalachia. In measures of education attainment, workforce participation, and child poverty, the gap between central Appalachia and the rest of the region increased dramatically.[60]

The downturn in the Appalachian economy represented more than just another bust in the long boom-and-bust cycle that had shaped the history of the region for more than a century. The new unemployment was structural, and jobs in coal mining, primary metals, textiles, and other industries would never return. Appalachia was caught in the middle of a larger transformation in the national economy. The old Appalachian economy was based on extractive resources and mature industry, but the postindustrial revolution pushed low-wage manufacturing jobs to Asia and Latin America while coal production shifted to lower-cost mines in the American West. The introduction of longwall mining equipment and new mountaintop removal techniques displaced thousands of skilled Appalachian underground miners. In 1981 and 1982 alone, the Appalachian region lost two and a half manufacturing jobs for every one it had gained in the 1970s.[61] The new service sector jobs paid only a fraction of the wages of manufacturing and unionized mining and usually provided no health benefits.

The recession in the mountain economy was only one part of the double whammy that struck most Appalachian states in the 1980s. Although the core social programs of the New Deal and Great Society survived the Reagan budget cuts, programs such as food stamps, job training, school lunches, and early childhood education received significant reductions in federal support, leaving it up to the states to manage the delivery of services from state revenues and block grants. West Virginia was hit especially hard by the reductions, ranking second in the United States in the loss of federal aid with total cuts of $1.8

billion between 1982 and 1986.[62] With a small tax base and few financial reserves, state government officials cut support for public schools, delayed Medicaid payments to health providers, and canceled community infrastructure projects. Almost bankrupt and mired in poverty and political corruption, the Mountain State was ignominiously labeled a "state of despair" by the *Wall Street Journal* in the fall of 1989.[63]

The situation was equally dire in other parts of central Appalachia. A series of articles in the *Knoxville News-Sentinel* in 1985 described Appalachian east Tennessee as a "land of pain and poverty," a place where official unemployment was as high as 23 percent and transfer payments (such as Social Security, black lung, and Aid to Families with Dependent Children) amounted to 21 percent of personal income. Reporter Fred Brown described inadequate housing conditions, poor sanitation, and "desperate families" who were barely able to fight off "the beast of hunger" in communities that had changed little since the days of the War on Poverty.[64] A year later, an investigation in the coalfields of southwest Virginia for the Commission on Religion in Appalachia found similar conditions, and the author professed little hope for the region's young people despite the recovery of the national economy. Mechanization and internationalization of area coal mines had reduced the number of operating mines by a third, and the new industrial parks built to attract industry had failed to provide enough low-wage jobs to replace those lost in mining. Unemployment in southwest Virginia averaged 20 percent, and the proportion of seventeen- to twenty-four-year-olds who had dropped out of high school was 38 percent, one of the highest in the nation. Whereas the economies in valley towns like Bristol, Johnson City, and Kingsport were better, the young people of the interior rural coal counties faced a bleak future—or the difficult choice of out-migration.[65]

The contrast between economic opportunities in the cities and those in surrounding rural counties mirrored the growing gap between rural and urban places within Appalachia. A study released by the University of Kentucky Appalachian Center in 1994 found not only that Appalachian Kentucky as a whole had fallen further behind the rest of the commonwealth in the 1980s but also that poverty was concentrated in certain places within the mountains. According to 1990 data, twenty-nine of the thirty poorest counties in Kentucky were in eastern Kentucky, and thirty-eight of the forty-nine ARC counties in the commonwealth were officially listed as distressed. Between 1980 and 1990, per capita income in Appalachian Kentucky declined from 67 to 60 percent of the national average, and almost one in three citizens of the region lived below the nationally established poverty level.[66]

The study revealed that rates of poverty were higher than the national average across eastern Kentucky, but distress was more severe in the ten interior counties than in peripheral counties along Interstates 64 and 75 and in coal-producing counties along the state's eastern border. The peripheral counties contained growth centers, such as Pikeville, Prestonsburg, Paintsville, Hazard, Harlan, London, Corbin, Richmond, and Winchester, where poverty was high but less pervasive. The group of ten interior counties, stretching from Morgan in the north to McCreary in the south, was overwhelmingly rural and contained some of the highest concentrations of America's persistently poor people. Although the extremes of poverty had been ameliorated, little had changed on a comparative basis in these counties since the 1960s. Together the counties had an average poverty rate of 42 percent and a per capita income of less than $6,500, compared to a national average of $17,500. Clustered within these counties, moreover, were communities of even greater distress that crossed county boundaries. Examination of subcounty census tract data revealed communities lying along the edges of these severely distressed counties that contained poverty rates from 46 to 63 percent, child poverty rates averaging more than 54 percent, and unofficial unemployment rates of more than 50 percent. In these poorest of poor communities, only one in three citizens had completed high school, nine out of ten children in female-headed households lived below the poverty level, and 26 percent of residents lived in trailers, compared with 1 percent of people in the state as a whole.

Geographic information system mapping of the patterns of distress in these communities identified a number of common characteristics that bound them together in poverty. Most of the poorest census tracts were located on the edges of their counties, far from the county seats and miles from regional growth centers. These clusters of communities were overwhelmingly rural and culturally traditional, although the economies of some were based on coal and others on agriculture and logging. Almost all had witnessed the loss of local schools because of county-wide consolidation, and few had access to public water and sewer systems. Existing at the periphery of county political and economic life, they were the backyards of poor counties. Although these cross-county clusters often included natural geographic or social communities, their division among a number of small county government and service units further limited their development opportunities. Between 1965 and 1990, they had received lower per capita ARC expenditures than their urban counterparts, and their counties had received fewer ARC investments for community development than had their more populous and politically powerful neighbors. Over the twenty-five-year period, for example, Owsley County and Wolfe County—the two poorest counties in Kentucky and among the ten poorest counties in the United States—received ARC funding of only $472, 914 and $704,091 respectively. Conditions in Kentucky reflected the loss of momentum in the effort to bring economic growth to Appalachia, but they also reflected the mounting disparities between rural places and urban places and between traditional communities and more modern communities within the region. By 1990 the influence of ARC growth center strategies, structural shifts in the national economy, and the weight of local and national politics had combined to generate significant change in the mountains. For some communities, the construction of highways, industrial parks, shopping centers, hospitals, and education facilities had produced better economic conditions, and, despite the recession of the early 1980s, they continued to experience population growth and assimilation into the global economy. For others, less touched by government development programs and less prepared for the new economy, modernization brought increased dependence and fueled a further decline of community-based jobs and institutions.

Those communities that were located along the interstate and Appalachian corridor highway systems and were more integrated into the national market economy gradually regained their economic energy and joined the rest of the nation in the march to a postindustrial society. Some Appalachian towns and villages, especially those that functioned as regional government service centers, improved access to telecommunications and higher education and shared in the technological boom that swept the country in the 1990s. Others expanded as amenity centers in response to tourism and second-home development. Those more remote communities in the coalfields and the rural areas, however, continued to suffer from high unemployment, environmental decay, poverty, and the loss of youth to out-migration. Increasingly, some parts of Appalachia looked just like any other suburban place in modern America, but many other places in the region continued to reflect the economic despair, if not the old lifestyles, that had set them apart in an earlier day.

The ARC weathered the storm of the Reagan budget cuts and was eventually reauthorized by Congress. Allocations to the regional agency, however, remained at only a fraction of their former levels and reflected the loss of national interest in poverty and in Appalachia. The ARC struggled throughout the 1990s to recover from reduced budgets and tepid presidential support. With its survival assured, the commission refocused its energies, pledging to complete the unfinished portions of the Appalachian highway system and to assist mountain communities in the transition to the new economy. In 1991 the ARC revised its code to authorize expenditures from the distressed counties allocation for education and other human service projects. Previously those expenditures had been limited to water and sewer investments. During the Clinton administration, the commission renewed its commitment to helping the distressed counties and, after some debate, increased the portion of its overall allocations dedicated to the distressed counties program.

As governor of Arkansas, Bill Clinton had admired the structure and resources that the ARC provided for Appalachian development. As president he established the Mississippi Delta Commission to bring ARC-type development to his home region and appointed Jesse White, former head of the Southern Growth Policies Board, as federal cochair of the ARC. White, a Mississippi-born economist, attempted to revitalize the Appalachian program and established new regional initiatives to encourage entrepreneurship and telecommunications to better equip the region for the new economy. White also hoped to restore a commitment to the original ARC goal of regional planning by engaging the states in a comprehensive strategic planning process and by sponsoring a series of economic development conferences. In 1996 the ARC produced its first regional strategic plan in more than twenty years, establishing goals in the areas of job creation, infrastructure development, health, highways, and education. For the first time in its history, the ARC also placed a priority on developing civic leadership in the mountains, although it allocated very limited resources to this goal.

Like other federal cochairs before him, White struggled to engage the active interest of the governors in the work of the ARC but failed to generate much enthusiasm for multistate planning. Except for the governors who served on an annually alternating basis as the states cochair, most governors delegated their ARC responsibilities to lower-level staff members, who were reluctant to take policy initiatives or endorse alternative or politically sensitive approaches to development. Among the general population of the region, the ARC remained a distant and almost unknown government agency.

With few resources and limited guidance coming from the states, the commission fell back into the mode of project management, building much-needed infrastructure and funding beneficial human service programs but providing little leadership to address the region's persisting social and economic problems. Even President Clinton's well-publicized trip to Appalachia in the summer of 1999 failed to generate significant new resources or development strategies for the region. Touring communities in eastern Kentucky in the manner of Lyndon Johnson more than thirty years earlier, Clinton attempted to rally support for his "new markets" initiative to stimulate private investment in distressed rural and inner-city areas. Despite the return of prosperity to the national economy, the number of officially distressed counties in Appalachia had grown from 60 in 1982 to 108 in 1999. Accompanied by Kentucky governor Paul Patton, several cabinet secretaries, and Jesse Jackson, Clinton hoped to attract support for his pending legislation and to renew Johnson's commitment to Appalachia.

The president's visit to Appalachia dramatized the dilemma facing the ARC and the region at the turn of the century: how to stem the widening gap between those mountain communities that were growing and those that were not. The ARC had helped to bring new roads, schools, health care facilities, water and sewer systems, and other improvements to many in the region, but it had failed to eliminate the "hardcore pockets of poverty" that were, as one reporter noted, "seemingly oblivious to all efforts at improving their lot."[67] Throughout the region there were communities of people who were better educated, better fed, and better housed than their parents. Some counties on the fringes of the mountains had even attained socioeconomic levels above national averages, but there were as many places of despair, scarcity, and frustration.

The route of the president's journey into Appalachian Kentucky illustrated the disparity that divided Appalachia. Clinton's entourage of reporters, business leaders, and government dignitaries landed in Lexington before boarding helicopters for rural Jackson County. Among the crowd that met Air Force One in Lexington were many who had migrated from eastern Kentucky to the Bluegrass decades before in search of jobs and educational opportunities. A good number of the shopping centers, housing developments, and small businesses that had helped to turn the small university town into a growth center in the 1970s had been constructed with "coal money," acquired by mountain entrepreneurs during the boom years and invested in Lexington, where the promise of financial return was greater than in the rural eastern Kentucky communities that had generated the wealth.

The president's helicopter passed over Interstate 75 and Madison County before heading east into the mountains to land at an elementary school in the small community of Tyner in Jackson County. Madison County, on the edge of the region, was home to the growing cities of Richmond and Berea, which had taken advantage of their location along the interstate to attract branch manufacturing plants and expand education, health, and retail services. Berea College, long a champion of Appalachian uplift and traditional culture, had broadened its student body to reach larger numbers of poor and minority students outside the mountains and had become one of the leading liberal arts colleges in the nation. Even the small school at Tyner was a new, multigraded facility, worlds apart from the one- and two-room schools that once dotted rural landscapes throughout Appalachia. Graduates of the Tyner school were bused to the modern, consolidated high school twelve miles away in the county seat, McKee. Fifty percent of those who graduated from Jackson County High School now went on to college, but one in two elementary students failed to complete high school, and 43 percent of the adult population had not finished the ninth grade.[68]

From the Tyner school, the president's motorcade drove into Whispering Pines, a cluster of small trailer homes with about one hundred residents. There Clinton sat briefly in a plastic lawn chair and talked with sixty-nine-year-old Ray Pennington, a retired laborer with emphysema who kept a portable oxygen tank at his side. In a conversation that echoed the visit of another president to the porch of a cabin in nearby Martin County in 1964, the two men shared stories of growing up in rural places and talked about the need for jobs that might reduce the outflow of the area's young people. "Pennington's daughter Jean Collett told Clinton that since she had to quit her job at the Dairy Queen to care for her recently widowed father, the family relie[d] heavily on her son-in-law's paycheck from the nearby Mid-South plant."[69] The local electric components assembly plant was one of several that benefited from new tax incentives, and it now employed almost five hundred people.

After touring the Mid-South Electronics plant, the president greeted onlookers at a local Stop-N-Go and an Auto Mart before flying on to Hazard, deep in the coalfields. The sixty-five-mile journey would have taken Clinton two hours by car through Clay County, one of the poorest counties in the United States, and along the Daniel Boone Parkway, a link in the Appalachian Development Highway System. By air, the president traversed countryside of rugged hills and narrow hollows, substantially unchanged since the 1960s. Along the winding but now paved roads were modest homes, rehabilitated cabins, nearly abandoned coal camps, and the occasional tiny country store. Beneath the forest vegetation lay hidden patches of marijuana, a major source of income in the new underground economy of the area. The schools and many of the churches and other public buildings had long ago migrated to the "big road" communities, along with the young people and the jobs.

As the president approached Hazard, he crossed miles of devastated ridgetops, flattened by the new surface mining process of mountaintop removal. The technique, a legal loophole in the Surface Mining Control and Reclamation Act, decapitated thousands of square miles of the surrounding mountains, dumping the soil and rock from above the coal seams into nearby hollows and streams and creating vast acreages of level land. A small portion of the mined land was set aside for industrial parks and other anticipated development, but the vast majority of the barren plateaus were reserved as "wildlife sanctuaries." Local residents complained about the destruction of the water tables, the pollution of well water, the contamination of creeks, and the destruction to homes and fields from blasting and high levels of dust, but the mines operated twenty-four hours a day, providing fuel for the nation's growing energy demands. Overloaded coal trucks hauled their product to nearby railheads or low-country generating plants across the Appalachian corridor highways that also carried rural workers to jobs and services in distant growth centers.

In Hazard, the president told a crowd of almost five thousand that Appalachia and other poor places in America needed more help from government and more investment in private industry if they were to share the prosperity of the rest of the nation. "If we, with the most prosperous economy of our lifetimes, cannot make a commitment to improve the economy of poor areas," he said before departing for Lexington, "we will have failed to meet a moral obligation, and we also will have failed to make the most of America's promise."[70] People in the crowd were enthusiastic and polite as they "sat on the hot streets of Hazard . . . drinking bottled water and wearing Old Navy," but most had heard these promises before.[71] The town, of course, had changed—it now boasted a new regional hospital, a fine community college, a Wal-Mart shopping center, dozens of retail outlets, and even several modern housing developments—but not far away, up the hollows and in the dying coal towns, was another Appalachia, one that sustained the old stereotypes of poverty and backwardness. That Appalachia persisted in the shadows of the new.

6

THE NEW APPALACHIA

In the heart of the mountains and along the northern and southern fringes of the region, the new Appalachia and the old survived side by side. During the years since the War on Poverty and the creation of the special program for Appalachian development, some communities had prospered and grown, while others had languished and declined. Everywhere the region's people were drawn into the web of a more modern and complex world. Growth centers and hollows alike had developed a greater dependence on the national economy and culture, although some communities had benefited from government-sponsored programs more than had others. Despite the transformation of places like Hazard and significant improvement by almost every gauge of region-wide socioeconomic performance, Appalachia still lagged behind the rest of the country in measures of income, health, education, and job security.

At the close of the twentieth century, the region was a much more diverse place. The modern highways, vocational schools, health facilities, and other public infrastructure projects funded by the ARC had altered the mountain landscape, reshaping much of Appalachia in the pattern of American consumer society. Appalachian teenagers wore the same clothing styles and listened to the same music as their counterparts in the rest of the nation, and local Wal-Marts carried an abundance of cheap, internationally made goods. Hidden within this new society, however, were old Appalachian problems that government initiatives had failed to address. An inadequate tax base, a low-wage economy, environmental abuse, civic fraud, political corruption, absentee landownership, and corporate irresponsibility continued to weaken the region and to limit the lives of its residents. The physical destruction of the mountains, rising drug dependence, and the loss of traditional values and culture, moreover, threatened to destroy those things that had made the region distinct. Appalachia was rapidly joining the cultural and economic mainstream, and that prospect raised a new set of uncertainties.

In the popular mind, Appalachia continued to represent the other America—an isolated place of backwardness and poverty ironically rich in romance and tradition. President Clinton's trip to eastern Kentucky, media fascination with mountain culture during coal mining tragedies, and the persistence of stereotypes in plays, television, and movies continued to dramatize the popular belief that Appalachia was somehow different from the rest of the country. The mountains and mountain people had served as counterpoints to American identity for over a hundred years, and the failure of the War on Poverty and economic expansion to abolish the perceived differentness of Appalachia only reinforced old images and perceptions. The idea of Appalachia as a place in, but not of, America continued because Americans needed to believe in Appalachia's existence as part of the ongoing debate over national identity itself.

Modern Appalachia, however, increasingly reflected the social divisions and the divergent dreams of the larger society. The growing gap between mountain middle-class and working-class people, between rural places and suburban communities, and between local families and neo-Appalachians raised troubling questions about the direction of American culture and the equity of unregulated development. The new Appalachia was as tied to material consumption and mass culture as was any part of the country, but in rural areas one could still find people who kept gardens, visited neighbors, and attended family churches. In the shadow of the new artist colonies, golf courses, and gated communities that increasingly dotted the hillsides of the Great Smoky Mountains and the Blue Ridge stood the trailer homes of families who struggled to hold on to farms that had nurtured their ancestors. Some of the wealthy newcomers admired mountain music and supported local craftspeople, but much of the talent and natural wealth of the region continued to flow out of the hills, along with many of the native youth.

Appalachia had been drawn closer to the rest of America, but the fundamental problems of the region remained: issues of land use and ownership, taxation and public responsibility, environmental quality, economic security, civic leadership, human rights, and respect for cultural diversity. Despite decades of behavior modification strategies, welfare management practices, and infrastructure development, the gap between the rich and the poor within Appalachia and the loss of land and community by longtime residents continued. In part, these public strategies designed to address the "Appalachian problem" failed not only because they did not confront the structural inequities behind the conditions but also because Appalachian problems were fundamentally those of the rest of the nation.

The Appalachian economy, for example, had always been tied to national markets, despite popular images of the region as isolated and underdeveloped. The postwar effort to modernize the mountains came at a time of rapid transition in the national economy, but politics and misperceptions of the region's history limited the actions of planners and policy makers to playing games of economic catch-up rather than to designing a sustainable, place-based economy for a changing world. During the 1970s and 1980s, as promoters of Appalachian development were building industrial parks, supporting the expansion of coal mining, and chasing runaway branch plants, the United States was undergoing a fundamental change from a manufacturing-based economy to a service-based economy. At a time when Appalachian leaders were struggling to recruit labor-intensive, low-wage manufacturing plants to an underdeveloped region, technology and globalization were moving these older forms of industrial growth abroad. Traditional industrial recruitment strategies not only perpetuated the long pattern of wealth flowing out of the mountains but also failed to provide a sustainable economic foundation or to protect the region's sensitive environmental resources. Branch plant economies provided jobs but created little permanent wealth in the communities where they operated. As the rest of the nation invested in expanding higher education, improving environmental quality, and encouraging creativity for a higher-tech and more service-based world, the core communities of Appalachia remained tied to the old, extractive economy.

This pattern of economic change without the benefits of diversity, forethought, and social equity was apparent throughout the region, but nowhere was it more evident than in the central coalfields. Despite the short-lived boom of the mid-1970s, employment in the coal industry continued to decline steadily throughout the final decades of the twentieth century. The introduction of new mining technologies, the depletion of easily accessible coal seams, competition from western U.S. and South American mines, and government regulation of air quality standards combined to restructure coal industry ownership and to shift production from underground mines to surface operations. Rural communities that had survived decades of uncertain employment in deep mines now found those remaining jobs disappearing, probably forever.

At least part of the decline in coal mining jobs was the result of the utilization of new technologies, especially robotics. Just as automated cutting and loading machines had displaced thousands of miners in the years immediately after World War II, the introduction of continuous mining equipment and remotely operated longwall machines revolutionized underground mining, allowing for increased production with still fewer employees. By the early 1980s, larger, more heavily capitalized companies were adopting the new technologies. Smaller operators, less able or willing to invest in the latest machinery, found it difficult to compete. In an era of energy industry consolidation, scores of smaller, locally owned companies sold out. Many operators moved their families and their wealth to Lexington, Roanoke, Knoxville, and other urban centers within the region.

The introduction of modern mining machinery reflected fundamental changes in the ownership structure of the coal industry, as a few large energy conglomerates came to dominate Appalachian coal production. Big operating companies such as Massey Energy, Arch Coal, and Consol Energy could afford to invest in the latest equipment, but the arrival of the energy corporations gave new meaning to the long legacy of absentee ownership of Appalachian resources. Less productive mines could be closed with little regard for local economies, and the application of new technologies was disproportionately weighted to increase production rather than to improve the health and safety of miners. Distant corporate executives and international stockholders were even less concerned with the future of declining coalfield communities than their predecessors had been.

As a result of globalization, technology, and the extension of the federal Clean Air Act in 1970, coal production within Appalachia shifted heavily toward the lower-sulfur coalfields of southern West Virginia and eastern Kentucky and toward cheaper surface-mined coal. With the decline of the American steel industry as a result of offshore competition, demand for metallurgical coal dried up, and production overwhelmingly shifted to steam coal. Older metallurgical mines in central West Virginia, southwest Virginia, and some areas of eastern Kentucky closed, leaving thousands of underground miners unemployed. In 2002, Appalachia still produced nearly 40 percent of the nation's coal, enough to generate about half of the electricity used in the United States, but region-wide production levels were on the decline, and the industry was concentrated in a few counties.[1]

The restructuring of the coal industry was especially hard on southwest Virginia. Coal production dropped so rapidly in Buchanan, Dickenson, and Wise counties during the 1990s that the total number of coal miners reached an all-time low of 6,900 in 1996, fewer than half of those employed in 1982. In nearby eastern Kentucky, the number of mining jobs declined from 35,000 to 15,000 during the same period. In counties where mining was once the dominant, if not the sole, source of employment, coal mining accounted for less than 15 percent of the jobs, behind construction and general trade positions. Harlan County, which had supported nearly 20,000 miners earlier in the century, employed only 1,200 in 2002. During the last two decades of the twentieth century, the number of coal mining jobs throughout all of Appalachia declined by 70 percent, falling from 159,000 to 46,000.[2]

Miners had lost their jobs before in the coalfields, which had always endured booms and busts in the coal market, but the disappearance of jobs in the 1980s and 1990s was permanent. Not only had technology altered the demand for underground miners, but the industry had already tapped the best seams of coal, and the deeper, thinner seams were more expensive to mine. Geologists in government agencies and universities increasingly predicted that the supply of mineable coal in Appalachia was running out and that declining reserves would limit future production. The Kentucky Geological Survey, for example, reported in 1989 that minable coal in some areas might be exhausted in twenty years. In many places, companies were already down to mining seams that had narrowed from seventy inches to as little as twelve inches, and these thin seams were full of impurities.[3] Despite the confidence of engineers that they would develop new technologies to reach deeper and thinner seams and the assurances of mine owners that the geologists were wrong, miners began to recognize that the era of big coal was gone and that fewer of the region's workers would again find employment in the industry.

The declining number of miners reflected changes in the politics and environment of coal communities. The once powerful UMWA almost disappeared as a political force in some areas of Appalachia, replicating the decline of union membership generally throughout the United States. After the election of Richard Trumka as president of the UMWA in 1982 and the ascendancy of conservative, probusiness interests in the Reagan White House, the union adopted a policy of supporting selective strikes rather than launching national strikes to shut down the entire coal industry. Trumka hoped to bring stability to the coalfields and to preserve jobs by helping American companies compete more efficiently with imported coal, but this policy of cooperation failed to halt sliding union membership. Then the A. T. Massey Coal Company in 1984–1985 and later the Pittston Coal Company in 1989–1990 broke away from industry-wide agreements in order to advance lower-wage and nonunion operations. The latter confrontation erupted as a spontaneous strike in southwest Virginia when Pittston refused to sign the union contract and brought in strikebreakers to replace picketing UMWA members. The strike resulted in the arrests of thousands of miners and their supporters and spread to more than fifty thousand miners in eleven states before reaching a compromise settlement. Pittston was permitted to continue to employ nonunion miners and to set a twenty-four-hour-a-day, seven-day-a-week work schedule. The Pittston strike signaled to smaller mining companies in Appalachia that they too could break their union contracts, and nonunion mines proliferated.[4]

The loss of jobs in underground mines and the decline of union membership sucked the economic lifeblood from scores of rural mountain communities. Few of the coalfield communities had benefited much from the infrastructure and industrial development efforts of the 1970s, and the limited service jobs and branch plants that had come to nearby towns and villages paid significantly less than a miner's wage and often provided no health or retirement benefits. A small number of miners found employment driving coal trucks and bulldozers at surface mines that began to expand in parts of southern West Virginia and eastern Kentucky, but many more left their homes seeking work in the new growth centers or in towns on the perimeter of the region. Those who were able to find work in the remaining nonunion deep mines labored under deteriorating work conditions and declining enforcement of federal mining laws, with fewer health benefits.

Even the landscape itself was altered by the changing structure of the coal industry. In the heart of the coalfields, the expansion of surface mining leveled thousands of acres of mountaintops, filling in the valleys between ridges and covering the heads of creeks with rubble. Blasts from these massive operations polluted or destroyed the well water of nearby homes, cracked foundations, and raised clouds of dust that settled everywhere. The new mining technique, known as mountaintop removal, emerged through a loophole in the Surface Mining Control and Reclamation Act of 1977 that allowed mine owners to circumvent regulations requiring the restoration of land to its approximate original contour if the reclaimed land could be put to "a higher and better use." The coal industry was quick to recognize the potential of mountaintop removal as a cheap and efficient way to create level land for economic development, and in an era when policy makers were feverish for industrial recruitment, the promise of flat, developable land in the mountains was enough to ease mining permits through the state regulatory agencies and the Army Corps of Engineers. With few exceptions, however, the promised developments never materialized, and communities were left with miles of deserted, treeless plateaus, poisoned water tables, and a permanently altered landscape. Most mountaintop removal sites were remote, and in the small number of cases where strip-mined sites were located close to population centers, the construction of shopping centers, hospitals, hotels, and small manufacturing facilities on old mine sites often ran into problems with unstable, shifting land.

Aside from the environmental destruction, increased production from surface mining generated few jobs, destroyed the area's potential for sustainable timber and tourism development, and pushed another generation of Appalachian youth out of their rural communities. By 2000 almost half of the coal mined in Appalachia came from mountaintop removal, but the growing industry's appetite for land seemed unlimited. As environmental writer Erik Reece put it, there were "now enough flattened mountains in Eastern Kentucky to set down the cities of Louisville and Lexington."[5] Despite the efforts of industry and government officials to recruit manufacturing plants to these so-called industrial parks, most remained abandoned or were later designated as wildlife sanctuaries. One site became the location of a federal prison, and another the home of a herd of elk transplanted from the western United States.

Local, state, and federal governments heavily invested public funds in making some of these mining sites suitable for development. At one valley fill location near Hazard, Kentucky, for example, more than $209 million in grants, tax credits, and local bonds were committed to build a fabricating plant that utilized timber from other surface mining sites in the production of glued wood trusses. Contractors spent $1 million of that amount to dig twenty feet down to find ground that was solid enough to build the facility.[6] Several years later, the commonwealth provided another incentive package to construct a four-thousand-square-foot aluminum building for a Florida-based computer call center, which left in 2003 after the tax abatement expired, taking its 393 low-paying jobs to El Salvador.[7] The wave of mountaintop destruction that swept across the central Appalachians as a result of growing urban demands for cheap electricity generated few jobs for mountain people but left a permanently scarred and wasted landscape.

As coal employment withered, attempts to recruit manufacturing facilities to the coalfields and nearby rural Appalachian communities intensified. Anxious government leaders diverted millions of dollars of public resources into the effort, but their plans were generally met with disappointment in an era of national economic transition. After taking advantage of incentive packages and tax rebates, most of the branch textile, shoe, food processing, and other small plants attracted to Appalachia in the 1980s and 1990s left the region by the end of the century, shifting their production to offshore, even-lower-wage facilities in Latin America and Asia. A study conducted for the ARC concluded that manufacturing in Appalachia, relative to the rest of the country, looked much the same in 1992 as it had in 1967—lower wages, lower productivity, and much more reliant on branch plants.[8]

The fever for manufacturing recruitment, of course, was not limited to Appalachian leaders. State governments across the South expanded their marketing programs and incentive packages to bring outside jobs into rural communities. Most of the funds and the employment opportunities, however, flowed into the more prosperous regions of those states rather than into the distressed mountain counties. A study of North Carolina's economic development programs in 2003 revealed that only 7 percent of the state's industrial recruitment funds were invested in western North Carolina, despite the loss of 6,700 regional industrial jobs in that year alone.[9] A similar investigation in Kentucky found that barely more than 6 percent of the corporate income tax credits granted by the commonwealth for rural economic development between 1990 and 1997 went to eastern Kentucky.[10] Nevertheless, Appalachian leaders were often among the strongest proponents of these incentive programs, and by the mid-1990s, almost every mountain county had developed its own industrial park in hopes of succeeding in the increasingly competitive hunt for runaway companies.

Enthusiasm for industrial recruitment was especially strong in Appalachian Kentucky, where local officials hoped to combat job loss by attracting low-wage industry. Under the leadership of Paul Patton, a former coal operator and Pike County judge executive who was elected governor in 1992, eastern Kentucky counties launched aggressive campaigns to develop industrial sites on flat, often strip-mined land and to build speculation buildings at public expense. Patton's statewide incentive program allowed recruited companies to keep their corporate income taxes and the state income taxes paid by their workers, but even these incentives failed to fill industrial parks or to retain many of the businesses that agreed to relocate. Frequently these companies fell short of the number of jobs specified in their contracts with the state, or they closed after a few years of operation.

Harlan County's experience with industrial recruitment was typical. Beginning in the early 1990s, the state approved more than $11 million in tax breaks and incentives to recruit manufacturing companies to the county in the wake of declining coal employment. Four of the seven companies that received subsidies closed or never opened, and two more employed far fewer people than projected.[11] One North Carolina company, United Glove, defaulted on its promise to provide 100 jobs after securing a $1 million tax credit and left the state. Another plant, the Sunshine Valley Farms biscuit factory, opened in 1994 promising to create 106 jobs. After employing only 7 people five years later, the company was sued by the state to recover the public's half-million-dollar investment.[12] Sunshine Valley Farms was owned by two Kentucky nonprofit corporations created during the War on Poverty, the Kentucky Highlands Investment Corporation (KHIC) and the Christian Appalachian Project. Other questionable coalfield development schemes involved investments by local politicians, business leaders, and even coal-related interests. A Harlan County sock factory that had received more than $1.5 million in grants and loans failed soon after one of its owners was elected to the state senate in 1998. In Governor Patton's Pike County, the state spent $15 million over a decade to recruit, and lose, seven manufacturing facilities at a forty-three-acre industrial park, including one short-lived company that built aluminum dump trailers for hauling coal.[13]

The frenzy for industrial recruitment spawned dozens of private, nonprofit organizations across Appalachia designed to reduce the region's poverty by offering venture capital loans for plant construction and relocation. Among the most successful was KHIC, which, despite its Sunshine Valley Farms failure, helped to bring dozens of small plants to southeastern Kentucky in the 1980s and 1990s. Launched in 1968, KHIC initially utilized federal grant money to provide loans to companies that would create jobs in poor communities. In the 1980s it transitioned into a venture capital investment corporation, and in 1994 it wrote and received one of three Clinton administration rural empowerment zone (EZ) grants for $40 million. The only EZ grant awarded in Appalachia, it provided the pretext for Clinton's poverty visit to eastern Kentucky in 1999.[14]

According to one of the chief architects of the federal EZ program, the goal of the initiative was to "move beyond categorical investments in infrastructure and businesses inside the community boundaries to building rural communities themselves, through holistic and integrative strategies."[15] Although the EZ philosophy emphasized community building through widespread participation in the planning and implementation processes, KHIC had little experience in community organizing. The Kentucky Highlands EZ was initiated, drafted, and managed by the staff of the KHIC in collaboration with a cadre of local officials who were more than happy to participate. Consequently the $40 million proposal reflected primarily the development interests of the corporation and a few powerful leaders in the three scattered rural counties.

Most of the federal investment in the EZ went to infrastructure, "downtown improvement," job training, and the Kentucky Highlands EZ Venture Fund for loans to industry. A planned 113-acre lake failed to materialize in severely distressed Jackson County, but the EZ recruited more than 3,000 jobs, mostly in Clinton and Wayne counties, south of Lake Cumberland. Employers in the latter included a number of luxury houseboat manufacturers and Cagle's-Keystone Foods, which employed more than 1,500 workers in a chicken processing facility.[16] Critics charged the EZ with using public funds to bring low-wage, dangerous jobs to the area and with employing large numbers of Hispanics and other workers from outside the county, but KHIC pointed to Cagle's-Keystone and to plants like the Mid-South Electronics facility that President Clinton visited in Jackson County as evidence of successful economic development.[17] Five years after Clinton visited the Mid-South plant, however, the company closed its Appalachian operations following a fire, leaving 700 employees without work.[18] Such plant closings were repeated again and again throughout the region as textiles, leather, and other small manufacturing operations abandoned the United States for cheaper offshore production.[19]

Despite the booming national economy in the 1990s, rural Appalachian communities struggled to keep pace with changing global markets. The decline of coal mining and manufacturing employment and the loss of supplemental income from tobacco farming left rural mountain families with few options in an era of rising consumption and technological change. Some families opted to commute long distances to service and trade jobs in regional growth centers. The new interstate and Appalachian corridor highways were clogged each morning and evening with workers from rural communities streaming to and from low-paying jobs elsewhere. Other mountain families chose to subsist on Social Security or disability assistance in hollows and coves that were populated more and more by older residents. Many individuals, especially the young, migrated permanently to the education, employment, and social opportunities of distant cities.

Government policies that encouraged short-term growth at the expense of more sustainable development, that facilitated investment in some communities over others, and that allowed a few private interests to feed liberally at the public trough continued to fuel the growing inequities between the new and the old Appalachia. Rather than investing limited public resources in community-based educational improvement, sustainable agriculture, small-business enhancement, and the development of a regionally integrated economy, policy makers diverted millions of dollars to the creation of jobs that were disappearing in the rest of the nation. Rather than focusing civic energies on the improvement of housing, higher education, culture, recreation, and health facilities that would enhance the quality of life for local workers and encourage creativity and entrepreneurship, leaders continued to look to external models of development that perpetuated old dependences on outside markets and absentee capital.

At one level, of course, government growth strategies achieved measurable success. Poverty rates for the ARC region as a whole were cut in half between 1960 and 2000, and the gap in per capita income between Appalachia and the rest of the country narrowed. In 1960 nearly one-third of the region's residents lived in poverty, compared with one-fifth of all Americans; by 2000 poverty rates in Appalachia had declined to a regional average of only 13.6 percent, compared with 12.3 percent for the rest of the nation. Per capita income in the Appalachian region at the turn of the twenty-first century reached almost 84 percent of the national average, unemployment rates declined, and the number of severely distressed counties fell from 223 to 89.[20] With equally impressive improvements in the number of health care and education facilities, government agencies such as the ARC were proud to point to the evidence of progress that had been made in reducing the gap between Appalachia and the rest of the nation.

These cumulative data, however, obscured the reality of economic differences within the region. Measures of economic distress improved significantly across the United States between 1960 and 2000, but improvements in central Appalachia lagged behind the rest of Appalachia and the nation. While poverty rates in northern and southern Appalachia were only 12.8 percent in 2000, slightly above the national average of 12.3 percent, rates in the heart of Appalachia were 22.1 percent, almost twice the national average. Eastern Kentucky and southern West Virginia contained five of the poorest twenty-five counties in the United States, counties where one in three residents lived below the poverty level. In Martin County, Kentucky, for example, where President Johnson had tried to rouse support for the War on Poverty in 1964, the per capita income had risen from 34 percent to 55 percent of the national level. The majority of the counties on the ARC distressed counties list were in central Appalachia, and eighty-five of the counties that were economically distressed in 1960 were still listed as distressed four decades later. In contrast, Appalachian sections of six ARC states (Alabama, Georgia, Mississippi, New York, North Carolina, and South Carolina) had poverty rates in 2000 that were lower than those of the non-Appalachian counties in their states.[21] Appalachia was still one of the poorest places in the United States, and the deepest and most persistent poverty was still concentrated in the core of the region in amounts that far exceeded national averages.

Such measures of economic well-being also obscured social inequalities that cut across the region. Throughout Appalachia the income gap between rural communities and metropolitan communities widened significantly. Most of the new jobs that came to the mountains in the late twentieth century were in services, retail trade, and government, and the majority of these were located in or adjacent to the metropolitan areas, the growth centers connected by ARC corridors and interstate highways. Family income in rural Appalachia in 1999 averaged only 70 percent of that in metropolitan areas of the region and 65 percent of family income in the United States.[22]

Like the rest of the country, moreover, the gap between the rich and the poor grew substantially in the last decades of the century, as those with greater access to education, capital, and political power prospered in the growing service and retail centers of the region. Most evident in the nonmetropolitan counties adjacent to major cities and in the tourist-based counties of the Blue Ridge, the new mountain professional class thrived on the expansion and relocation of education, health, retail, and government services in the larger towns. In some places a growing population of nonnative retirees added to the income disparity, further increasing the demand for public services and driving up land values in rural areas. The gated housing developments, ethnic restaurants, BMWs, and Volvos that one could increasingly find in some mountain counties were ever present reminders of the gap between those with the resources to succeed in the new Appalachia and those without them. According to a study by the Center on Budget and Policy Priorities, in West Virginia the incomes of the richest families climbed substantially between 1980 and 2000, while the incomes of the middle- and lower-income families saw only modest increases. The growth in income inequality between the richest 20 percent and the poorest 20 percent of the population in the Mountain State was the sixth largest in the nation.[23]

Women and children carried the heaviest burden of poverty and income disparity. Although mountain women were quick to take advantage of the job training programs and community college facilities, many of the new jobs that opened up in the service sector paid low wages and were usually located far from workers' home communities. Child care was difficult to find, public transportation nonexistent, and maintaining a car expensive. Women in Appalachia, as elsewhere, had substantially lower incomes than men, earning on average about two-thirds of men's income. The highest poverty rates in the region were among female-headed households. In the most persistently distressed counties of central Appalachia, nearly 70 percent of female-headed households with children under six years old had incomes below the national poverty level in 2000.[24]

When Congress enacted welfare reform legislation in 1996 with the goal of moving individuals from welfare to work, the initiative was met with widespread skepticism in Appalachia. Low educational levels, the lack of available jobs, and the distances to child care and other public services made the implementation of the act difficult in most rural mountain communities, where poverty and disability rates were already high. Despite these challenges, welfare caseloads were reduced by over 70 percent in Appalachia over the next decade as thousands of families were squeezed into an already glutted workforce or onto government disability programs such as Supplemental Security Income. The lack of available jobs and the migration of public services to the larger towns and villages placed a double burden on the rural poor, contributing to the persistently high rates of unemployment, underemployment, and poverty.[25]

Efforts by public and private agencies to ease poverty and income disparity in Appalachia met with some success in the 1990s. Under the leadership of Jesse White, the ARC adopted policies to encourage local entrepreneurship, job training programs, and the clustering of higher-tech industries that would advance regional competitiveness in the global economy and wean policy makers from their reliance on branch plant recruitment. The Ford Foundation launched a $10 million national effort, the Rural Community College Initiative, to help a dozen community colleges in Appalachia, the Delta, the Southwest, and Native American communities to become catalysts for local community development. A number of small, nonprofit organizations established programs to train and support local entrepreneurs, and one, the New Opportunity School for Women, won national recognition for its efforts to improve the educational, employment, and financial status of low-income Appalachian women. Such programs expanded the income potential for hundreds of individuals across the region, but they were usually underfunded, and they failed to alter traditional structures and patterns of development in the most distressed counties. By the turn of the century, for example, there was only one facility in all of central Appalachia designed to incubate small businesses and encourage creativity, in contrast to dozens that had been established in the more affluent northern and southern sections of the region.

The uneven benefits of economic development not only limited the opportunities for some individuals but narrowed the options for alternative patterns of community development as well. The absence of public and private initiatives to encourage locally owned small businesses and the marketing of regionally produced goods and services left mountain communities even more tied to global markets than they had been earlier in the century. Policies that recruited outside industries and utilized former mine sites for megacorporate chains such as

Wal-Mart not only facilitated the transfer of wealth out of the region, contributing to the decline of smaller, community-based businesses, but also drained public resources that might have nurtured local entrepreneurs and encouraged innovative, sustainable alternatives to the delivery of goods and services. In a region desperate for better housing, health care, education, and cultural amenities, community-based solutions for development were often bypassed in favor of externally controlled businesses and institutions that were more interested in growth than development.

This bias in favor of traditional, market-based solutions to regional problems was not limited to state or federal policy makers; it also influenced the economic visions of local mountain elites and shaped their attitudes toward the poor. Most Appalachian leaders welcomed growth of any kind, hoped to replicate mainstream symbols of material progress in their own communities, and were defensive about media portrayals of Appalachia as backward and distressed. Having benefited directly from the government investments that had helped to create the new Appalachia, mountain business leaders and professionals were proud of the transformations that had reshaped their communities, and they were sometimes indignant at suggestions that Appalachia was still a land of the poor.

During President Clinton's visit to eastern Kentucky in 1999, the economic and ideological gap between the rich and the poor was manifest in the response of local leaders. Most dignitaries and public officials who met with the president were honored to have the nation's leader in the mountains promoting the need for private investment in Appalachia, but some were insulted that his visit was part of a poverty tour. "I'm a Republican, and I really think he did us a good honor," Hazard mayor Bill Gorman told a *New York Times* reporter. "The greatest problem I've seen with people [in the mountains] is the lack of hope. You give them hope and they will conquer the world." Gorman, who had been mayor for the past twenty-three years and whose brother was a leading banker and coal operator in the area, had invited the president two months earlier to visit Hazard to demonstrate how well Appalachia was doing in the new economy. "Appalachia has a lot of problems," he informed reporters as they toured the local Wal-Mart and the new off-track betting facility, U Bet. "But the quality of life here is no different than it is anywhere in the country." Charlie Hammonds, another Hazard official, added, "We're just the same as most places." But he worried that "the president spent a little too much time in places where the old stereotypes of Appalachia persists [sic]—on rural roads, out where families have little education or work."[26]

The faith of local leaders in the potential of postwar models of growth ignored historical and systemic inequities that continued to divide the region. The truth, of course, was that too many Appalachian families still had inadequate education, little hope for employment, and insufficient health care, and the institutional structures that had evolved since the 1960s had done little to alter existing class and political relationships. The loss of jobs to mechanization and global competition and the rise of technology and a knowledge-based national economy left many older, uneducated farmers, miners, and unskilled workers with nowhere to turn. Opportunities expanded for individuals who were positioned to take advantage of the new economy, but the reduction in federal job training programs during the 1980s, the lack of start-up capital and technical assistance for small businesses, and the anxieties of interacting with impersonal bureaucracies in distant growth centers forced many rural residents to fall back on old survival skills and the support of the extended family.

The politics of growth in the mountains, who won and who lost as a result of government investments, was nowhere more evident than in the arenas of education and health care. Long a weakness in Appalachia, public education underwent revolutionary change as a result of state and federal initiatives in the post–World War II years. The region's schools were modernized and restructured at every level, and measures of education from literacy to college graduation rates improved. By 2000 the old one- and two-room country schools had been replaced throughout the mountains by new consolidated schools, and access to higher education had expanded with state and federal investments in community and technical colleges. The percentage of Appalachian adults who had completed high school rose steadily, reaching 77 percent in 2000, compared with 81 percent for the rest of the nation, and the percentage of those who had attained college degrees reached almost 18 percent, compared with 25 percent nationally. Educational gains, however, like economic gains, were not distributed equally across the region. While metropolitan areas and the northern and southern subregions made gains that sometimes exceeded national averages, central Appalachia and rural areas throughout the mountains continued to trail far behind national averages. In 2000 only 64 percent of adults in central Appalachia and 65 percent of adults in rural areas within the region had completed high school. Moreover, the gap in postsecondary education levels between Appalachia and the United States actually increased as the rate of college graduates in the rest of the nation grew faster than that in Appalachia.[27] The gain in college graduates was slowest in the coal counties and in other rural areas, in part because of the continued gap in per capita income in those communities but also because of the growing challenges of transportation and cultural alienation in the new education system.

As with strategies for economic development, efforts to improve education in Appalachia usually followed the pattern established by national and urban norms. The closing of rural community schools and the construction of modern consolidated schools with better classrooms, laboratories, and vocational training facilities not only provided an environment that looked like schools in suburban America but offered a broader variety of courses and the promise of more successful sports programs and extracurricular activities. By the new millennium, Appalachian schools looked much like those of the rest of the nation. Most of the consolidated high schools, however, were centrally located near county seats or metropolitan communities, requiring rural children to be bused (sometimes up to three hours a day) to and from school and limiting their participation in after-school activities.

Rural communities often paid the highest price for the consolidation of county schools. It was more difficult for students and their parents to participate in school programs, and the rural community lost a center for community life, pride, and identity. Modern, technical approaches to learning that rewarded individual competition rather than collaborative work; large, impersonal classes; and a school culture that emphasized access to consumer goods rather than traditional values and culture frequently distanced poorer, rural youth from the education system. Rural children, rather than their urban classmates, were among the first to drop out of school after the ninth grade, and those rural students who finished high school were less likely to move on to higher education. Time and again, those who did succeed in the new system were drawn away permanently from their home communities to colleges, universities, and jobs elsewhere. From the perspective of some rural parents, improved educational facilities at the new consolidated schools enhanced the economic opportunities of county officials and their families but only facilitated the exodus of talented students from rural areas.

Many of the young people, especially women, who adapted to the new secondary education system took advantage of the modern community colleges that opened across the region and secured degrees as computer programmers, nurses, accountants, and other mid-level technicians for expanding government agencies in nearby towns. A few attended four-year colleges and universities, but many who did failed to return to the region because of the lack of employment opportunities in their specialty fields. Thus for larger numbers of mountain young people, higher education became a real possibility, but for many it also became another highway out of the mountains. Rather than serving as an economic engine that might power creativity, security, and innovation as it did in other areas of the nation, higher education in Appalachia too often served to sustain the existing system or to drain away the region's human assets.

Despite the opening of a law school in Grundy, Virginia, and a new medical school at Pikeville College in eastern Kentucky, for example, graduate and professional schools and institutes for scientific and medical research were scarce in central Appalachia, leaving most of the region's professionals to be educated outside the mountains and denying localities the economic and civic benefits that such institutions provide to dynamic communities. During an era when job creation was often linked to information exchange, knowledge management, and innovation, there was not a single rank-one research university in all of central Appalachia, between Morgantown, West Virginia, and Knoxville, Tennessee, and between Blacksburg, Virginia, and Lexington, Kentucky. Large research institutions on the perimeter of the region and a number of excellent small colleges and regional universities expanded their linkages with the rural interior counties during this period, but the intellectual and economic impact of higher education on Appalachia remained limited.

The mixed benefits of improvements in education were mirrored in health care, which also underwent dramatic change in the last decades of the twentieth century. The expansion of emergency facilities and primary care clinics provided better access to medical care, but income and transportation barriers often limited the use of these facilities by the rural poor. Although primary care facilities were available within thirty miles of almost every Appalachian family by the turn of the century, access to higher-level care usually required travel to a distant university medical center or urban facility. The advent of medical helicopters improved the travel time for emergency treatment, but the economic benefits of advances in health care flowed to the external medical centers rather than expanding the local economy and institutional base. Specialized care, particularly in mental health and obstetrics, was sparse in central Appalachian communities, leaving most rural families to seek advanced services or treatment outside the region.

As a result of federal programs to recruit health professionals to rural counties, the number of primary care physicians serving Appalachia increased between 1965 and 2000, but two-thirds of mountain counties were still listed as "health professional shortage areas" at the turn of the century. The shortage was especially severe in the rural, economically distressed counties of central Appalachia. Those counties were least likely to have full-service hospitals, and the primary health care needs of residents were most often served by federally subsidized community health centers. Many small hospitals in the mountains closed during the 1980s, after the federal government altered the Medicaid-Medicare reimbursement formula to favor larger, urban hospitals, and in the 1990s one in four hospitals in Appalachia was facing severe financial challenges. Rural counties suffered from shortages of dentists, obstetricians, and substance abuse treatment centers as well.[28]

As in other areas of the United States, life expectancy increased and infant mortality and maternal death rates decreased significantly in Appalachia during the last decades of the century, but such measures, which are often used to assess health status, hid disparities that continued to place mountain residents at greater risk than other Americans. Inadequate health insurance, higher levels of poverty and unemployment, and lack of education and of preventive care led to higher instances of illness and death from some diseases in Appalachia, especially those related to diet and stress. Mountain residents were more likely than other Americans to suffer from heart and other cardiovascular diseases; diabetes; cervical, breast, and lung cancers; and work disability. Moreover, rural Appalachians suffered higher mortality rates from these conditions than did urban Appalachians.[29]

While the prevalence of a disease among any population group may have complex origins, there is little doubt that poverty contributed to the persistence of these health disparities in Appalachia. As one researcher observed, lower-income people in the mountains experienced "a combination of decreased access to health care, increased risk to occupational and environmental hazards, and a greater tendency toward lifestyle habits that correlate with a low sense of control over one's destiny."[30] Income uncertainty and the lack of job opportunities, for example, elevated levels of stress, anxiety, and feelings of powerlessness that sometimes resulted in drug dependence, obesity, and depression. The maladies of heart disease, diabetes, and lung cancer in Appalachia were linked to persistently high rates of tobacco consumption, which was in turn associated with stress and with the region's rural heritage. West Virginia and Kentucky had the highest rates of heart disease in the nation, and eastern Kentucky, where 43 percent of adults smoked, led the country in lung cancer mortality rates.[31]

Emphysema, asthma, and other lung-related illnesses remained particularly high in coal counties. Within the region, coal mining had always been the most dangerous form of employment. Disability and poor health had gone hand in hand with work in underground mines. The passage of the Federal Coal Mine Health and Safety Act of 1969 and the Black Lung Benefits Act of 1972 increased hopes that the health and survival of miners would improve, but as late as 2007, a national study found severe black lung disease on the rise among younger miners in eastern Kentucky and southwestern Virginia. The report concluded that a lack of enforcement and compliance with dust-control regulations was placing larger numbers of miners at risk. Black lung disease was still listed as the underlying cause of death for an average of more than six hundred former miners each year in Appalachia between 1999 and 2004, more than thirty years after the passage of federal mine safety laws.[32]

Despite state and federal mine safety legislation and the precipitous decline in coal employment in the last decades of the twentieth century, coal mining remained one of the most hazardous occupations in the United States. Between 1996 and 2005, 320 workers were killed in American coal mines. An even larger number were injured or permanently disabled by mine accidents. Most deaths and injuries occurred in individual incidents of roof falls, equipment misuse, or ventilation problems, most of which, one study claimed, could have been avoided if existing regulations had been followed.[33] Only when multiple lives were taken by dramatic mine explosions did the nation's attention refocus on mine safety issues. After 16 miners died in unrelated explosions in three mines in West Virginia and eastern Kentucky in the spring of 2006, three separate Labor Department reports accused the Mine Safety and Health Administration of overlooking obvious violations and of failing to take serious enforcement actions against the coal companies involved.[34] Critics charged the Mine Safety and Health Administration and state regulators with a long history of failing to enforce legislation, issuing nominal fines, and ignoring unsafe roof conditions, inadequate ventilation, and deficient safety procedures.

Just as coal mining continued to be hazardous to miners' health, living in the new Appalachia also brought a rise in tobacco, alcohol, and drug abuse usually associated with suburban and inner-city life. High rates of accidents and disease, elevated levels of worker disability, persistent unemployment, income uncertainty, and the growing availability of prescription painkillers contributed to rising levels of drug dependence in many mountain communities. An older population with more chronic disease and more chronic pain increasingly pressured medical providers for pain prescriptions, and more and more young people, lacking hope in the future of their own communities, turned to illegally obtained prescription drugs as a means of escape. According to one study, drugstores, hospitals, and other legal outlets in central Appalachia received more prescription painkillers than did any other area of the country.[35]

By the 1990s the illegal use of prescription narcotics such as Oxy-Contin and Vicodin had become an epidemic. Marketed by national drug companies as less addictive and less subject to abuse than other drugs and almost casually prescribed by scores of mountain doctors, these narcotics rapidly became the drugs of choice among illegal drug traffickers and users in Appalachia. Possession and sales of these illegal substances jumped 348 percent from 1997 through 2001 in eastern Kentucky, and from 2000 to 2002, more than 1,300 drug-related deaths occurred in the mountains of the Bluegrass State. The *Lexington Herald-Leader* labeled that area "the prescription-painkiller capital of the United States." With parts of Appalachia experiencing drug-related deaths at four times the rate of the rest of the country, even the ARC became involved, helping to fund the regional Coalition on Appalachian Substance Abuse Policy and encouraging states to strengthen drug abuse programs and to build more treatment facilities. "Not only is substance abuse a public health problem," an ARC report pointed out to Appalachian policy makers, "studies show it impacts education, economic development and family life."[36]

The rise of the prescription drug culture in rural Appalachia was a tragic symbol of the arrival of modern America in the mountains. The new highways, shopping centers, consolidated schools, and industrial parks had reduced the perceived otherness of Appalachia, but the new economy failed to provide security, hope, and meaning for the lives of many of the region's residents. Persistent disparities in income, education, and health status limited the life possibilities of young and old alike and hastened the disintegration of the once strong Appalachian family and culture. As the region entered a new century, communities throughout Appalachia again confronted the dilemmas of modernization: how to define progress, how to grow with equity and fairness, and how to change without losing the strengths of identity and tradition.

Debate over growth and development had divided mountain communities for generations. At least since the late nineteenth century, some in Appalachia had advocated growth through industrialization as the way to enhance individual opportunities and wealth, and they looked to the greater connections with mainstream society and markets as the paths to regional progress. Others sought to sustain a more communal way of life that valued stability, security, and independence. After a century of economic change, first as a result of private and corporate investment in the region's resources and later as a consequence of government initiatives, the old debate remained. Many communities, faced with job losses and the out-migration of youth, searched for alternative ways to survive; a few, confronted with rapid growth, looked to control the process of change and to protect fast-disappearing cultural and natural resources. Most places struggled with conflicting ideas about the good life and with differing notions of the role of government in shaping that life.

The character and strength of that struggle intensified in the new Appalachia, in part because of the consequences of technology and global change and in part because of educational opportunities presented by government programs. The growth of world markets, the shift of manufacturing jobs abroad, and escalating demand for cheap energy added to existing pressure on the economy and the land. The expansion of the professional class, rising numbers of neo-Appalachians who migrated to the mountains in search of alternative lifestyles, and higher education levels among native residents increased the civic capacity and the diversity of critical voices within the region. Greater access to higher education in the 1960s and 1970s, moreover, produced a new generation of cultural and political leaders that was more educated and more willing to challenge existing power structures. A few began to look beyond the old economies of coal and branch plant manufacturing for more sustainable, alternative strategies for development. Coalitions of the new leadership often came together around issues related to the environment, health care, and cultural heritage, but their ideas frequently met resistance from institutions and politicians comfortable with the status quo.

Ironically, the political culture that had evolved with the arrival of industrialization decades earlier now proved to be the greatest barrier to structural change. Mountain residents had always felt a sense of separateness from mainstream society that reinforced their passion for freedom and independence. This pride in things local and familiar was more than just a defensive reaction to outside stereotypes, for it fueled a cooperative community spirit that allowed families to survive during hard times. It also provided a pretext, though, to resist change, and eventually it was utilized by mountain elites to maintain long established political dynasties. A certain deference for authority, for example, sustained by religious traditions and gender roles, strengthened the power of influential local males, who often controlled access to jobs and family security, and it contributed to an acceptance of the political process as an extension of private economic interest. In a world of uncertainty and economic insecurity, challenging existing patriarchy could be especially risky. The good old boys who still dominated much of Appalachian economic, cultural, and political life at the end of the twentieth century disdained criticism, innovation, and wider participation in civic life just as much as those who had controlled the political system on behalf of outside corporate interests decades earlier. They continued to use patronage, fear, and prejudice to maintain privilege and power in their modern little kingdoms.

Most Appalachian families tended to separate public from private life unless some imminent threat challenged their fragile security. As a result, the old cadre of power brokers continued to dominate local governments and institutions, too often utilizing the public sector to achieve personal gain or to reward relatives and friends. Despite increased oversight by state and federal authorities, corruption and election fraud persisted in many mountain counties, and advocates of political and economic reform found their efforts repeatedly frustrated. Programs to improve the quality of leadership and enhance civic participation blossomed in the 1990s and met with some success in bringing women, youth, and minorities into the public process. The ARC even added civic capacity to its list of regional development goals, but these programs were limited and slow to alter the prevailing political culture.

Fraud, corruption, and self-interest were not unique to Appalachia, but in a region plagued with persistent social and economic inequalities, the paucity of honest and creative leadership added an additional barrier to systemic reform. Politicians in some of the most distressed counties of the region were accused regularly of complicity in tolerating poor schools and social services to maintain their control over the local job market, which in turn assured their own political survival. The consolidation of schools and the growth of federal human service programs provided an ever expanding pool of patronage jobs and government contracts that could be channeled to friends and family, and control of the law enforcement system afforded additional cover for other profitable but illegal activities. Mingo County, West Virginia, for example, attracted national attention in the late 1980s when sixty-two local officials were indicted for corruption within a two-year period. Among those convicted of drug trafficking were two sheriffs, a police chief, and the fire chief. Federal prosecutors charged another local leader, who served as the president of the school board and the director of the poverty program, with drug conspiracy, obstruction of justice, and fraud. The man had personally handed out more than 2,400 jobs in a county where the total number of jobs was 8,700.[37]

In other mountain counties, elected officials were charged with bribery, the illegal use of public funds to pave private roads, nepotism (including the extension of no-bid contracts for county services to relatives), and theft of public property, but the most frequent indictments were for election fraud. A grand jury in Appalachia, Virginia, in Wise County, indicted the mayor, a council member, and twelve others for buying votes to elect three members of a five-member council. Once in office, the new council members had helped to appoint the head of a police department that trafficked drugs and took money and personal possessions from residents.[38] Across the border in Knott County, Kentucky, the county judge executive was convicted of voter fraud and sent to jail. Two years later the county was under new leadership, but the Kentucky state auditor accused the new Knott County fiscal court of gross mismanagement of public funds. An audit found more than $13 million of questionable expenditures for illegal activities ranging from the use of public money to pave private roads to the overpayment of contractors, some of whom were related to county officials.[39]

In spite of the persistence of corruption and the continued power of special interest groups such as coal and banking, a few of the new leaders were able to rise above the quagmire of mountain politics and, for a time, attempted to chart a different direction. One former coal miner in Letcher County, Kentucky, Carroll Smith, brought door-to-door recycling to county homes and union representation to county employees when he was elected county judge executive in the state's fifth-largest coal-producing county. Soon after taking office, Smith, a Republican, proposed an ordinance to limit logging that was damaging county land and roads. He also proposed a bottle recycling bill, an ordinance to ban smoking in public buildings, and a bill to raise the minimum wage above the federal level. None of the latter proposals won the approval of the fiscal court, but Smith developed a strong regional reputation for independence and for his efforts to promote open government and economic diversification. Unlike other politicians in the area, Smith refused to take donations from the coal industry.[40] He was narrowly defeated by a coal-supported candidate in 2006 after three terms in office.

Community leaders like Smith increasingly challenged the old political structures in Appalachia at the turn of the twenty-first century. They represented a rising number of residents who were frustrated with poor schools, insufficient job opportunities, inadequate health care, and deterioration of the environment. Many were professionals: doctors, lawyers, teachers, and artists. Some were new to the mountains, but others were native sons and daughters who had been educated outside the region and returned home to raise their own children. A few ran for office, but frequently they chose to avoid the sullied political process and to join citizen-based associations for change. For example, after the fifth congressional district in southeast Kentucky was identified as the least-educated congressional district in the country, more than 1,500 local people joined Forward in the Fifth, a grassroots organization established to work with teachers and children to improve educational outcomes in the schools.[41] Others joined multi-issue groups like Western North Carolina Tomorrow, Kentuckians for the Commonwealth, and the Kentucky Appalachian Council. Many focused their efforts on protecting the region's fragile and threatened environment, forming multistate networks such as the Southern Appalachian Forest Coalition, the Ohio Valley Environmental Coalition, and the Citizens Coal Council. More and more these organizations provided countervailing voices to the calls for growth at any cost, and they helped to draw public attention to the neglected problems of the region.

Nowhere was opposition to the old order greater than in the arena of the environment. Land, water, and forest resources had always shaped the quality of human life in the mountains, and this relationship was even more evident at the end of the twentieth century. Nothing brought out ideological conflicts over the future of the region more than disputes about land use, and nothing reflected old disparities of income, health, and political power quite as vividly as efforts to enforce environmental regulations. As America confronted the challenges of global warming, energy dependence, and urban sprawl, the mountains of Appalachia once again provided a stage for national debate.

The pursuit of quick and easy profit and the insatiable demand for cheap energy and developable land fueled the physical devastation of the mountains at an even more rapid pace than earlier in the twentieth century. The rising cost of foreign oil and the escalating demand for electricity increased the price of coal and expanded production from surface mining across central Appalachia. The growth of regional service centers and shopping facilities, the spread of suburban neighborhoods, and the explosion of recreational and second-home development intensified pressure on traditional land use practices and threatened sensitive ecosystems. Efforts to preserve the landscape and to protect the natural environment challenged head-on the modern values of growth, individualism, and consumption. Environmental battles often pitted giant corporations against private individuals and community groups, but more often than not the conflicts cut across class lines. In Appalachia, as much as in any other part of America, the false choice between jobs and the environment divided communities, pitting personal economic interests against the common good, short-term gain against long-term survival.

Some of the most dramatic examples of this conflict over land use occurred in the wake of the heavy rains that periodically drench the region. One of the oldest and most diverse forest ecosystems in the world, the Appalachian range contains the headwaters for most of the streams that drain the eastern United States. Blanketed by a forest that includes more species of deciduous trees, other plants, and wildlife than any other region of North America, the Appalachian woodlands functioned for thousands of years as a natural sponge that filtered and harnessed water resources and moderated runoff and soil erosion. The impact of industrial development in this temperate rain forest during the past century left increasingly large portions of the landscape cutover by logging, strip mined for coal and other minerals, and paved over for roads, housing, and suburban growth. Flooding became a major problem in mountain communities after the turn of the twentieth century and played a role in the establishment of the national forests in Appalachia during the 1920s, the TVA in the 1930s, and the special Appalachian development programs of the 1960s. The absence of logging regulations on private land, the lack of zoning ordinances, and the expansion of strip mining, however, led to persistent disasters from periodic flooding and revealed deep social and political anxieties about environmental protection in a growth-oriented economy.

The great Appalachian flood of 1977, for example, contributed to the passage of the federal Surface Mining Control and Reclamation Act, but the compromise legislation did little to slow the destruction of mountain hillsides, and the act contained within it the seeds of an even more devastating mining practice, mountaintop removal. Coming just five years after the Buffalo Creek disaster in Logan County, West Virginia, that killed 125 people, the April 1977 flood ravaged four Appalachian states, destroying more than 1,700 homes and displacing almost 25,000 residents. Striking fourteen counties in the middle of the coalfields, the record flooding was most severe along smaller tributary streams at the heads of hollows where strip mining was most intense, but state and federal officials were reluctant to attribute the loss of life and property to mining practices for fear of alienating the coal industry. Governor Julian Carroll of Kentucky acknowledged that silt and debris from mining might have clogged up the streams and reservoirs but claimed that "farming, housing development, and the wind, which scatters soil" had contributed equally to the flooding.[42] An intensive investigation by the group Appalachia—Science in the Public Interest later found that strip mining had played "a significant role" in the latest disaster, especially on tributary streams where heavy sediment and the absence of vegetation had caused floodwaters to rise faster and without warning.[43]

Twenty-five years later, residents of the coalfields still complained about the ineffectiveness of the 1977 legislation, and the region continued to suffer from the destructive effects of mining on mountain water resources. After another massive flood ripped through the central Appalachian coalfields in the spring of 2001, killing six and wrecking

4,600 homes in West Virginia alone, that state's governor, Bob Wise, ordered state authorities once again to investigate how much of the devastation was attributable to rapid runoff from mining and timbering sites. Ten months later, after flood waters had ravaged poor communities in McDowell County, West Virginia, for a second time in a year, reporters found that legislators had refused to attend the committee hearings that Wise had established and that state regulators had resisted federal requirements mandating flood runoff protection on mining sites for the past twelve years.[44]

The failure of regulators to enforce existing mining laws was tragically illustrated again in October 2000, when a 2.2-billion-gallon coal slurry pond in Martin County, Kentucky, collapsed, spilling 300 million gallons of sludge into two neighboring creeks and creating what the Environmental Protection Agency (EPA) called one of the worst environmental disasters ever in the southeastern United States. One of hundreds of coal slurry ponds constructed in the mountains to hold residue from washing coal before shipment, the Martin County impoundment was similar to the earthen dam that collapsed at Buffalo Creek in 1972. After the Buffalo Creek disaster, the Mine Safety and Health Administration had begun regulating the design and maintenance of these coal waste dams, which contained toxic heavy metals and which frequently leaked or overflowed. The Martin County impoundment, owned by a subsidiary of Massey Energy, broke through the abandoned mine over which it had been constructed and spewed toxic, black sludge up to eight feet deep along tributaries to the Tug Fork and the Big Sandy River, contaminating drinking water for eighty miles downstream. The spill was twenty times larger than the 1989 *Exxon Valdez* oil spill in Alaska. Investigators later determined that Massey Energy had failed to follow up on recommendations to repair the slurry pond after a smaller leak in 1994, and regulators at the Mine Safety and Health Administration had failed to enforce their own recommendations. Although the coal company claimed that the accident was an unfortunate "act of God" and denied legal responsibility for the disaster, a team of engineers appointed by the Mine Safety and Health Administration afterward to investigate the spill found sufficient evidence to issue citations against the Massey subsidiary for willful and criminal negligence. Before the investigation could be completed, however, the new George W. Bush administration replaced the team leadership and narrowed the scope of the investigation. A final report eventually cited the company for two minor violations and issued a fine of $100,000. A judge later reduced that fine to $55,000, but not before a member of the original investigating team, Jack Spadaro, revealed the government negligence and the cover-up of the violations to the national media. Spadaro, who had served as an investigator following the Buffalo Creek flood in 1972, was demoted from his position as head of the National Mine Health and Safety Academy and forced out of government for his criticism of the administration and the coal industry.[45]

Environmental disasters like those at Buffalo Creek and Martin County dramatized the growing tragedy of surface mining in the mountains and the unwillingness of most politicians to challenge the power of the coal industry or to confront the real costs of energy consumption in the United States. The lack of oversight by regulators, the collusion between the industry and political leaders, and the growing demand for coal as a replacement for foreign oil exposed the mountains and mountain people to some of the worst environmental devastation in the history of the region. Even the massive deforestation of Appalachia by the American logging industry at the turn of the twentieth century had not altered the landscape in the permanent manner that mountaintop removal did. By the turn of the twenty-first century, hundreds of miles of ridgeline in southern West Virginia, eastern Kentucky, southwest Virginia, and east Tennessee had been leveled, the tops of the mountains dumped into adjacent valleys, creating vast, desert-like plateaus. Nearly one thousand miles of streams had been buried, and entire ecosystems had been dismantled, the forests and wildlife permanently replaced by lespedeza and sandstone rubble. Almost five hundred mountains in the heart of Appalachia had been decapitated, and more were being lost every day.

Fearing that Appalachia was fast becoming a national sacrifice area in the quest for energy independence, mountain residents increasingly challenged mountaintop removal in the courts. In 1998 regional environmentalists, led by the Ohio Valley Environmental Coalition and the West Virginia Highlands Conservancy, filed a federal lawsuit claiming that the practice of filling mountain valleys with the overburden from mountaintop removal operations violated the Clean Water Act. A federal judge in southern West Virginia agreed and prohibited mining within one hundred feet of a flowing stream. When the decision was overturned upon appeal, KFTC filed its own lawsuit seeking to prohibit the Army Corps of Engineers from granting permits to deposit mine waste into valley streams. The same federal judge ruled against the coal industry again, but in 2003 the U.S. Court of Appeals for the Fourth Circuit overturned this decision as well, declaring that the Clean Air Act's prohibition of waste in streambeds referred only to "garbage and sewage" and not to mine waste.[46]

Opponents of mountaintop removal received little help from state and federal authorities, who were generally more concerned with protecting coal production even if they hoped to mitigate the harshest effects of mining on the land and the people. During the 1980s, the Reagan administration cut the Office of Surface Mining's budget for enforcement and directed a smaller staff to provide "regulatory relief" to the coal industry. President Clinton slashed the office's budget again, limiting inspection and enforcement staff by one-third and eliminating six field offices. Under George W. Bush, the agency became even less vigilant, replacing recalcitrant staff members such as Spadaro and focusing more on speeding up mining permits than on regulating the industry.[47]

The struggle to protect the mountains was left to a few environmental organizations and to individuals like Larry Gibson. The self-proclaimed "keeper of the mountains," Gibson became a popular symbol of resistance to mountaintop removal in Appalachia after he organized neighbors in his southern West Virginia community to fight the destruction of Kayford Mountain by Massey Energy bulldozers. Gibson's 50-acre farm, which had been in his family for almost two hundred years, stood like a defiant oasis in a dead sea, surrounded by 180,000 acres of one of the largest mountaintop removal operations in Appalachia.[48] The man and his land became a focal point for environmental activists in the region; he seemed a fitting heir to Dan Gibson, Jink Ray, and Ollie Combs.

Throughout Appalachia, citizens like Gibson continued to challenge the destruction of their communities by corporate greed and governmental neglect. In the 1980s residents of Bell County, Kentucky, fought a decade-long battle to clean up the sewage and industrial waste being dumped into Yellow Creek by the Middlesboro Tanning Company and by a substandard municipal water treatment facility. Before winning a settlement among the City of Middlesboro, the tannery, and the EPA, the Yellow Creek Concerned Citizens confronted local and state officials, held rallies and demonstrations, and inundated federal agencies with letters of support from government officials in developing countries around the world who were concerned with the industrial pollution of streams in poor communities. Nearby, the Harlan County Concerned Citizens against Toxic Waste forced a Texas company to clean up a former industrial site polluted with cancer-causing PCBs that was then being used as a mobile home park. After toxic solvents and waste oils were found to have fouled at least fourteen drinking wells in the community of Dayhoit and to have leaked into groundwater a mile away, the company agreed to remove contaminated soil and to pay for the construction of a new water line.[49]

One struggle raised tensions between two states when economic activities in North Carolina destroyed a river flowing into Tennessee and may have contributed to high rates of cancer in a community lying along the border. Since 1906, the Champion Paper Company had provided more than two thousand jobs in Haywood County, North Carolina, at its Canton paper mill, but the company dumped tons of carcinogenic pollutants into the Pigeon River, effectively killing the once clean-flowing mountain stream and turning it dark brown below the mill. By the mid-1980s, residents of the small Cocke County, Tennessee, town of Hartford, downstream from the paper mill, had started to notice a disproportionately high rate of deaths from cancer, especially among men who swam or lived near the river. The town had long been nicknamed Widowville, and an informal survey of the town's 500 residents revealed an alarming 167 cancer cases. In 1985 local residents formed the Dead Pigeon River Council to pressure Tennessee and North Carolina to enforce water quality standards and to clean up and restore the Pigeon River. In federal court, the EPA became involved and refused to renew operating permits for the Champion plant unless the problem was fixed. Relationships between the two states became contentious. North Carolina and Haywood County feared the loss of jobs; Tennessee, Cocke County, and the EPA demanded that the river be brought up to Tennessee water quality standards. Champion finally agreed to modernize its Canton plant, and in 1990 the EPA issued a new permit. The company later consented to pay Cocke County property owners $6.5 million in compensation and to endow environmental education projects in the area. Following the agreement, however, the Connecticut-based company sold the North Carolina plant and moved its production facilities abroad. A much-reduced labor force continued to operate the Canton mill as a partially worker-owned company, Blue Ridge Paper Products. After the installation of new equipment and bleaching processes, water quality improved, and fish and other wildlife returned to the river. Within a decade a thriving river-based recreational industry had developed in Hartford, and the community was on the road to recovery.[50]

Struggles for environmental justice were common across Appalachia at the end of the twentieth century. The region's poverty, politics, and long history of industrial exploitation subjected mountain communities to disproportionate threats from health hazards and environmental damage. Local citizens' groups organized to fight acid mine drainage, pesticide contamination, toxic landfills, timber clearcutting, nuclear dump sites, waste incinerators, hydroelectric dams, and other threats. As urban Americans gained a greater awareness of the dangers of waste disposal in their own environments, low-income rural areas in Appalachia became prime targets for commercial landfills, waste incinerators, and toxic storage facilities. The availability of comparatively cheap land, abandoned deep mines, lax environmental regulations, and receptive local politicians made it cost effective for large companies to haul solid waste from cities in the Northeast to dump sites in rural communities in Appalachia, especially in Virginia and West Virginia. Citizens' organizations such as the Blue Ridge Environmental Defense League challenged the landfill developers in court and often succeeded in limiting the volume of the landfill, if not defeating the project itself.

Less confrontational organizations, often supported by government and business leaders, emerged as well to improve environmental quality, reduce unsightly trash, and educate children about local ecosystems. Groups such as Eastern Kentucky PRIDE, created in 1997 by U.S. Representative Hal Rogers and Kentucky Department of Natural

Resources secretary James Bickford to promote "personal responsibility in a desirable environment," energized schools, parents, civic organizations, and businesses to clean up creeks, rivers, and highways and to protect the natural beauty of their neighborhoods. Eastern Kentucky PRIDE mobilized thousands of volunteers to clean up streams and illegal trash dumps, and it encouraged the building of outdoor classrooms, greenhouses, and nature trails in almost every county in southeastern Kentucky. With the assistance of federal grants to improve water quality, the organization helped to install over seven thousand septic systems and to modernize sewage treatment facilities serving over twenty thousand homes. Most of the streams of eastern Kentucky had long since ceased to be healthy and viable as a result of mine drainage, straight pipe sewage disposal, and other nonpoint pollution. Eastern Kentucky PRIDE hoped to restore water quality and to create a more attractive environment for economic development by advocating personal responsibility for waste and educating children to prevent pollution in the future.

Ultimately, rising concern about the environment, especially among middle-class groups like Eastern Kentucky PRIDE, reflected a growing cultural crisis in Appalachia over land use and its relationship to traditional values and identities. As a result of the expansion of highways, retail centers, industrial parks, and other indicators of modern sprawl, many mountain communities now faced the same dilemmas of economic growth that challenged other areas of the United States, such as how to protect open space, how to preserve communities, and how to provide meaning to life in a changing world. In Appalachia, however, the land had always shaped human relationships and personal identity. It had always defined cultural meaning. The loss of farms and of farm life, the enclosure of the forests for private use, the pollution of streams, the uprooting of families, and the congestion of people in once quiet places were for many Appalachians high costs to pay for material convenience and comfort.

The environmental and cultural consequences of uncontrolled growth were evident in both urban and rural Appalachia. Mountain families who lived near metropolitan centers on the perimeter of the region and those who resided in the larger towns and growth centers witnessed with mixed feelings the spread of housing developments, shopping malls, restaurants, motels, and chain stores. Modern services provided access to consumer products and amenities, but the service economy created few well-paying jobs, and the distance between home, shopping, school, and work left little time for community and family life. Suburban sprawl converted limited agricultural bottomland into housing and retail developments, and extensive paving and floodplain construction increased flood levels and groundwater contamination. The expansion of metropolitan centers such as Atlanta, Charlotte, and Knoxville into adjoining rural counties and the spread of tourism and second-home development deeper into coves and hollows increased traffic congestion, property values, and taxes in once remote communities. Rural residents, who had benefited least from the new economy, now faced displacement, the loss of their land, and the disappearance of their way of life.

For some Appalachian communities, the growth of tourism during the last decades of the twentieth century provided a hopeful alternative to environmentally destructive industries such as mining and timbering, but recreational development brought its own problems. Traffic congestion, visual pollution, low-wage jobs, and increased demand on local public services tempered the economic benefits of tourism. Megadevelopments associated with theme parks, outlet malls, and internationally based hotels at places like Pigeon Forge and Gatlinburg, Tennessee, not only transformed these communities entirely but leaked many of the dollars spent by tourists back to absentee corporate owners. Outdoor recreational activities associated with the free-range riding of motorcycles and all-terrain vehicles rutted trails, polluted streams, and disturbed wildlife. The unregulated spread of rental cabins and second-home communities along ridgetops and hillsides altered mountain ecosystems and views, threatening the landscape that had sustained local culture and attracted tourists to the region in the first place.

The growing popularity of ecotourism and heritage tourism, on the other hand, contained the potential for building an alternative economy, one that promised greater monetary returns for local residents, the preservation of rural traditions, and the protection of sensitive natural resources. At least 115 million Americans lived within a day's driving distance of Appalachia, and the region's water, forests, and cultural resources increasingly appealed to urban hikers, campers, kayakers, fishermen, and families seeking relaxation and cultural enrichment. In parts of the region less scarred by environmental destruction, outfitters, bed and breakfast accommodations, restaurants, and other small businesses multiplied to serve urban tourists seeking outdoor adventure. Festivals celebrating mountain music and crafts and fairs promoting local farm products, homecomings, historical reenactments, and community gatherings of all kinds brought dollars into local economies, supported local shop owners, and sustained a sense of local pride.

In some communities struck hard by the decline of manufacturing and mining jobs, ecotourism and other community-based forms of small business development became important strategies for renewal. Community leaders in western North Carolina, for example, built on that area's long history of handcraft production to organize independent artists into a marketing network that was environmentally sustainable and took advantage of the international economy. Handmade in America, as the effort was called, not only provided guidebooks and other marketing tools for mountain artists, galleries, inns, farmers' markets, and historical sites in the Carolina Blue Ridge but developed technical assistance programs that helped small towns identify local assets, share community building strategies, and promote entrepreneurship. Such programs sought to capture the growing suburban interest in handmade products and alternative services and to channel wealth back to local communities and producers, reversing the historical pattern in which assets flowed out of the mountains. These efforts attempted to build distinctive and sustainable communities that enhanced the human and natural resources of the region. They sought to turn the commodification of the land into something that could preserve the land and the cultural meanings that derived from close relationships to that land.

Thus, in an ironic way, Appalachia at the turn of the twenty-first century was a microcosm of the contradictions confronting modern American life. The flood of suburban tourists seeking to renew their relationship with the natural world passed young people along the highway leaving the mountains in search of better lives in the cities from which the urban refugees had fled. Flatland exiles seeking to possess a piece of the mountains and to control the views from the ridgetops clashed with local families who resented fence lines and no-trespassing signs and who struggled to find work and adequate housing. Insiders and outsiders alike consumed the electricity generated by coal from surface mines that destroyed forests and decapitated the mountains forever. Everyone searched for some connection to place. Some hoped to find it in the new Appalachia. Others clung to the memory of the old.

On the morning of August 13, 2007, fifty demonstrators gathered outside the downtown Asheville, North Carolina, branch of the Bank of America to protest the bank's investment policies in Massey Energy and in Arch Coal, two of the largest producers of surface-mined coal in Appalachia. Protesters hoped to draw public attention to Bank of America energy investments that not only promoted the use of coal, the largest single contributor to global warming, but supported the destructive practice of mountaintop removal that was devastating the land and way of life in the heart of the mountains. In the weeks ahead, demonstrations would spread to other Bank of America branches and even to the bank's annual investors' conference in California, where protesters also criticized company support of Peabody Energy, whose Black Mesa mine in Arizona had damaged the land and water of indigenous Navajo and Hopi communities. Some of the same environmental activists who confronted the Bank of America had helped earlier to sideline plans for two coal-fired electricity-generating plants being proposed for western North Carolina, but at the time of the Asheville demonstration, plans were on the books for the construction of almost 160 more coal plants nationwide.[51]

The event in Asheville, however, symbolized an important change in the way America understood Appalachia. Asheville was an unlikely place to find demonstrations against the coal industry. That no coal was mined within a hundred miles of the old Blue Ridge town, which had become a prosperous cultural and recreational icon of the new southern highlands, signified both the acceptance of a broader regional identity since the 1960s and a shift in popular perceptions of regional distinctiveness. No longer was Appalachia defined primarily by poverty and cultural backwardness; the region now had become a symbol of the larger dilemma of people's relationship to the land and responsibilities to each other. Appalachians and neo-Appalachians alike increasingly acknowledged that the quality of life in the mountains was inexorably tied to the use of the land and that Appalachia's problems were both systemic and universal. The Appalachian experience reflected the social, environmental, and cultural consequences of unrestrained growth, and it echoed the voices of powerless people struggling to survive in a changing world. Saving Appalachia now meant confronting the larger structures of global injustice as well as challenging local power brokers, corporate greed, and government apathy.

No one articulated more clearly the plight of the mountains and mountain people in the new era than Larry Gibson. The hero of activists in the heart of the region who were fighting mountaintop removal and the expansion of coal production that was destroying forests, streams, and the future of communities, Gibson spoke for another generation of mountain families who had witnessed progress, the coming of government programs to uplift mountain people, and the tapping of mountain resources to better connect Appalachia to the mainstream economy. Standing on the precipice of the three-hundred-foot cliff that marked the boundary between his farm and the strip mine that had destroyed his mountain, he lamented what had been lost. "We have a history here," he told a group of visitors as he picked up a broken miner's lamp that he had discovered in his surviving woods.

> We have a conversation with the land here. The land will talk to us. It will tell us things. Nothing comes easy for people in the mountains. This is a symbol of what the history of the mountains is about. We are a little worn. We are a little bent. We are a little broken. But we are real, and we are here. And we are tired of being collateral damage, a sacrificial zone for rich people and other people to be comfortable in their life. . . . This is life for us. We don't have a choice here in the coalfields. We are either going to be an activist or we are going to be annihilated. And I am tired of seeing my people being annihilated. So we are fighting back. It's the only thing that we have.[52]

In his lifetime, Gibson had witnessed the rediscovery of the mountains by the national media, the arrival of idealistic poverty warriors, and the enactment of a special program to promote economic development in the region. He had traveled the new highways, visited the new hospitals, and placed his children on the buses that carried them to the new consolidated schools. Many of his neighbors had left for jobs in the new urban centers, where they could find shopping centers, housing developments, and all of the material goods of modern life. For Gibson and many others, growth had indeed come to the mountains, with its uneven benefits and hidden inequalities. But whether or not that growth had fulfilled the promise of the Great Society was a matter of debate. In that respect, the uneven ground of Appalachia was no longer the other America. It *was* America, and the region's uncertain destiny stood as a warning to the rest of the nation.

NOTES

INTRODUCTION

1. Michael Harrington, *The Other America: Poverty in the United States* (New York: Macmillan, 1962).

1. RICH LAND—POOR PEOPLE

Epigraph: Harriette Arnow, *The Dollmaker* (New York: Macmillan, 1954), 24–25.

1. See Ronald D Eller, *Miners, Millhands, and Mountaineers: The Industrialization of the Appalachian South, 1880–1930* (Knoxville: University of Tennessee Press, 1982).

2. Alva W. Taylor, "Up a Kentucky Mountain Cove," *Mountain Life and Work*, Winter 1942, 19.

3. Wayne T. Gray, "Mountain Dilemmas: Study in Mountain Attitudes," *Mountain Life and Work*, April 1936, 1. See also J. Wesley Hatcher, "Glimpses of Appalachian America's Basic Conditions of Living," pts. 1 and 2, *Mountain Life and Work*, October 1938, 1–5; January 1939, 1–9.

4. Rexford G. Tugwell, "The Resettlement Administration and Its Relation to the Appalachian Mountains," *Mountain Life and Work*, October 1935, 3.

5. Quoted in Eller, *Miners, Millhands, and Mountaineers*, 242.

6. "National Defense and Mountain Communities," *Mountain Life and Work*, Winter 1942, 1–15.

7. Ibid., 12.

8. Olaf F. Larson, "Wartime Migration and the Manpower Reserve on Farms in Eastern Kentucky," *Rural Sociology* 8, no. 2 (1943).

9. Taylor, "Kentucky Mountain Cove," 20.

10. Harry M. Caudill, *Night Comes to the Cumberlands: A Biography of a Depressed Area* (Boston: Little, Brown, 1963), 223.

11. Jerry Wayne Napier, "Mines, Miners, and Machines: Coal Mine Mechanization and the Eastern Kentucky Coal Fields, 1890–1990" (PhD diss., University of Kentucky, 1997), 42, 48.

12. Ibid., 41.

13. Quoted in Caudill, *Night Comes*, 228.

14. Curtis Seltzer, *Fire in the Hole: Miners and Managers in the American Coal Industry* (Lexington: University Press of Kentucky, 1985), 61; Napier, "Mines, Miners, and Machines," 62–63.

15. Seltzer, *Fire in the Hole*, 59–63; Napier, "Mines, Miners, and Machines," 62–66; Joseph E. Finley, *The Corrupt Kingdom: The Rise and Fall of the United Mine Workers* (New York: Simon and Schuster, 1972), 168–70. See also Thomas N. Bethell, "Conspiracy in Coal," in *Appalachia in the Sixties: Decade of Reawakening*, ed. David S. Walls and John B. Stephenson (Lexington: University Press of Kentucky, 1972).

16. Napier, "Mines, Miners, and Machines," 56.

17. Ibid., 75.

18. Appalachian Regional Commission, *Appalachian Data Book* (Washington, DC: ARC, 1967); U.S. Bureau of Labor Statistics, *Technology, Productivity, and Labor in the Bituminous Coal Industry 1950–79*, Bulletin 2072 (Washington, DC: GPO, 1981).

19. Clyde B. McCoy and James S. Brown, "Appalachian Migration to Midwestern Cities," in *The Invisible Minority: Urban Appalachians*, ed. William W. Philliber and Clyde B. McCoy (Lexington: University Press of Kentucky, 1981), 36, table 3.1. See also Chad Berry, *Southern Migrants, Northern Exiles* (Urbana: University of Illinois Press, 2000).

20. James S. Brown and Harry K. Schwarzweller, "The Appalachian Family," in *Appalachia: Its People, Heritage, and Problems*, ed. Frank S. Riddel (Dubuque, IA: Kendall/Hunt, 1974), 71.

21. Clyde B. McCoy and Virginia McCoy Watkins, "Stereotypes of Appalachian Migrants," in Philliber and McCoy, *Invisible Minority*, 29.

22. Quoted in Jack T. Kirby, "The Southern Exodus, 1910–1960: A Primer for Historians," *Journal of Southern History* 49, no. 4 (1983): 598.

23. Bob Downing, "Akron, West Virginia," *Mountain Review*, May 1976, 2–4; David Giffels and Steve Love, "Appalachia to Akron," *Akron Beacon Journal*, February 9, 1997; *Akron Beacon Journal*, August 2, 1937.

24. Albert N. Votaw, "The Hillbillies Invade Chicago," *Harper's*, February 1958, 64.

25. Harry W. Ernst, "Appalachians in a Hostile World," *Charleston (WV) Gazette-Mail*, October 9, 1966.

26. For the origins of Appalachian stereotypes and the associated "idea of Appalachia," see Henry David Shapiro, *Appalachia on Our Mind: The Southern Mountains and Mountaineers in the American Consciousness* (Chapel Hill: University of North Carolina Press, 1978).

27. Votaw, "Hillbillies Invade Chicago," 67.

28. McCoy and Watkins, "Stereotypes of Appalachian Migrants," 22.

29. Ibid., 24.

30. W. L. Hamilton, F. C. Collignon, and C. E. Carlson, "The Causes of Rural to Urban Migration among the Poor," in Riddel, *Appalachia*, 187; Hal Bruno, "Chicago's Hillbilly Ghetto," *Reporter*, June 4, 1964, 28.

31. Roscoe Giffin, "From Cinder Hollow to Cincinnati," *Mountain Life and Work*, Winter 1956, 16.

32. See John R. Hundley, "The Mountain Man in Northern Industry," *Mountain Life and Work*, Summer 1955, 33–38; B. H. Luebke and John Fraser Hart, "Migration from a Southern Appalachian Community," *Land Economics* 34, no. 1 (1958); and Bruno, "Chicago's Hillbilly Ghetto," 28–31.

33. Ernst, "Appalachians in a Hostile World."

34. Michael Maloney, "The Prospects for Urban Appalachians," in Philliber and McCoy, *Invisible Minority*, 168. See also Giffin, "From Cinder Hollow," 11–20, and Ronald D Eller, "Lost and Found in the Promised Land: The Education of a Hillbilly," in *One Hundred Years of Appalachian Visions*, ed. Bill Best (Berea, KY: Appalachian Imprints, 1997), 125–30.

35. John D. Photiadis, "Occupational Adjustment of Appalachians in Cleveland," in Philliber and McCoy, *Invisible Minority*. See also James N. Gregory, *The Southern Diaspora: How the Great Migrations of Black and White Southerners Transformed America* (Chapel Hill: University of North Carolina Press, 2007).

36. "The Southern Mountaineer in Cincinnati," *Mountain Life and Work*, Fall 1954, 23.

37. Ora Spaid, "Southerners Shuttle North, Back," *Louisville Courier-Journal*, October 21, 1959; Bruno, "Chicago's Hillbilly Ghetto," 31.

38. James S. Brown and George A. Hillery Jr., "The Great Migration, 1940–1960," in *The Southern Appalachian Region: A Survey*, ed. Thomas R. Ford (Lexington: University of Kentucky Press, 1962), 59.

39. Ibid., 39, 59–60.

40. Appalachian Regional Commission, *Appalachian Data Book*.

41. Roy E. Proctor and T. Kelley White, "Agriculture: A Reassessment," in Ford, *Southern Appalachian Region*.

42. U.S. Bureau of the Census, *Census of Population, 1950* (Washington, DC: GPO, 1952); U.S. Bureau of the Census, *Census of Population, 1960* (Washington, DC: GPO, 1962).

43. Appalachian Regional Commission, *Appalachian Data Book*.

44. Kentucky Agricultural Development Board, *Economic Data on Eastern Kentucky Coal Field* (Frankfort: Commonwealth of Kentucky, 1956), 9.

45. U.S. Bureau of the Census, *Census of Population, 1950*; U.S. Bureau of the Census, *Census of Population, 1960*.

46. President's Appalachian Regional Commission, *Appalachia: A Re-*

port by the President's Appalachian Regional Commission (Washington, DC: PARC, 1964), 1–3; William E. Cole, "Social Problems and Welfare Services," in Ford, *Southern Appalachian Region*, 245; Appalachian Regional Commission, *Appalachia: Twenty Years of Progress* (Washington, DC: ARC, 1985), 13.

47. Appalachian Regional Commission, *Twenty Years of Progress*, 13.

48. Orin Graff, "The Needs of Education," in Ford, *Southern Appalachian Region*, 190.

49. President's Appalachian Regional Commission, *Report*, 10.

50. Ibid., 13; U.S. Bureau of the Census, *Census of Population, 1960*.

51. Harry W. Ernst, "For 300,000 West Virginians: A Starvation Diet?" *Mountain Life and Work*, Spring 1959.

52. Caudill, *Night Comes*, 275.

53. Paul F. Cressey, "The Changing Highlands," *Mountain Life and Work*, Fall 1951, 45.

54. For mountain politics, see Frank Duff, "Government in an Eastern Kentucky Coal County" (master's thesis, University of Kentucky, 1950); Richard A. Ball, "Social Change and Power Structure: An Appalachian Case," in *Change in Rural Appalachia: Implications for Action Programs*, ed. John D. Photiadis and Harry K. Schwarzweller (Philadelphia: University of Pennsylvania Press, 1970), 156–58; H. Dudley Plunckett and Mary Jean Bowman, *Elites and Change in the Kentucky Mountains* (Lexington: University Press of Kentucky, 1973); Caudill, *Night Comes*, 280–83; Harry M. Caudill, "The Permanent Poor: The Lesson of Eastern Kentucky," *Atlantic*, June 1964, 49–53; Harry M. Caudill, *Theirs Be the Power: The Moguls of Eastern Kentucky* (Urbana: University of Illinois Press, 1983); Harry M. Caudill, *The Senator from Slaughter County* (Boston: Little, Brown, 1973); and Lester Perry, *Forty Years of Mountain Politics* (Parsons, WV: McClain, 1971).

55. Ken Hechler, "TVA Ravages the Land," *Environmental Journal*, July 1971, 16.

56. Eller, *Miners, Millhands, and Mountaineers*, 55; Caudill, *Night Comes*, 73, 306. See also Robert Wiese, *Grasping at Independence: Debt, Male Authority, and Mineral Rights in Appalachian Kentucky, 1850–1915* (Knoxville: University of Tennessee Press, 2001).

57. Harry M. Caudill, "The Mountaineers in the Affluent Society," *Environmental Journal*, July 1971, 19.

58. Harry M. Caudill, "The Rape of the Appalachians," *Atlantic*, April 1962, 41–42; Caudill, *Night Comes*, 318–21; Hechler, "TVA Ravages the Land," 15–16; James Branscome, *The Federal Government in Appalachia* (New York: Field Foundation, 1977), 15–16.

59. U.S. Forest Service, Eastern Region, *Tri-State Floods, January 29–30, 1957: Disaster through Land Misuse*, n.d., Special Collections and Ar-

chives, Hutchins Library, Berea College, Berea, KY; Caudill, *Night Comes*, 322–23; "Floods Must Be Controlled," *Mountain Life and Work*, Spring 1957, 35–36.

60. Caudill, *Night Comes*, 322.

61. U.S. Forest Service, *Tri-State Floods*, 5–8.

62. Thomas J. Kiffmeyer, "From Self-Help to Sedition: The Appalachian Volunteers and the War on Poverty in Eastern Kentucky, 1964–1970" (PhD diss., University of Kentucky, 1998), 14–62; David E. Whisnant, *Modernizing the Mountaineer: People, Power, and Planning in Appalachia* (Boone, NC: Appalachian Consortium Press, 1980), 3–25; Morris R. Mitchell, "Dare the School Build a Community?" *Mountain Life and Work*, July 1938, 1–3.

63. Gerald Griffin, "The Truth about Eastern Kentucky," *Mountain Life and Work*, Winter 1955.

64. Luebke and Hart, "Migration," 53.

65. See Eller, *Miners, Millhands, and Mountaineers*, 120.

66. Harry W. Ernst and Charles H. Drake, "The Lost Appalachians: Poor, Proud and Primitive," *Nation*, May 30, 1959, 492.

67. Caudill, *Night Comes*, 371.

68. George S. Mitchell, "Let's Unite the Pie," *Mountain Life and Work*, Spring 1951, 19–20.

69. "The Council Resolves," *Mountain Life and Work*, Fall 1959, 37.

70. W. D. Weatherford, "The Southern Appalachian Studies: Their Final Form and Potential," *Mountain Life and Work*, Winter 1959, 27–30.

71. Napier, "Mines, Miners, and Machines," 129; Glen Taul, "A Seed Is Planted" (unpublished paper, 1998), in the author's possession, 3.

72. Taul, "Seed Is Planted," 5–17.

73. Kentucky Junior Chamber of Commerce, *Annual Report, 1956–57* (Louisville: Kentucky Junior Chamber of Commerce, 1957); *Lexington Herald*, September 7, 1956.

74. Eastern Kentucky Regional Planning Commission, *Program 60* (Frankfort: Eastern Kentucky Regional Planning Commission, 1959), A2. The history of the Eastern Kentucky Regional Development Council is detailed in Taul, "Seed Is Planted," 9–27.

75. Eastern Kentucky Regional Planning Commission, *Program 60*, C1.

76. Ibid., A3; Taul, "Seed Is Planted," 24.

77. Eastern Kentucky Regional Planning Commission, *Program 60*, A3.

78. Ibid., E1–H4.

79. Taul, "Seed Is Planted," 38–39.

80. Ibid., 42–43.

81. Eastern Kentucky Regional Planning Commission, *Program 60*, B1.

82. "Eastern Kentucky Needs More Than What Washington Offers," *Louisville Courier-Journal*, February 7, 1959.

2. The Politics of Poverty

Epigraph: "Kentucky," *Time*, February 23, 1959.

1. See, for example, *Louisville Courier-Journal*, February 15, 19, March 10, 12, 1960.

2. Harry W. Ernst, *The Primary That Made a President: West Virginia 1960* (New York: McGraw-Hill, 1962), 5.

3. The best accounts of the 1960 West Virginia primary are Ernst, *Primary*, and Theodore H. White, *The Making of the President, 1960* (New York: Atheneum, 1961).

4. The conference was organized by the Maryland Department of Economic Development, whose director, George W. Hubley, was until early 1960 the commissioner of economic development for Kentucky and was familiar with the East Kentucky Development Commission and *Program 60*. See David A. Grossman and Melvin R. Levin, *The Appalachian Region: A Preliminary Analysis of Economic and Population Trends in an Eleven State Problem Area* (Annapolis: Maryland Department of Economic Development, 1960).

5. Robert L. Riggs, "Philosophy Conflict Blocks Seven-State Pact," *Louisville Courier-Journal*, May 21, 1960.

6. Council of State Governments, *Summary: Conference of Appalachian Governors* (Atlanta, 1960), 6, John D. Whisman Papers, box 56, file 928, Special Collections Library, University of Kentucky, Lexington (hereafter cited as Whisman Papers).

7. Hugh Morris, "States Differ on Need for U.S. Aid to Area," *Louisville Courier-Journal*, May 18, 1960.

8. Conference of Appalachian Governors, "A Resolution Subscribing to and Supporting a Declaration for Action Regarding the Appalachian Region," in Council of State Governments, *Summary*, 32–33.

9. Ibid., 32.

10. Ibid., 32–33.

11. Irwin Unger, *The Best of Intentions: The Triumph and Failure of the Great Society under Kennedy, Johnson, and Nixon* (New York: Doubleday, 1996), 23.

12. "Kennedy Names 11 to Draft Aid Plan for Depressed Areas," *Louisville Courier-Journal*, December 5, 1960; Fred W. Luigart Jr., "Kentuckian Is Joining Depressed-Area Group," *Louisville Courier-Journal*, December 7, 1960.

13. John D. Whisman to Appalachian Commission Members, n.d., in the author's possession; "The Kennedy Task Force on Area Redevelopment," *Congressional Record*, 86th Cong., December 27, 1960, 10–13, Whisman Papers, box 41, file 642.

14. Whisnant, *Modernizing the Mountaineer*, 71–72; James E. Anderson,

"Poverty, Unemployment, and Economic Development: The Search for a National Antipoverty Policy," *Journal of Politics* 29 (February 1967): 78–79.

15. Anderson, "Poverty, Unemployment," 79. See also Branscome, *Federal Government in Appalachia*, 23–24.

16. Conference of Appalachian Governors, *A Proposal to the Area Redevelopment Administration for a Technical Assistance Project to Formulate Development Programming for the Appalachian Region* (June 1961), in the author's possession.

17. Michael Bradshaw, *The Appalachian Regional Commission: Twenty-five Years of Government Policy* (Lexington: University Press of Kentucky, 1992), 30–31; Branscome, *Federal Government in Appalachia*, 24; Whisnant, *Modernizing the Mountaineer*, 73–74.

18. Whisnant, *Modernizing the Mountaineer*, 75–87.

19. Caudill, *Night Comes*, 390.

20. *Louisville Courier-Journal*, February 18, 1962.

21. Eastern Kentucky Regional Planning Commission, *Program 60: Report* (Frankfort: Eastern Kentucky Regional Planning Commission, 1962), 8.

22. John Kenneth Galbraith, *The Affluent Society* (Boston: Houghton Mifflin, 1958). See also Unger, *Best of Intentions*, 32.

23. Michael Harrington, "Our Fifty Million Poor: Forgotten Men of the Affluent Society," *Commentary*, July 1959, 26.

24. Julius Duscha, "A Long Trail of Misery Winds the Proud Hills," *Washington Post*, August 7, 1960.

25. David A. Grossman and Melvin R. Levin, "The Appalachian Region: A National Problem Area," *Land Economics* 38 (1961).

26. Ford, *Southern Appalachian Region*.

27. Harrington, *Other America*.

28. See Leon Keyserling, "Two-Fifths of a Nation," *Progressive*, June 1962, 11–14.

29. Thomas B. Morgan, "Portrait of an Underdeveloped Country," *Look*, December 4, 1962.

30. Caudill, introduction to *Night Comes*, xii–xiii.

31. Homer Bigart, "Kentucky Miners: A Grim Winter," *New York Times*, October 20, 1963.

32. See Bernie Bookbinder, "Appalachia: The Desperate Americans," *Newsday*, December 17, 1963.

33. John Ed Pearce, "The Superfluous People of Hazard, Kentucky," *Reporter*, January 3, 1963, 33–35.

34. Carl M. Brauer, "Kennedy, Johnson, and the War on Poverty," *Journal of American History* 69, no. 1 (1982): 103; Unger, *Best of Intentions*, 31–34.

35. Dwight MacDonald, "Our Invisible Poor," *New Republic*, January 19, 1963, 134.

36. Michael L. Gillette, *Launching the War on Poverty: An Oral History* (New York: Twayne, 1996), 1–11.

37. Brauer, "Kennedy, Johnson," 102–3.

38. *Lexington Herald*, March 18, 1963; *Louisville Courier-Journal*, March 19, 1963; *Whitesburg (KY) Mountain Eagle*, March 20, 1963.

39. John D. Whisman, "Origin and Development of the Program, 1955–1975," memorandum to Appalachian Commission Members, 1976, 23–24, Whisman Papers, box 203, file 2859.

40. Advisory Policy Board to Area Redevelopment Administration and Conference of Appalachian Governors, transcript of the joint meeting, Washington, DC, April 9, 1963, 1–4, Whisman Papers, box 58, file 959.

41. Ibid., 12–21.

42. Ibid., 21–22.

43. John D. Whisman, interview by Glen Edward Taul, May 5, 1995, quoted in Glen Edward Taul, "Poverty, Development, and Government in Appalachia: Origins of the Appalachian Regional Commission, 1956–1965" (PhD diss., University of Kentucky, 2001), 256. See also Advisory Policy Board to Area Redevelopment Administration and Conference of Appalachian Governors, 75.

44. Benjamin Chinitz, "Signs of Hope in the Graveyard of the American Dream," *Pitt*, January 1964, 1.

45. Bradshaw, *Appalachian Regional Commission*, 34.

46. Bigart, "Kentucky Miners."

47. Fred Luigart, "Mountains Get Aid from JFK Order," *Louisville Courier-Journal*, December 24, 1963.

48. Unger, *Best of Intentions*, 77–78.

49. Taul, "Poverty, Development," 287–89.

50. John L. Sweeney, interview by Glen Edward Taul, June 6, 1997, quoted in Taul, "Poverty, Development," 287.

51. For more detail, see Taul, "Poverty, Development," 290–92.

52. See Sweeney, interview, and Taul, "Poverty, Development," 301–2.

53. President's Appalachian Regional Commission, *Report*, 16.

54. Ibid., 31.

55. Ibid., 65.

56. *Louisville Courier-Journal*, April 25, 1964.

57. Sweeney, interview, quoted in Taul, "Poverty, Development," 315.

58. *Louisville Courier-Journal*, April 25, 1964.

59. Sweeney, interview, quoted in Taul, "Poverty, Development," 316.

60. Governor William Scranton, letter of endorsement, President's Appalachian Regional Commission, *Report*, vi–vii.

61. Senate Committee on Environment and Public Works, *Summary and Analysis of the Legislative History of the Appalachian Regional Develop-*

ment Act of 1965 and Subsequent Amendments, report prepared by Douglas Reid Weimer, 99th Cong., 1st sess., 1985, Committee Print 14, 5.

62. Ibid., 8.

63. Taul, "Poverty, Development," 375–76; Sweeney, interview.

64. Lyndon B. Johnson, "Remarks of the President at Signing Ceremony on the Appalachia Bill in the Rose Garden, March 9, 1965," Appalachian Regional Commission Archives, box 8, folder 6, Special Collections Library, University of Kentucky, Lexington (hereafter cited as ARC Archives).

65. Lyndon B. Johnson, commencement address (University of Michigan, Ann Arbor, May 22, 1964), quoted in Robert Dallek, *Flawed Giant: Lyndon Johnson and His Times, 1961–1973* (New York: Oxford University Press, 1998), 82.

66. Lyndon B. Johnson, "Remarks of the President and Mrs. Johnson upon Departure from Tri-State Airport, Huntington, WV, April 24, 1964," Statements of Lyndon B. Johnson, container 102, 2, Lyndon Baines Johnson Library and Museum, Austin, Texas.

67. See correspondence and memoranda, Office Files of Bill Moyers, boxes 16, 130, Lyndon Baines Johnson Library and Museum, Austin, Texas.

68. "Poverty and Urban Policy" (transcript of group discussion of the Kennedy administration urban poverty programs and policies), 162–63, John F. Kennedy Library, quoted in James T. Patterson, *America's Struggle against Poverty, 1900–1980* (Cambridge, MA: Harvard University Press, 1981), 134.

69. See, for example, M. Murphy, "The Valley of Poverty," *Life*, January 31, 1964; James Reston Jr., "Appalachia: No Place for the Young," *Chicago Daily News*, February 1, 1965; Ben B. Seligman, "Appalachia as Symbol," *Nation*, February 22, 1965; Reese Cleghorn, "Appalachia: Poverty, Beauty and Poverty," *New York Times Magazine*, April 25, 1965; and Jack E. Weller, "Is There a Future for Yesterday's People?" *Saturday Review of Literature*, October 16, 1965.

3. Developing the Poor

1. David M. Potter, *People of Plenty: Economic Abundance and the American Character* (Chicago: University of Chicago Press, 1954).

2. Alice O'Connor, *Poverty Knowledge: Social Science, Social Policy, and the Poor in Twentieth-Century U.S. History* (Princeton, NJ: Princeton University Press, 2001), 100.

3. O'Connor, *Poverty Knowledge*, 102–23.

4. Harrington, "Our Fifty Million Poor," 25; Harrington, *Other America*, 167.

5. Quoted in Unger, *Best of Intentions*, 78.

6. Dallek, *Flawed Giant*, 76–79; Unger, *Best of Intentions*, 80–83; Gillette, *Launching the War*, 26–31.

7. Anderson, "Poverty, Unemployment," 82–84; Sar A. Levitan, *The Design of Federal Antipoverty Strategy* (Ann Arbor: Institute of Labor and Industrial Relations, University of Michigan, 1967), 8–10.

8. Dallek, *Flawed Giant*, 60; Unger, *Best of Intentions*, 78–79; Gillette, *Launching the War*, 72–73.

9. Unger, *Best of Intentions*, 78.

10. Gillette, *Launching the War*, 74; Dallek, *Flawed Giant*, 80.

11. Nicolas Lemann, *The Promised Land: The Great Black Migration and How It Changed America* (New York: Vintage, 1992), 97–103.

12. Oscar Lewis, *The Children of Sanchez: Autobiography of a Mexican Family* (New York: Random House, 1961); Oscar Lewis, *La Vida: A Puerto Rican Family in the Culture of Poverty* (New York: Random House, 1966). See also O'Connor, *Poverty Knowledge*, 117–21, and Unger, *Best of Intentions*, 29–30.

13. Rupert Vance, "The Region: A New Survey," in Ford, *Southern Appalachian Region*, 7–8.

14. Harrington, *Other America*, 146.

15. Frank Mankieitz quoted in Gillette, *Launching the War*, 90.

16. Ibid., 87.

17. Arnold Toynbee, *A Study of History* (New York: Oxford University Press, 1947), 2:312.

18. Jack E. Weller, *Yesterday's People: Life in Contemporary Appalachia* (Lexington: University of Kentucky Press, 1965), 7.

19. Rupert Vance, introduction to ibid., ix.

20. Branscome, *Federal Government in Appalachia*, 32.

21. See Richard L. Hoffman, "Community Action: Innovative and Coordinative Strategies in the War on Poverty" (PhD diss., University of North Carolina, 1969).

22. Carrie Celia Mullins, "Poverty and Politics: One Kentucky County's Version of the War on Poverty" (unpublished graduate student essay, 1994), in the author's possession, 6–10.

23. Willis A. Sutton Jr., "Differential Perceptions of the Impact of a Rural Anti-Poverty Campaign," *Social Science Quarterly* 50 (1969); Bill Peterson, "Poor-People Power," *Louisville Courier-Journal*, June 11, 1972. See also Paul Street et al., *Community Action in Appalachia: An Appraisal of the War on Poverty in a Rural Setting in Southeastern Kentucky*, 3 vols. (Lexington: University of Kentucky Center for Developmental Change, 1965–1968).

24. See Huey Perry, *"They'll Cut Off Your Project": A Mingo County Chronicle* (New York: Praeger, 1972).

25. Douglass Arnett, "Eastern Kentucky and the Politics of Dependency and Development" (PhD diss., Duke University, 1978), 172.

26. O'Connor, *Poverty Knowledge*, 168.

27. Unger, *Best of Intentions*, 152.

28. O'Connor, *Poverty Knowledge*, 13.

29. *New York Times*, April 26, 1960; J. Allan Smith, "Action Program for Mountain Counties," *Mountain Life and Work*, Summer 1961, 12–18; *Louisville Courier-Journal*, June 16, 1963.

30. Thomas Parrish, "Speakers Rouse Council in Annual Conference," *Mountain Life and Work*, Summer 1964, 12.

31. William H. Miller, *Annual Report of the Resource Development Specialist in Community Services, 1964* (Eastern Kentucky Resource Development Project, University of Kentucky Cooperative Extension Service), in the author's possession, 1.

32. Malcolm H. Holliday (executive director of the Kentucky River Area Development District) to Dr. Lewis Cochran (vice president of the University of Kentucky), October 29, 1970, in the author's possession.

33. I taught on the faculty at Mars Hill College from 1975 to 1985, shortly after the college received national recognition for a new core curriculum that emphasized the "behavioral outcomes" of a liberal arts education.

34. *ALCOR Decade, 1969–1979: Appalachian Leadership and Community Outreach, Inc.* (Pippa Passes, KY, 1980), in the author's possession, 3.

35. Ibid., 13.

36. "Teamwork Does the Job," *Mountain Life and Work*, Spring 1964, 17; Whisnant, *Modernizing the Mountaineer*, 187–88; Thomas J. Kiffmeyer, "From Self-Help to Sedition: The Appalachian Volunteers in Eastern Kentucky, 1964–1970," *Journal of Southern History* 64, no. 1 (1998): 70–71.

37. "Teamwork Does the Job," 18.

38. Quoted in Whisnant, *Modernizing the Mountaineer*, 188.

39. Kiffmeyer, "From Self-Help to Sedition," *Journal of Southern History*, 71.

40. John Fetterman, "Young Samaritans in Appalachia," *Louisville Courier-Journal*, March 19, 1964.

41. Clark Miller, "Era of Change: Volunteers Helped Appalachia," *Louisville Courier-Journal*, May 15, 1988.

42. Whisnant, *Modernizing the Mountaineer*, 190.

43. Quoted in Kiffmeyer, "From Self-Help to Sedition," *Journal of Southern History*, 77.

44. Whisnant, *Modernizing the Mountaineer*, 192–95.

45. Max E. Glenn, "The Commission on Religion in Appalachia: Its Origin, Purpose, and Current Status," in *Proceedings—CORA 1966: A United Approach to Fulfilling the Church's Mission in Appalachia* (Knoxville, TN: Commission on Religion in Appalachia, 1966); Jack E. Weller, "Look at What You've Done," in *Unite: A CORA War on Poverty Commemoration* (Knoxville, TN: Commission on Religion in Appalachia, 1986), 3–7.

46. Glenn, "Commission on Religion," 27.

47. "CAP Organizational History," attachment to *Faith and Actions: An-*

nual Report of the Christian Appalachian Project, 1987 (Lancaster, KY: CAP, 1987).

48. *Faith and Actions*, 18.

49. Gil Rosenberg, "The Selling of Bobbie Sue" (unpublished graduate student essay, 1989), in the author's possession. Rosenberg was a former CAP employee.

50. Reverend Ralph Beiting, CAP fund-raising letter, n.d., in the author's possession. See also Rosenberg, "Selling of Bobbie Sue."

51. Helen M. Lewis and Monica Appleby, introduction to *Mountain Sisters: From Convent to Community in Appalachia* (Lexington: University Press of Kentucky, 2003), xiv–xv.

52. Lewis and Appleby, *Mountain Sisters*, 148–197.

53. For details of these and other activities of the former Glenmary Sisters in Appalachia, see ibid.

54. Catholic Committee of Appalachia, *This Land Is Home to Me: A Pastoral Letter on Powerlessness in Appalachia by the Catholic Bishops of the Region* (Whitesburg, KY: Catholic Committee of Appalachia, 1975), 30.

4. Confronting Development

1. James Ridgeway, "Why the Poverty War Seems a Muddle," *New Republic*, October 9, 1965, 7. See also C. E. Silberman, "Mixed-up War on Poverty," *Fortune*, August 1965, 156–61, and C. E. Silberman, "More Boon Than Doggle: Predictable Patterns of Controversy, Red Tape and Scandal," *Time*, October 15, 1965, 33.

2. Unger, *Best of Intentions*, 167, 196.

3. Richard W. Boone, "Working with the Poor," *New Republic*, November 9, 1965, 39.

4. "The War within the War," *Time*, May 13, 1966, 25; *U.S. News and World Report*, December 13, 1965, 29.

5. "War within the War," 25.

6. Joe Malloy, interview by Thomas Kiffmeyer, quoted in John M. Glen, "The War on Poverty in Appalachia: Oral History from the Top Down and the Bottom Up," *Oral History Review* 22, no. 1 (1995): 84.

7. Ibid., 84–85.

8. For a fuller assessment and critique of Caudill's perspective on Appalachia, see Ronald D Eller, "Harry Caudill and the Burden of Mountain Liberalism," in *Critical Essays in Appalachian Life and Culture: Proceedings of the Fifth Annual Appalachian Studies Conference*, ed. Rick Simon (Boone, NC: Appalachian Consortium Press, 1982).

9. Harry M. Caudill, "Misdeal in Appalachia," *Atlantic*, June 1965, 44.

10. Ibid.

11. Harry Caudill to Milton Ogle, May 4, 1966, Appalachian Volunteers

Records, box 21, Southern Appalachian Archives, Special Collections and Archives, Hutchins Library, Berea College, Berea, Kentucky.

12. Naomi Weintraub Cohen, interview by Gibbs Kinderman, "Voices from the Sixties," August 16, 1987, quoted in Glen, "War on Poverty," 85.

13. "979 Community Action Council" (typescript of fund-raising history, ca. 1970), in the author's possession.

14. *Hawkeye*, September 1968.

15. "Eastern Kentucky Welfare Rights Organization" (ca. 1970), in the author's possession.

16. Maxine Kenny, "Mountain Health Care: Politics, Power and Profits," *Mountain Life and Work*, April 1971, 14–17.

17. Whisnant, *Modernizing the Mountaineer*, 191–95.

18. Kyle Vance, "Poor Mobilize in Appalachia: Talk of March," *Louisville Courier-Journal*, February 19, 1967.

19. Senate Committee on Labor and Public Welfare, Subcommittee on Employment, Manpower, and Poverty, *Examination of the War on Poverty*, 90th Cong., 1st sess., 1967, 52–57, 279–90.

20. Vance, "Poor Mobilize in Appalachia."

21. Whisnant, *Modernizing the Mountaineer*, 193–94.

22. K. W. Lee, "Fair Elections in West Virginia," in Walls and Stephenson, *Appalachia in the Sixties*.

23. Clark Miller, "Era of Change: Volunteers Helped Appalachia and Vice Versa," *Louisville Courier-Journal*, May 15, 1988; Lee, "Fair Elections," 170.

24. Lee, "Fair Elections," 168–70.

25. Chad Montrie, *To Save the Land and People: A History of Opposition to Surface Coal Mining in Appalachia* (Chapel Hill: University of North Carolina Press, 2003), 72–74.

26. Ibid., 63–65.

27. Ibid., 75–78.

28. The following account of Combs's story is drawn from a number of sources, including "Strip Mining, January 10, 1965–December 23, 1965," Anne and Harry Caudill Papers, box 19, folder 4, Special Collections Library, University of Kentucky, Lexington; Guy Carawan and Candie Carawan, *Voices from the Mountains* (New York: Knopf, 1975), 44–48; Montrie, *To Save the Land*, 79; and "Mrs. Ollie Combs Family Scrapbook." I wish to thank the Combs family for use of a CD copy of the latter collection of photographs and newspaper clippings.

29. Harry M. Caudill, *The Watches of the Night: A New Plea for Appalachia* (Boston: Little, Brown, 1976), 42.

30. Montrie, *To Save the Land*, 87–88.

31. Joe Mulloy, "The Appalachian Story," *Bill of Rights Journal*, December 1969, 31.

32. Anne Braden, "The McSurely Case and Repression in the 1960s," *Southern Exposure*, September–October 1983, 24; Caudill, *Watches of the Night*, 47.

33. "Sedition Is Laid to Three in Kentucky," *New York Times*, August 13, 1967; Braden, "McSurely Case," 24.

34. Braden, "McSurely Case," 26.

35. Charles Young, "The Trial of Alan and Margaret McSurely," *Southern Exposure*, September–October 1983, 19.

36. James Tunnell, "Un-American Activities Unit Voted," *Louisville Courier-Journal*, March 9, 1968.

37. Bill Peterson, "Witness Scolds AV Probers for Attacks," *Louisville Courier-Journal*, December 4, 1968; Whisnant, *Modernizing the Mountaineer*, 207; Bill Peterson, "Fighting Splits Pikeville as KUAC Probe Nears," *Louisville Courier-Journal*, October 10, 1968.

38. Peterson, "Fighting Splits Pikeville."

39. Peter Schrag, "Appalachia: Again the Forgotten Land," *Saturday Review*, January 27, 1968, 14.

40. "Kennedy Hears of Need for Jobs during Two-Day Mountain Tour," *Whitesburg (KY) Mountain Eagle*, February 15, 1968.

41. Schrag, "Appalachia," 16, 18.

42. The complete text of Caudill's testimony is reprinted in the *Whitesburg (KY) Mountain Eagle*, February 15, 1968.

43. *Whitesburg (KY) Mountain Eagle*, February 15, 1968.

44. *To Save the Land and People*, dir. Anne Lewis (Whitesburg, KY: Appalshop Inc., 1999).

45. Schrag, "Appalachia," 16.

46. See Bill Peterson, "Political Battle Brewing on Anti-Poverty Program," *Louisville Courier-Journal*, September 20, 1969, and "Poverty: Feud in the Hills," *Time*, September 12, 1969, 21.

47. K. W. Lee, "Catalyst of the Black Lung Movement," in Walls and Stephenson, *Appalachia in the Sixties*, 201–9.

48. Carawan and Carawan, *Voices from the Mountains*, 172–80.

49. Richard P. Mulcahy, *A Social Contract for the Coal Fields: The Rise and Fall of the United Mine Workers of America Welfare and Retirement Fund* (Knoxville: University of Tennessee Press, 2000), 147–48; Caudill, *Watches of the Night*, 53–55.

50. Caudill, *Watches of the Night*, 147–72.

51. George Vecsey, "Ideal of Unity Stirs Appalachian Poor," *New York Times*, April 23, 1972.

52. For the history of the MFD movement, see George W. Hopkins, "The Miners for Democracy: Insurgency in the United Mine Workers of America, 1970–1972" (PhD diss., University of North Carolina, 1976); Seltzer, *Fire in*

the Hole; and Paul J. Nyden, "Miners for Democracy: Struggle in the Coal Fields" (PhD diss., Columbia University, 1974).

53. The best history of the struggle against surface mining in Appalachia is Montrie, *To Save the Land.*

54. Montrie, *To Save the Land*, 102.

55. Ibid., 104–5, 149.

56. See Thomas N. Bethell and Davitt McAteer, *The Pittston Mentality: Manslaughter on Buffalo Creek* (Huntington, WV: Appalachian Movement Press, 1972), and Kai T. Erikson, *Everything in Its Path: Destruction of Community in the Buffalo Creek Flood* (New York: Simon and Schuster, 1976).

57. *Mountain Life and Work*, June–July 1972, 20–22; Montrie, *To Save the Land*, 149–51.

58. Ben A. Franklin, "President Signs Strip Mining Bill, but Cites Defects," *New York Times*, August 4, 1972.

59. *Mountain Life and Work*, November 1971, 22–30, June–July 1972, 20–21.

60. *Mountain Life and Work*, March 1972, 10.

61. *Mountain Life and Work*, January 1970, 8.

62. Bryan Woolley, "Challenge for a Mountain Man," *Louisville Courier-Journal*, September 27, 1970.

63. *Mountain Life and Work*, June–July 1972, 22.

64. *Mountain Life and Work*, November 1972, 27.

65. *Mountain Life and Work*, October 1977, 40, September 1977, 46, August 1977, 46.

66. Appalachian Land Ownership Task Force, *Who Owns Appalachia? Landownership and Its Impact* (Lexington: University Press of Kentucky, 1983). See also Steve Fisher, ed., *A Landless People in a Rural Region: A Reader on Land Ownership and Property Taxation in Appalachia* (New Market, TN: Highlander Research and Education Center, 1979).

67. See Jim White, Ronald D Eller, and Debbie Auer, *Coal Severance Taxation: A Comparison of State Strategies for Collection and Distribution* (Lexington: University of Kentucky Appalachian Center, 1992).

68. Branscome, *Federal Government in Appalachia*, 37–39.

69. Virginia Wilson, *Economic Analysis of a Proposed Property Tax on Unmined Minerals in Kentucky*, Appalachian Center Occasional Paper Series no. 1 (Lexington: University of Kentucky Appalachian Center, 1983); Judy Jones, "Kentucky Lax on Coal Tax," *Lexington Herald-Leader*, October 27, 1998.

70. See Melanie Zuercher, ed., *Making History: The First Ten Years of the KFTC* (Prestonsburg, KY: Kentuckians for the Commonwealth, 1991).

71. *People's Appalachia* 1, no. 6 (1971): 3.

72. See Logan Brown et al., "ASA History," *Appalachian Journal* 31, no. 1 (2003).

73. Branscome quoted in Vecsey, "Ideal of Unity."

74. Michael Smathers, "Notes of a Native Son," *Vantage Point* 2 (1973): 6–7.

5. Growth and Development

1. Robert M. Collins, *More: The Politics of Economic Growth in Postwar America* (New York: Oxford University Press, 2000), 21, 38–39.

2. Walter Lippmann, *Washington Post*, March 19, 1964, quoted in Collins, *More*, 60.

3. Ralph R. Widner, "The Political Implementation of Regional Theory: The Appalachian Experience" (paper presented to the Southern Economic Association, November 13, 1970), 3, Research Reports, Administrative Research Library, Appalachian Regional Commission, Washington, DC (hereafter cited as ARL). See also John Friedman, "Regional Planning as a Field of Study," *Journal of the American Institute of Planners* 29 (August 1963), and John Friedman, "Regional Planning in Post-Industrial Society," *Journal of the American Institute of Planners* 30 (May 1964).

4. John L. Preston, "An Analysis of the Growth Center Strategy of the Appalachian Regional Commission" (Appalachian Regional Commission Division of Regional Program Planning and Evaluation Study Paper no. 13, March 1971), 7–8, Research Reports, ARL. See also Niles M. Hansen, *Intermediate-Size Cities as Growth Centers: Applications for Kentucky, the Piedmont Crescent, the Ozarks, and Texas* (New York: Praeger, 1971), 14–17, 26–28.

5. Widner, "Political Implementation," 3.

6. Quoted in Albert Solnit, "Deliberate Depopulation of Whole Areas: A Protest," *Whitesburg (KY) Mountain Eagle*, August 4, 1966.

7. Quoted in ibid.

8. "The Urban-Rural Growth Strategy in Appalachia" (commission staff summary report, September 1970), 13, Research Reports, ARL.

9. Widner, "Political Implementation," 5–6.

10. "Urban-Rural Growth Strategy," 14.

11. Ralph R. Widner, "Planning in Appalachia" (address to the Appalachian Water Development Coordinating Committee, June 15, 1967), 3, Research Reports, ARL.

12. John Fischer, "The Easy Chair: Can Ralph R. Widner Save New York, Chicago, and Detroit?" *Harper's*, October 1968.

13. "Urban-Rural Growth Strategy," 16, 17.

14. Ibid., 18.

15. Ralph R. Widner, "Science, Technology and Regional Development" (paper presented to the National Academy of Sciences, Washington, DC, May 12, 1967, and the University of Tennessee Space Sciences Seminar, Knoxville, TN, May 19, 1967), 8, Research Reports, ARL; Ralph R. Widner, "A Challenge for Action: Research and Planning for Regional Development" (paper presented to the Regional Conference on Research Related to Poverty and Development in Appalachia, Virginia Polytechnic Institute, Blacksburg, VA, July 17, 1968), 7, Research Reports, ARL.

16. Ralph R. Widner, "The Application of Systems Planning to Regional Development: The Appalachian Experience" (lecture at Northwestern University, Evanston, IL, April 23, 1969), 5, Research Reports, ARL.

17. Ralph R. Widner, "The Application of Systems Planning to Economic and Social Problems" (remarks to the Systems and Cybernetics Group, Institute of Electrical and Electronic Engineers, Washington DC, February 19, 1969), 4, Research Reports, ARL.

18. Ralph R. Widner, "Appalachia: America's Oldest or Newest Frontier" (convocation address at Union College, Barbourville, KY, October 1, 1970), 10, Appalachian Regional Commission Oral History Project conducted by Duke University, Research Reports, ARL.

19. Appalachian Regional Commission, *1971 Annual Report of the Appalachian Regional Commission* (Washington, DC: ARC, 1971), 25.

20. Bradshaw, *Appalachian Regional Commission*, 49.

21. Calvin G. Grayson, "Remarks to the Kentucky Appalachian Task Force" (Hazard, KY, March 29, 1994), in the author's possession. See also Alice J. Kinder, *William C. Hambley: The Mayor Who Moved a Mountain* (Berea, KY: Appalachian Imprints, 1988).

22. Appalachian Regional Commission, *Twenty Years of Progress*, 50; Bradshaw, *Appalachian Regional Commission*, 50–57.

23. Alvin Arnett, interview, July 5, 1983, audiovisual tape, ARC Archives; Donald Whitehead, interview, July 12, 1983, audiovisual tape, ARC Archives; John Whisman, interview, July 21, 1982, audiovisual tape, ARC Archives.

24. Charles Babcock, "Records Withheld in States' Probe of ARC Official: Irregularities Questioned," *Louisville Courier-Journal*, March 17, 1975.

25. Bradshaw, *Appalachian Regional Commission*, 58.

26. Arnett, interview.

27. Caudill, "Misdeal in Appalachia," 43–47.

28. Harriette Arnow, "The Gray Woman of Appalachia," *Nation*, December 28, 1970, 684–87.

29. Ben A. Franklin, "Appalachia Revisited: After Ten Years of Hope, Its Poor Still Waiting for That New Day Coming," *Louisville Courier-Journal*, December 8, 1970.

30. Bill Peterson, "The Appalachian Commission: Boon or Boondoggle?" *Louisville Courier-Journal*, April 8–11, 1973.

31. Phil Primack, "Depopulation Plan Advanced by ARC Director," *Whitesburg (KY) Mountain Eagle*, June 29, 1972. See also Phil Primack, "ARC: In Case You Were Wondering about ARC but Didn't Know Where to Look," *Mountain Life and Work*, March 1973, 6–8.

32. Howard Bray, "Appalachia: The View from Washington," *Progressive*, February 1975, 31–34.

33. ARC Accountability Project, *The Appalachian Regional Commission: Boon or Boondoggle—A Citizens' Handbook on the ARC* (Morgantown, WV: ARC Accountability Project, 1974), 68.

34. Ibid., 70.

35. Collins, *More*, 108; Bradshaw, *Appalachian Regional Commission*, 93.

36. See Appalachian Regional Commission, *Appalachia: A Reference Book* (Washington, DC: ARC, 1977).

37. Appalachian Alliance, *Appalachia 1978: A Protest from the Colony* (1978), in the author's possession.

38. John D. Rockefeller IV, interview, "What's Holding Up the Switch to Coal?" *U.S. News and World Report*, September 4, 1979, 26–27.

39. Quoted in Collins, *More*, 149.

40. Martha Cole, "ARC Approves $4 Million in Hospital Aid," *Lexington Herald*, May 17, 1978; Appalachian Regional Commission, *Twenty Years of Progress*, 50; *Lexington Leader*, August 9, 1978; "Task Force Investigates Landownership," *Mountain Life and Work*, September 1979, 22–23; Albert Smith, interview, May 1982, audiovisual tape, ARC Archives.

41. Cole, "ARC Approves."

42. *Lexington Leader*, August 9, 1978.

43. See "Women Coal Miners," special issue, *Mountain Life and Work*, July–August 1979.

44. John Egerton, "Appalachia's Absentee Landlords," *Progressive*, June 1981, 42–45. See also Appalachian Landownership Task Force, *Who Owns Appalachia*.

45. Egerton, "Appalachia's Absentee Landlords," 44; Gaventa quoted in ibid.

46. Tack Cornelius, "A Kentucky Success Story," *Appalachia: Journal of the Appalachian Regional Commission*, January–June 1983.

47. "Appalachia: The Economic Outlook through the Eighties," *Appalachia: Journal of the Appalachian Regional Commission*, November–December 1983, 4.

48. Doris Deakin, "Appalachia—on Our Way," *Appalachia: Journal of the Appalachian Regional Commission*, March–April 1979, 1, 8.

49. Appalachian Regional Commission, *Twenty Years of Progress*, 76.

50. "Economic Outlook," 3.

51. Deakin, "Appalachia," 12.

52. Quoted in Collins, *More*, 196.

53. Appalachian Regional Commission, *Twenty Years of Progress*, 29–30; Bradshaw, *Appalachian Regional Commission*, 105.

54. Appalachian Regional Commission, *Twenty Years of Progress*, 55–56.

55. Appalachian Governors, *A Report to Congress Concerning the Appalachian Regional Commission* (Washington, DC: ARC, 1981), 45.

56. Appalachian Regional Commission, *Twenty Years of Progress*, 68.

57. Ben A. Franklin, "Despite Twenty Years of Federal Aid, Poverty Still Reigns in Appalachia," *New York Times*, August 11, 1985.

58. Lee Mueller, "Can Eastern Kentucky Survive the Budget Cuts?" *Lexington Herald*, May 31, 1981.

59. Richard A. Couto, *An American Challenge: A Report on Economic Trends and Social Issues in Appalachia* (Dubuque, IA: Kendall/Hunt, 1994), 83, 105.

60. Ibid., 137, 145.

61. Ibid., 46.

62. Rick Steelhammer, "How Bad Is It? West Virginians Stand at an Economic Crossroads," *Charleston (WV) Gazette*, December 1989.

63. Claire Ansberry and Rick Wartzman, "State of Despair: West Virginia Mired in Poverty, Corruption, Battles a Deep Gloom," *Wall Street Journal*, September 21, 1989. See also Kate Long, "Almost Broke, West Virginia," *Southern Exposure*, Fall 1988, 56–59.

64. Fred Brown, "Appalachia: Land of Pain and Poverty," *Knoxville (TN) News-Sentinel*, January 5–11, 1985.

65. Francis J. Rivers, "People and Jobs in the Southwest Virginia Coalfields" (unpublished report prepared for the Commission on Religion in Appalachia and Community College Ministries, March 1989), in·the author's possession.

66. This and the following data are from Ronald D Eller et al., *Kentucky's Distressed Communities: A Report on Poverty in Appalachian Kentucky* (Lexington: University of Kentucky Appalachian Center, 1994).

67. James E. Casto, "Clinton Visits Appalachia," *Appalachia: Journal of the Appalachian Regional Commission*, May–August 1999, 4.

68. Eller et al., *Kentucky's Distressed Communities*.

69. Casto, "Clinton Visits Appalachia," 4.

70. Bill Estep, "More Jobs and Hope," *Lexington Herald-Leader*, July 6, 1999.

71. Don Edwards, "Looking Forward Instead of Backward," *Lexington Herald-Leader*, July 6, 1999.

6. The New Appalachia

1. Jack Hurst, "Business, Industry, and Technology," in *Encyclopedia of Appalachia*, ed. Rudy Abramson and Jean Haskell (Knoxville: University of Tennessee Press, 2006), 441.

2. John Hoke, "Coalfields in Decline," *Richmond (VA) Times-Dispatch*, February 28, 1996; "Coal Mining Only Top Industry Now Showing Job Loss," *Whitesburg (KY) Mountain Eagle*, July 1, 1996; Hurst, "Business, Industry," 441.

3. William Keesler, "Is Coal All There Is?" *Louisville Courier-Journal*, November 12, 1989; Hoke, "Coalfields in Decline."

4. See Shannon Jones, "In the Background of the Sago Mine Disaster," pt. 2, World Socialist Web Site, January 26, 2006, http://www.wsws.org/articles/2006/jan2006/mine-j26.shtml, and Richard A. Brisbin Jr., *A Strike like No Other Strike: Law and Resistance during the Pittston Coal Strike of 1989–1990* (Baltimore: Johns Hopkins University Press, 2002).

5. Erik Reece, *Lost Mountain: A Year in the Vanishing Wilderness; Radical Strip Mining and the Devastation of Appalachia* (New York: Riverhead, 2006), 63.

6. Jason Bailey and Liz Natter, *Kentucky's Low Road to Economic Development: What Corporate Subsidies Are Doing to the Commonwealth* (Lexington, KY: Democracy Resource Center, 2000), 25.

7. Reece, *Lost Mountain*, 58.

8. J. Bradford Jensen, *Birth and Death of Manufacturing Plants and Restructuring in Appalachia's Industrial Economy, 1963–1992: Evidence from the Longitudinal Research Database* (Washington, DC: ARC, 1998), 4.

9. Angie Newsome, "Region Struggles with Layoffs as Money for Incentive Programs Goes Elsewhere," *Asheville (NC) Citizen-Times*, November 27, 2005.

10. Bill Bishop, "Tax Incentives Do a Triple Flop," *Lexington Herald-Leader*, April 18, 1999.

11. Bill Estep and John Stamper, "Bad Breaks: Places like Harlan County Can't Hold Jobs or Plants for Long," *Lexington Herald-Leader*, November 13, 2005.

12. Lance Williams, "State Sues Harlan Factory for Failure to Provide Jobs," *Lexington Herald-Leader*, March 3, 2000.

13. Estep and Stamper, "Bad Breaks"; Bill Estep and John Stamper, "A Lot of Job Sites, Not So Many Jobs," *Lexington Herald-Leader*, November 20, 2005. See also Jason Bailey and Justin Maxson, *Accounting for Impact: Economic Development Spending in Kentucky* (Berea, KY: Mountain Association for Community Economic Development, 2006).

14. A cluster of communities around Clay County in West Virginia received an "enterprise community" award of $3 million.

15. J. Norman Reid, "Empowering the Way Out of Poverty: Why It Matters, How It Works" (paper delivered at the National Association of Resource Conservation and Development Councils Forum against Poverty, Tunica, MS, April 23, 2002). Reid was the acting deputy administrator of the USDA's Office of Community Development.

16. Kentucky Highlands Investment Corporation, *Kentucky Highlands Empowerment Zone 10 Year Report: A Common Belief That Progress Is Possible* (London, KY: KHIC, 2004), 1–34.

17. Ty Tagami, "Critics Assail Chicken Plant's Tax Incentives," *Lexington Herald-Leader*, April 29, 1999.

18. "Economic Incentives: Annville's Losses Revive Hard Questions," *Lexington Herald-Leader*, February 21, 2006.

19. See Eve S. Weinbaum, *To Move a Mountain: The Global Economy in Appalachia* (New York: Norton, 2004).

20. Kelvin M. Pollard, *Appalachia at the Millennium: An Overview of Results from Census 2000* (Washington, DC: ARC, 2003), 17–18; Lawrence E. Wood, *Trends in National and Regional Economic Distress, 1960–2000* (Washington, DC: ARC, 2005), 16.

21. Pollard, *Appalachia at the Millennium*, 20.

22. Deborah Thorne, Ann Tickameyer, and Mark Thorne, "Poverty and Income in Appalachia," *Journal of Appalachian Studies* 10 (2004): 345.

23. Jared Bernstein, Elizabeth McNichol, and Karen Lyons, *Pulling Apart: A State-by-State Analysis of Income Trends* (Washington, DC: Center on Budget and Policy Priorities, 2006), 20.

24. Thorne, Tickameyer, and Thorne, "Poverty and Income," 351.

25. See Leslie A. Whitener, Robert Gibbs, and Lorin Kusmin, "Rural Welfare Reform: Lessons Learned," *Amber Waves*, June 2003; Evelyn Nieves, "Job Market in W. Va. Defies Efforts to Reform Welfare," *Washington Post*, July 24, 2005; John Cheves, "Welfare Reform Swells SSI Lists," *Lexington Herald-Leader*, August 22, 2002; and Tammy Werner and Joanna Badagliacco, "Appalachian Households and Families in the New Millennium," *Journal of Appalachian Studies* 10 (2004): 387.

26. Evelyn Nieves, "Anger at Being Part of the Poverty Tour," *New York Times*, September 26, 2000.

27. Thomas C. Shaw, Allan J. DeYoung, and Eric Rademacher, "Educational Attainment in Appalachia: Growing with the Nation but Challenges Remain," *Journal of Appalachian Studies* 10 (2004).

28. Bruce Behringer, "Health Care Services in Appalachia," in *Sowing Seeds in the Mountains: Community-Based Coalitions for Cancer Prevention and Control*, ed. Richard A. Couto, Nancy K. Simpson, and Gale Harris (Bethesda, MD: Appalachia Leadership Initiative on Cancer, Cancer Control Sciences Program, Division of Cancer Prevention and Control, National Cancer Institute, 1994); Jeffrey Stensland, Curt Mueller, and Janet Sutton, intro-

duction to *An Analysis of Financial Conditions of Health Care Institutions in the Appalachian Region and Their Economic Impacts* (Washington, DC: ARC, 2002), iii–v.

29. Gary Burkett, "Status of Health in Appalachia," in Couto, Simpson, and Harris, *Sowing Seeds*, 66–67.

30. Ibid., 59.

31. Mike Stobbe, "Kentucky No. 2 in Rate of Heart Disease—Only West Virginia Is Worse," *Lexington Herald-Leader*, February 16, 2007; Burkett, "Status of Health," 55.

32. Laura Unger and P. G. Dunlap, "Black Lung Study Sees Growing Problems, Gaps in Safety," *Louisville Courier-Journal*, July 6, 2007.

33. Ken Ward Jr., "One by One Disasters Make Headlines, but Most Miners Killed on the Job Site Alone," *Charleston (WV) Gazette*, November 5, 2006.

34. Ken Ward Jr., "MSHA Report Finds Own Performance Unacceptable: Inspectors, Managers Failed in 2006 Deaths," *Charleston (WV) Gazette*, June 29, 2007.

35. Linda J. Johnson, "Eastern Kentucky: Painkiller Capital," *Lexington Herald-Leader*, January 19, 2003.

36. Ibid.; Appalachian Regional Commission, "Substance Abuse in Appalachia," http://www.arc.gov/index.do?nodeId=1750.

37. Claire Ansberry and Rick Wartzman, "State of Despair: West Virginia, Mired in Poverty, Corruption, Battles a Deep Gloom," *Wall Street Journal*, September 21, 1988.

38. Sue Lindsey, "Coal Town Seeks to Polish Image after Pork Rind Political Scandal," *Hampton (VA) Daily Press*, April 27, 2006.

39. Crit Luallen (auditor of public accounts, Commonwealth of Kentucky), "Knott County '06 Audit," news release, July 11, 2007.

40. Alan Maimon, "Letcher Official Doesn't Fear Backing Controversial Causes," *Louisville Courier-Journal*, December 3, 2005.

41. Gil Lawson, "A Crisis in Appalachia: Grassroots Reform Effort Shows Results," *Lexington Herald-Leader*, September 6, 1989.

42. Strat Douthat, "Strip Mining Halt Asked after West Virginia Floods," *Louisville Courier-Journal*, April 10, 1977; "Carroll Says Silt from Strip Mining Not a Major Cause of Heavy Flooding," *Louisville Courier-Journal*, April 8, 1977.

43. Jerry Hardt, *Harlan County Flood Report* (Livingston, KY: Appalachia—Science in the Public Interest, 1978); "Strip Mines Made Floods Worse," *Plow*, September 2, 1978, 2.

44. "Flood Causes: Get Serious with Studies," *Charleston (WV) Gazette*, May 8, 2002.

45. Phillip Barbich, "A Dirty Business: The Martin County Coal Mine Slurry Spill and the Bush Cover-up of an Environmental Disaster," *Salon*

.com, November 13, 2003; Lee Mueller, "Coal Company Calls Spill Act of God," *Lexington Herald-Leader*, November 30, 2000; "Sludge Inquiry Allegedly Hindered," *Lexington Herald-Leader*, April 4, 2004; David Hensley (general manager of Martin County Coal Corporation), "Errors Flood Slurry-Spill Reports," *Lexington Herald-Leader*, April 26, 2004.

46. Ken Ward Jr., "Mine Ruling Tossed: Haden's Valley Fills Ruling Overturned Again," *Charleston (WV) Gazette*, January 30, 2003.

47. Ken Ward Jr., "Thirty Years Later, Mine Law's Success Debated," *Charleston (WV) Gazette*, July 22, 2007.

48. *Keeper of the Mountains*, dir. B. J. Gudmundsson (Lewisburg, WV: Patchwork Films, 2006).

49. "Pollution Suit Names Tannery," *Lexington Herald-Leader*, May 17, 1983; "Agreement Settles Federal Suit," *Lexington Herald-Leader*, September 14, 1985; "Polluted Creek Draws International Concern," *Lexington Herald-Leader*, February 10, 1987; "Middlesboro Site of Battle over Sewage," *Lexington Herald-Leader*, April 3, 1990; "Activists Rally around Dayhoit," *Lexington Herald-Leader*, July 26, 1990.

50. Anna Manzo and Scott Harris, "The Dead Pigeon River," *Environmental Magazine*, May–June 1997; Daniel R. Varat, "Champion Fiber Company," in Abramson and Haskell, *Encyclopedia of Appalachia*, 467. See also Daniel Varat, "The Champion Family: Mountaineers in the Modern World" (PhD diss., University of Mississippi, 2002), and Richard A. Bartlett, *Troubled Waters: Champion International and the Pigeon River Controversy* (Knoxville: University of Tennessee Press, 1995).

51. "Protestors Shut Down Bank," *Asheville Citizen-Times*, August 14, 2007; Rainforest Action Network, "Protest and Picket Bank of America's 37th Annual Investor's Conference," September 7, 2007, http://www.indybay.org/newsitems/2007/09/07/18446200.php.

52. *Keeper of the Mountains*.

BIBLIOGRAPHY

MANUSCRIPT COLLECTIONS

Administrative Research Library, Appalachian Regional
Commission, Washington DC

> Minutes
> Research Reports
> Vertical Files

Special Collections and Archives, Hutchins Library,
Berea College, Berea, Kentucky

> Appalachian Volunteers Records
> Council of the Southern Mountains Records
> Vertical Files

Lyndon Baines Johnson Library and Museum, Austin, Texas

> Office Files of Bill Moyers
> Statements of Lyndon B. Johnson

Special Collections Library, University of Kentucky, Lexington

> Appalachian Regional Commission Archives
> Anne and Harry Caudill Papers
> Everette Tharp Papers
> John D. Whisman Papers

West Virginia State Archives, Division of Culture and History,
Charleston, West Virginia

> Special Collections
> Vertical Clipping Files

BIBLIOGRAPHY

West Virginia and Regional History Collection, Charles C. Wise Jr. Library, West Virginia University, Morgantown

West Virginia Newspapers on Microfilm Collection

GOVERNMENT PUBLICATIONS

"Appalachia: Economic Outlook through the Eighties." *Appalachia: Journal of the Appalachian Regional Commission*, November–December 1983.

Appalachian Governors. *A Report to Congress Concerning the Appalachian Regional Commission*. Washington, DC: ARC, 1981.

Appalachian Regional Commission. *Appalachia: A Reference Book*. Washington, DC: ARC, 1977.

———. *Appalachia: Twenty Years of Progress*. Washington, DC: ARC, 1985.

———. *Appalachian Data Book*. Washington, DC: ARC, 1967.

Casto, James E. "Clinton Visits Appalachia." *Appalachia: Journal of the Appalachian Regional Commission*, May–August 1999.

Cornelius, Tack. "A Kentucky Success Story." *Appalachia: Journal of the Appalachian Regional Commission*, January–June 1983.

Couto, Richard A., Nancy K. Simpson, and Gale Harris, eds. *Sowing Seeds in the Mountains: Community-Based Coalitions for Cancer Prevention and Control*. Bethesda, MD: Appalachia Leadership Initiative on Cancer, Cancer Control Sciences Program, Division of Cancer Prevention and Control, National Cancer Institute, 1994.

Deakin, Doris. "Appalachia—on Our Way." *Appalachia: Journal of the Appalachian Regional Commission*, March–April 1979.

Eastern Kentucky Regional Planning Commission. *Program 60*. Frankfort: Eastern Kentucky Regional Planning Commission, 1959.

———. *Program 60: Report*. Frankfort: Eastern Kentucky Regional Planning Commission, 1962.

Grossman, David A., and Melvin R. Levin. *The Appalachian Region: A Preliminary Analysis of Economic and Population Trends in an Eleven State Problem Area*. Annapolis: Maryland Department of Economic Development, 1960.

Jensen, J. Bradford. *Birth and Death of Manufacturing Plants and Restructuring in Appalachia's Industrial Economy, 1963–1992: Evidence from the Longitudinal Research Database*. Washington, DC: ARC, 1998.

Kentucky Agricultural Development Board. *Economic Data on Eastern Kentucky Coal Field*. Frankfort: Commonwealth of Kentucky, 1956.

Kentucky Junior Chamber of Commerce. *Annual Report, 1956–57*. Louisville: Kentucky Junior Chamber of Commerce, 1957.

Pollard, Kelvin M. *Appalachia at the Millennium: An Overview of Results from Census 2000.* Washington, DC: ARC, 2003.

President's Appalachian Regional Commission. *Appalachia: A Report by the President's Appalachian Regional Commission.* Washington, DC: PARC, 1964.

Stensland, Jeffrey, Curt Mueller, and Janet Sutton. *Analysis of Financial Conditions of Health Care Institutions in the Appalachian Region and Their Economic Impacts.* Washington, DC: ARC, 2002.

U.S. Bureau of the Census. *Census of Population, 1950.* Washington, DC: GPO, 1952.

———. *Census of Population, 1960.* Washington, DC: GPO, 1962.

———. *Census of Population, 1970.* Washington, DC: GPO, 1973.

———. *Census of Population, 1980.* Washington, DC: GPO, 1983.

———. *Census of Population, 1990.* Washington, DC: GPO, 1993.

———. *Census of Population, 2000.* Washington, DC: GPO, 2003.

U.S. Bureau of Labor Statistics. *Technology, Productivity, and Labor in the Bituminous Coal Industry, 1950–79.* Bulletin 2072. Washington, DC: GPO, 1981.

U.S. Congress. Senate. Committee on Environment and Public Works. *Summary and Analysis of the Legislative History of the Appalachian Regional Development Act of 1965 and Subsequent Amendments.* Report prepared by Douglas Reid Weimer. 99th Cong., 1st sess., 1985. Committee Print 14.

———. Committee on Labor and Public Welfare, Subcommittee on Employment, Manpower, and Poverty. *Examination of the War on Poverty.* 90th Cong., 1st sess., 1967.

Whitener, Leslie A., Robert Gibbs, and Lorin Kusmin. "Rural Welfare Reform: Lessons Learned." *Amber Waves*, June 2003.

Wood, Lawrence E. *Trends in National and Regional Economic Distress, 1960–2000.* Washington, DC: ARC, 2005.

DOCUMENTARY FILMS

Beyond Measure: Appalachian Culture and Economy. Directed by Herb E. Smith. Whitesburg, KY: Appalshop, 1994.

Buffalo Creek Flood: An Act of Man. Directed by Mimi Pickering. Whitesburg, KY: Appalshop, 1984.

Coalmining Women. Directed by Elizabeth Barret. Whitesburg, KY: Appalshop, 1982.

Fightin' for a Breath. Directed by Stephanie Wagner Whetstone. Whitesburg, KY: Appalshop, 1995.

Justice in the Coal Fields. Directed by Anne Lewis. Whitesburg, KY: Appalshop, 1995.

Keeper of the Mountains. Directed by B. J. Gudmundsson. Lewisburg, WV: Patchwork Films, 2006.

Long Journey Home. Directed by Elizabeth Barret. Whitesburg, KY: Appalshop, 1987.

Mud Creek Clinic. Directed by Anne Lewis. Whitesburg, KY: Appalshop, 1986.

On Our Own Land. Directed by Anne Lewis. Whitesburg, KY: Appalshop, 1988.

Ready for Harvest: Clearcutting in the Southern Appalachians. Directed by Anne Lewis. Whitesburg, KY: Appalshop, 1984.

Roving Pickets. Directed by Anne Lewis. Whitesburg, KY: Appalshop, 1991.

Sludge. Directed by Robert Salyer. Whitesburg, KY: Appalshop, 2004.

Strangers and Kin: A History of the Hillbilly Image. Directed by Herb E. Smith. Whitesburg, KY: Appalshop, 1984.

Stranger with a Camera. Directed by Elizabeth Barret. Whitesburg, KY: Appalshop, 2000.

Strip Mining: Energy, Environment, and Economics. Directed by Francis Morton and Gene DuBey. Whitesburg, KY: Appalshop, 1979.

To Save the Land and People. Directed by Anne Lewis. Whitesburg, KY: Appalshop, 1999.

THESES AND DISSERTATIONS

Arnett, Douglass. "Eastern Kentucky and the Politics of Dependency and Development." PhD diss., Duke University, 1978.

Duff, Frank. "Government in an Eastern Kentucky Coal County." Master's thesis, University of Kentucky, 1950.

Hoffman, Richard L. "Community Action: Innovative and Coordinative Strategies in the War on Poverty." PhD diss., University of North Carolina, 1969.

Hopkins, George W. "The Miners for Democracy: Insurgency in the United Mine Workers of America, 1970–1972." PhD diss., University of North Carolina, 1976.

Jensen, Richard J. "Rebellion in the United Mine Workers: The Miners for Democracy, 1970–1972." PhD diss., Indiana University, 1974.

Kiffmeyer, Thomas J. "From Self-Help to Sedition: The Appalachian Volunteers and the War on Poverty in Eastern Kentucky, 1964–1970." PhD diss., University of Kentucky, 1998.

Maggard, Sally Ward. "Eastern Kentucky Women on Strike: A Study of Gender, Class, and Political Action in the 1970s." PhD diss., University of Kentucky, 1988.

Napier, Jerry Wayne. "Mines, Miners, and Machines: Coal Mine Mechanization and the Eastern Kentucky Coal Fields, 1890–1990." PhD diss., University of Kentucky, 1997.

Nyden, Paul J. "Miners for Democracy: Struggle in the Coal Fields." PhD diss., Columbia University, 1974.

Taul, Glen Edward. "Poverty, Development, and Government in Appalachia: Origins of the Appalachian Regional Commission, 1956–1965." PhD diss., University of Kentucky, 2001.

Varat, Daniel. "The Champion Family: Mountaineers in the Modern World." PhD diss., University of Mississippi, 2002.

BOOKS AND ARTICLES

Abramson, Rudy, and Jean Haskell, eds. *Encyclopedia of Appalachia.* Knoxville: University of Tennessee Press, 2006.

Adams, Noah. *Far Appalachia: Following the New River North.* New York: Dell, 2002.

Anderson, James E. "Poverty, Unemployment, and Economic Development: The Search for a National Antipoverty Policy." *Journal of Politics* 29 (February 1967).

Appalachian Landownership Task Force. *Who Owns Appalachia? Landownership and Its Impact.* Lexington: University Press of Kentucky, 1983.

ARC Accountability Project. *The Appalachian Regional Commission: Boon or Boondoggle—A Citizens' Handbook on the ARC.* Morgantown, WV: ARC Accountability Project, 1974.

Arnow, Harriette. *The Dollmaker.* New York: Macmillan, 1954.

———. "The Gray Woman of Appalachia." *Nation,* December 28, 1970.

Bailey, Jason, and Justin Maxson. *Accounting for Impact: Economic Development Spending in Kentucky.* Berea, KY: Mountain Association for Community Economic Development, 2006.

Bailey, Jason, and Liz Natter. *Kentucky's Low Road to Economic Development: What Corporate Subsidies Are Doing to the Commonwealth.* Lexington, KY: Democracy Resource Center, 2000.

Ball, Richard A. "Social Change and Power Structure: An Appalachian Case." In Photiadis and Schwarzweller, *Change in Rural Appalachia.*

Bartlett, Richard A. *Troubled Waters: Champion International and the Pigeon River Controversy.* Knoxville: University of Tennessee Press, 1995.

Batteau, Alan, ed. *Appalachia and America: Autonomy and Regional Dependence.* Lexington: University Press of Kentucky, 1983.

Bernstein, Jared, Elizabeth McNichol, and Karen Lyons. *Pulling Apart: A State-by-State Analysis of Income Trends.* Washington, DC: Center on Budget and Policy Priorities, 2006.

Berry, Chad. *Southern Migrants, Northern Exiles.* Urbana: University of Illinois Press, 2000.

Bethell, Thomas N. "Conspiracy in Coal." In Walls and Stephenson, *Appalachia in the Sixties.*

Bethell, Thomas N., and Davitt McAteer. *The Pittston Mentality: Manslaughter on Buffalo Creek.* Huntington, WV: Appalachian Movement Press, 1972.

Billings, Dwight, and Kathleen Blee. *The Road to Poverty: The Making of Wealth and Hardship in Appalachia.* New York: Cambridge University Press, 2000.

Bookbinder, Bernie. "Appalachia: The Desperate Americans." *Newsday,* December 17, 1963.

Boone, Richard W. "Working with the Poor." *New Republic,* November 9, 1965.

Borman, Kathryn, and Phillip J. Obermiller. *From Mountain to Metropolis: Appalachian Migrants in American Cities.* Westport: Bergin and Garvey, 1994.

Braden, Anne. "The McSurely Case and Repression in the 1960s." *Southern Exposure,* September–October 1983.

Bradshaw, Michael. *The Appalachian Regional Commission: Twenty-five Years of Government Policy.* Lexington: University Press of Kentucky, 1992.

Branscome, James. *The Federal Government in Appalachia.* New York: Field Foundation, 1977.

Brauer, Carl M. "Kennedy, Johnson, and the War on Poverty." *Journal of American History* 69, no. 1 (1982).

Bray, Howard. "Appalachia: The View from Washington." *Progressive,* February 1975.

Brisbin, Richard A. *A Strike like No Other Strike: Law and Resistance during the Pittson Coal Strike of 1989–1990.* Baltimore: Johns Hopkins University Press, 2002.

Brown, James S., and George A. Hillery. "The Great Migration, 1940–1960." In Ford, *Southern Appalachian Region.*

Brown, James S., and Harry K. Schwarzweller. "The Appalachian Family." In Riddel, *Appalachia.*

Brown, Logan, Teresa Burchett-Anderson, Donavan Cain, and Jinny Turman Deal. "ASA History." *Appalachian Journal* 31, no. 1 (2003).

Bruno, Hal. "Chicago's Hillbilly Ghetto." *Reporter,* June 4, 1964.

Campbell, Tracy. *Deliver the Vote: A History of Election Fraud, an American Political Tradition, 1742–2004.* New York: Carroll and Graf, 2005.

Carawan, Guy, and Candie Carawan. *Voices from the Mountains.* New York: Knopf, 1975.

Carter, L. J. "The Appalachian Program: A Mechanism for a National Growth Policy?" *Science,* July 3, 1970.

Catholic Committee of Appalachia. *This Land Is Home to Me: A Pastoral*

Letter on Powerlessness in Appalachia by the Catholic Bishops of the Region. Whitesburg, KY: Catholic Committee of Appalachia, 1975.

Caudill, Harry M. *A Darkness at Dawn: Appalachian Kentucky and the Future.* Lexington: University Press of Kentucky, 1976.

———. "Misdeal in Appalachia." *Atlantic,* June 1965.

———. "The Mountaineers in the Affluent Society." *Environmental Journal,* July 1971.

———. *Night Comes to the Cumberlands: A Biography of a Depressed Area.* Boston: Little, Brown, 1963.

———. "The Permanent Poor: The Lesson of Eastern Kentucky." *Atlantic,* June 1964.

———. "The Rape of the Appalachians." *Atlantic,* April 1962.

———. *The Senator from Slaughter County.* Boston: Little, Brown, 1973.

———. *Theirs Be the Power: The Moguls of Eastern Kentucky.* Urbana: University of Illinois Press, 1983.

———. *The Watches of the Night: A New Plea for Appalachia.* Boston: Little, Brown, 1976.

Chinitz, Benjamin. "Signs of Hope in the Graveyard of the American Dream." *Pitt,* January 1964.

Christian Appalachian Project. *Faith and Actions: Annual Report of the Christian Appalachian Project, 1987.* Lancaster, KY: CAP, 1987.

Cleghorn, Reese. "Appalachia: Poverty, Beauty and Poverty." *New York Times Magazine,* April 25, 1965.

Cole, William E. "Social Problems and Welfare Services." In Ford, *Southern Appalachian Region.*

Collins, Robert M. *More: The Politics of Economic Growth in Postwar America.* New York: Oxford University Press, 2000.

Commission on Religion in Appalachia. *Proceedings—CORA 1966: A United Approach to Fulfilling the Church's Mission in Appalachia.* Knoxville, TN: Commission on Religion in Appalachia, 1966.

———. *Unite: A CORA War on Poverty Commemoration.* Knoxville, TN: Commission on Religion in Appalachia, 1986.

Couto, Richard A. *Making Democracy Work Better: Mediating Structures, Social Capital, and the Democratic Prospect.* Chapel Hill: University of North Carolina Press, 1999.

———. *An American Challenge: A Report on Economic Trends and Social Issues in Appalachia.* Dubuque, IA: Kendall/Hunt, 1994.

Cressey, Paul F. "The Changing Highlands." *Mountain Life and Work,* Fall 1951.

Dallek, Robert. *Flawed Giant: Lyndon Johnson and His Times, 1961–1973.* New York: Oxford University Press, 1998.

Downing, Bob. "Akron, West Virginia." *Mountain Review,* May 1976.

Drake, Richard. *A History of Appalachia*. Lexington: University Press of Kentucky, 2001.

Duncan, Cynthia M. *Worlds Apart: Why Poverty Persists in Rural America*. New Haven, CT: Yale University Press, 1999.

Egerton, John. "Appalachia's Absentee Landlords." *Progressive*, June 1981.

Eller, Ronald D. "Harry Caudill and the Burden of Mountain Liberalism." In *Critical Essays in Appalachian Life and Culture: Proceedings of the Fifth Annual Appalachian Studies Conference*, edited by Rick Simon. Boone, NC: Appalachian Consortium Press, 1982.

———. "Lost and Found in the Promised Land: The Education of a Hillbilly." In *One Hundred Years of Appalachian Visions*, edited by Bill Best. Berea, KY: Appalachian Imprints, 1997.

———. *Miners, Millhands and Mountaineers: The Industrialization of the Appalachian South, 1880–1930*. Knoxville: University of Tennessee Press, 1982.

Eller, Ronald D, Phillip Jenks, Christopher Jasparro, and Jerry Napier. *Kentucky's Distressed Communities: A Report on Poverty in Appalachian Kentucky*. Lexington: University of Kentucky Appalachian Center, 1994.

Erikson, Kai T. *Everything in Its Path: Destruction of Community in the Buffalo Creek Flood*. New York: Simon and Schuster, 1976.

Ernst, Harry W. "For 300,000 West Virginians: A Starvation Diet?" *Mountain Life and Work*, Spring 1959.

———. *The Primary That Made a President: West Virginia 1960*. New York: McGraw-Hill, 1962.

Ernst, Harry W., and Charles H. Drake. "The Lost Appalachians: Poor, Proud and Primitive." *Nation*, May 30, 1959.

Ewen, Lynda Ann. *Which Side Are You On? The Brookside Mine Strike in Harlan County, Kentucky, 1973–1974*. Chicago: Vanguard, 1979.

Finley, Joseph E. *The Corrupt Kingdom: The Rise and Fall of the United Mine Workers*. New York: Simon and Schuster, 1972.

Fischer, John. "The Easy Chair: Can Ralph R. Widner Save New York, Chicago, and Detroit?" *Harper's*, October 1968.

Fisher, Stephen L., ed. *Fighting Back in Appalachia: Traditions of Resistance and Change*. Philadelphia: Temple University Press, 1993.

———, ed. *A Landless People in a Rural Region: A Reader on Land Ownership and Property Taxation in Appalachia*. New Market, TN: Highlander Research and Education Center, 1979.

Ford, Thomas R., ed. *The Southern Appalachian Region: A Survey*. Lexington: University of Kentucky Press, 1962.

Friedman, John. "Regional Planning as a Field of Study." *Journal of the American Institute of Planners* 29 (August 1963).

———. "Regional Planning in Post-Industrial Society." *Journal of the American Institute of Planners* 30 (May 1964).

Fritsch, Al, and Kristin Johannsen. *Ecotourism in Appalachia: Marketing the Mountains.* Lexington: University Press of Kentucky, 2004.

Galbraith, John Kenneth. *The Affluent Society.* Boston: Houghton Mifflin, 1958.

Gaventa, John, Barbara Ellen Smith, and Alex Willingham. *Communities in Economic Crisis: Appalachia and the South.* Philadelphia: Temple University Press, 1990.

Giffin, Roscoe. "From Cinder Hollow to Cincinnati." *Mountain Life and Work*, Winter 1956.

Gillette, Michael L. *Launching the War on Poverty: An Oral History.* New York: Twayne, 1996.

Glen, John M. "The War on Poverty in Appalachia: Oral History from the Top Down and the Bottom Up." *Oral History Review* 22, no. 1 (1995).

Graff, Orin. "The Needs of Education." In Ford, *Southern Appalachian Region.*

Gray, Wayne T. "Mountain Dilemmas: Study in Mountain Attitudes." *Mountain Life and Work*, April 1936.

Gregory, James N. *The Southern Diaspora: How the Great Migrations of Black and White Southerners Transformed America.* Chapel Hill: University of North Carolina Press, 2007.

Griffin, Gerald. "The Truth about Eastern Kentucky." *Mountain Life and Work*, Winter 1955.

Grossman, David A., and Melvin R. Levin. "The Appalachian Region: A National Problem Area." *Land Economics* 38 (1961).

Hamilton, W. L., F. C. Collignon, and C. E. Carlson. "The Causes of Rural to Urban Migration among the Poor." In Riddel, *Appalachia.*

Hansen, Niles M. *Intermediate-Size Cities as Growth Centers: Applications for Kentucky, the Piedmont Crescent, the Ozarks, and Texas.* New York: Praeger, 1971.

Hardt, Jerry. *Harlan County Flood Report.* Livingston, KY: Appalachia—Science in the Public Interest, 1978.

Harrington, Michael. "Appalachia, beyond Free Enterprise: The Appalachian Regional Development Act." *Commonweal*, May 7, 1965.

———. *The Other America: Poverty in the United States.* New York: Macmillan, 1962.

———. "Our Fifty Million Poor: Forgotten Men of the Affluent Society." *Commentary*, July 1959.

Hatcher, J. Wesley. "Glimpses of Appalachian America's Basic Conditions of Living." Pts. 1 and 2. *Mountain Life and Work*, October 1938, January 1939.

BIBLIOGRAPHY

Hechler, Ken. "TVA Ravages the Land." *Environmental Journal*, July 1971.

Hinsdale, Mary Ann, Helen Lewis, and Maxine Waller. *It Comes from the People: Community Development and Local Theology.* Philadelphia: Temple University Press, 1995.

Howell, Benita J., ed. *Culture, Environment, and Conservation in the Appalachian South.* Urbana: University of Illinois Press, 2002.

Hundley, John. "The Mountain Man in Northern Industry." *Mountain Life and Work*, Summer 1955.

Hurst, Jack. "Business, Industry, and Technology." In Abramson and Haskell, *Encyclopedia of Appalachia.*

Kenny, Maxine. "Mountain Health Care: Politics, Power and Profits." *Mountain Life and Work*, April 1971.

Kentucky Highlands Investment Corporation. *Kentucky Highlands Empowerment Zone 10 Year Report: A Common Belief That Progress Is Possible.* London, KY: KHIC, 2004.

Keyserling, Leon. "Two-Fifths of a Nation." *Progressive*, June 1962.

Kiffmeyer, Thomas J. "From Self-Help to Sedition: The Appalachian Volunteers in Eastern Kentucky, 1964–1970." *Journal of Southern History* 64, no. 1 (1998).

Kinder, Alice J. *William C. Hambley: The Mayor Who Moved a Mountain.* Berea, KY: Appalachian Imprints, 1988.

Kirby, Jack T. "The Southern Exodus, 1910–1960: A Primer for Historians." *Journal of Southern History* 49, no. 4 (1983).

Kopkind, A. "Revolt of the Poor." *New Statesman*, April 22, 1966.

Larson, Olaf F. "Wartime Migration and the Manpower Reserve on Farms in Eastern Kentucky." *Rural Sociology* 8, no. 2 (1943).

Lee, K. W. "Fair Elections in West Virginia." In Walls and Stephenson, *Appalachia in the Sixties.*

Lemann, Nicholas. *The Promised Land: The Great Black Migration and How It Changed America.* New York: Vintage, 1992.

Levitan, Sar A. *The Design of Federal Antipoverty Strategy.* Ann Arbor: Institute of Labor and Industrial Relations, University of Michigan, 1967.

Lewis, Helen M., and Monica Appleby. *Mountain Sisters: From Convent to Community in Appalachia.* Lexington: University Press of Kentucky, 2003.

Lewis, Helen Matthews, Linda Johnson, and Donald Askins, eds. *Colonialism in Modern America: The Appalachian Case.* Boone, NC: Appalachian Consortium Press, 1978.

Lewis, Oscar. *Children of Sanchez: Autobiography of a Mexican Family.* New York: Random House, 1961.

———. *La Vida: A Puerto Rican Family in the Culture of Poverty.* New York: Random House, 1966.

Long, Kate. "Almost Broke, West Virginia." *Southern Exposure*, Fall 1988.

Luebke, B. H., and John Fraser Hart. "Migration from a Southern Appalachian Community." *Land Economics* 34, no. 1 (1958).

MacDonald, Dwight. "Our Invisible Poor." *New Republic*, January 19, 1963.

Maloney, Michael. "The Prospects for Urban Appalachians." In Philliber and McCoy, *Invisible Minority*.

Manzo, Anna, and Scott Harris. "The Dead Pigeon River." *Environmental Magazine*, May–June 1997.

Marshall, Suzanne. *"Lord, We're Just Trying to Save Your Water": Environmental Activism and Dissent in the Appalachian South*. Gainesville: University Press of Florida, 2002.

McCoy, Clyde B., and James S. Brown. "Appalachian Migration to Midwestern Cities." In Philliber and McCoy, *Invisible Minority*.

McCoy, Clyde B., and Virginia McCoy Watkins. "Stereotypes of Appalachian Migrants." In Philliber and McCoy, *Invisible Minority*.

Mitchell, George S. "Let's Unite the Pie." *Mountain Life and Work*, Spring 1951.

Mitchell, Morris R. "Dare the School Build a Community?" *Mountain Life and Work*, July 1938.

Montrie, Chad. *To Save the Land and People: A History of Opposition to Surface Coal Mining in Appalachia*. Chapel Hill: University of North Carolina Press, 2003.

Morgan, Thomas B. "Portrait of an Underdeveloped Country." *Look*, December 4, 1962.

Mulcahy, Richard P. *A Social Contract for the Coal Fields: The Rise and Fall of the United Mine Workers of America Welfare and Retirement Fund*. Knoxville: University of Tennessee Press, 2000.

Mulloy, Joe. "The Appalachian Story." *Bill of Rights Journal*, December 1969.

Murphy, M. "The Valley of Poverty." *Life*, January 31, 1964.

"National Defense and Mountain Communities." *Mountain Life and Work*, Winter 1942.

O'Connor, Alice. *Poverty Knowledge: Social Science, Social Policy, and the Poor in Twentieth-Century U.S. History*. Princeton, NJ: Princeton University Press, 2001.

Parrish, Thomas. "Speakers Rouse Council in Annual Conference." *Mountain Life and Work*, Summer 1964.

Patterson, James T. *America's Struggle against Poverty, 1900–1980*. Cambridge, MA: Harvard University Press, 1981.

Pearce, John Ed. "The Superfluous People of Hazard, Kentucky." *Reporter*, January 3, 1963.

Perry, Huey. *"They'll Cut Off Your Project": A Mingo County Chronicle.* New York: Praeger, 1972.

Perry, Lester. *Forty Years of Mountain Politics.* Parsons, WV: McClain, 1971.

Philliber, William W. *Appalachian Migrants in Urban America: Cultural Conflict or Ethnic Group Formation?* New York: Praeger, 1981.

Philliber, William W., and Clyde B. McCoy, eds. *The Invisible Minority, Urban Appalachians.* Lexington: University Press of Kentucky, 1981.

Photiadis, John D. "Occupational Adjustment of Appalachians in Cleveland." In Philliber and McCoy, *Invisible Minority.*

Photiadis, John D., and Harry K. Schwarzweller, eds. *Change in Rural Appalachia: Implications for Action Programs.* Philadelphia: University of Pennsylvania Press, 1970.

Plunckett, H. Dudley, and Mary Jean Bowman. *Elites and Change in the Kentucky Mountains.* Lexington: University Press of Kentucky, 1973.

Proctor, Roy E., and T. Kelley White. "Agriculture: A Reassessment." In Ford, *Southern Appalachian Region.*

Reece, Eric. *Lost Mountain: A Year in the Vanishing Wilderness; Radical Strip Mining and the Devastation of Appalachia.* New York: Riverhead, 2006.

Riddel, Frank S., ed. *Appalachia: Its People, Heritage, and Problems.* Dubuque, IA: Kendall/Hunt, 1974.

Ridgeway, James. "Sedition in Kentucky." *New Republic,* September 2, 1967.

———. "Why the Poverty War Seems a Muddle." *New Republic,* October 9, 1965.

Rockefeller, John D., IV. Interview. "What's Holding up the Switch to Coal?" *U.S. News and World Report,* September 4, 1979.

Schrag, Peter. "Appalachia: Again the Forgotten Land." *Saturday Review,* January 27, 1968.

Seligman, Ben B. "Appalachia as Symbol." *Nation,* February 22, 1965.

Seltzer, Curtis. *Fire in the Hole: Miners and Managers in the American Coal Industry.* Lexington: University Press of Kentucky, 1985.

Shapiro, Henry David. *Appalachia on Our Mind: The Southern Mountains and Mountaineers in the American Consciousness.* Chapel Hill: University of North Carolina Press, 1978.

Shaw, Thomas C., Allan J. DeYoung, and Eric Rademacher. "Educational Attainment in Appalachia: Growing with the Nation but Challenges Remain." *Journal of Appalachian Studies* 10 (2004).

Silberman, C. E. "Mixed-up War on Poverty." *Fortune,* August 1965.

Smathers, Michael. "Notes of a Native Son." *Vantage Point* 2 (1973).

Smith, Barbara Ellen. *Digging Our Own Graves: Coal Miners and the Strug-*

gle over Black Lung Disease. Philadelphia: Temple University Press, 1987.

Smith, J. Allan. "Action Program for Mountain Counties." *Mountain Life and Work*, Summer 1961.

Stafford, Thomas F. *Afflicting the Comfortable: Journalism and Politics in West Virginia.* Morgantown: West Virginia University Press, 2005.

Starnes, Richard D. *Creating the Land of the Sky: Tourism and Society in Western North Carolina.* Tuscaloosa: University of Alabama Press, 2005.

Street, Paul, Lowndes F. Stephens, Stephen R. Cain, James W. Gladden, Morris K. Caudill, Lewis Donohew, Willis A. Sutton Jr., Ottis Murphy, and Thomas P. Field. *Community Action in Appalachia: An Appraisal of the War on Poverty in a Rural Setting of Southeastern Kentucky.* 3 vols. Lexington: University of Kentucky Center for Developmental Change, 1965–1968.

Sutton, Willis A., Jr. "Differential Perceptions of the Impact of a Rural Anti-Poverty Campaign." *Social Science Quarterly* 50 (1969).

Taylor, Alva W. "Up a Kentucky Mountain Cove." *Mountain Life and Work*, Winter 1942.

Thorne, Deborah, Ann Tickameyer, and Mark Thorne. "Poverty and Income in Appalachia." *Journal of Appalachian Studies* 10 (2004).

Toynbee, Arnold. *A Study of History.* Vol. 2. New York: Oxford University Press, 1947.

Tugwell, Rexford G. "The Resettlement Administration and Its Relation to the Appalachian Mountains." *Mountain Life and Work*, October 1935.

Unger, Irwin. *The Best of Intentions: The Triumph and Failure of the Great Society Under Kennedy, Johnson, and Nixon.* New York: Doubleday, 1996.

Votaw, Albert N. "The Hillbillies Invade Chicago." *Harper's*, February 1958.

Wakefield, D. "In Hazard Kentucky." *Commentary*, September 1963.

Walls, David S., and John B. Stephenson, eds. *Appalachia in the Sixties: Decade of Reawakening.* Lexington: University Press of Kentucky, 1972.

Weatherford, W. D. "The Southern Appalachian Studies: Their Final Form and Potential." *Mountain Life and Work*, Winter 1959.

Weinbaum, Eve S. *To Move a Mountain: The Global Economy in Appalachia.* New York: Norton, 2004.

Weise, Robert S. *Grasping at Independence: Debt, Male Authority, and Mineral Rights in Appalachian Kentucky, 1850–1915.* Knoxville: University of Tennessee Press, 2001.

Weller, Jack E. "Is There a Future for Yesterday's People?" *Saturday Review of Literature*, October 16, 1965.

———. *Yesterday's People: Life in Contemporary Appalachia.* Lexington: University of Kentucky Press, 1965.

Werner, Tammy, and Joanna Badagliacco. "Appalachian Households and Families in the New Millennium." *Journal of Appalachian Studies* 10 (2004).

Whisnant, David E. *Modernizing the Mountaineer: People, Power, and Planning in Appalachia.* Boone, NC: Appalachian Consortium Press, 1980.

White, Jim, Ronald D Eller, and Debbie Auer. *Coal Severance Taxation: A Comparison of State Strategies for Collection and Distribution.* Lexington: University of Kentucky Appalachian Center, 1992.

White, Theodore H. *The Making of the President, 1960.* New York: Atheneum, 1961.

Williams, John Alexander. *Appalachia: A History.* Chapel Hill: University of North Carolina Press, 2001.

Wilson, Virginia. *Economic Analysis of a Proposed Property Tax on Unmined Minerals in Kentucky.* Appalachian Center Occasional Papers Series no. 1. Lexington: University of Kentucky Appalachian Center, 1983.

Young, Charles. "The Trial of Alan and Margaret McSurely." *Southern Exposure,* September–October 1983.

Zuercher, Melanie, ed. *Making History: The First Ten Years of the KFTC.* Prestonsburg, KY: Kentuckians for the Commonwealth, 1991.

INDEX

acculturation, 100–101, 127

acid mine drainage, 254

activism, grassroots Appalachian
against CAAs, 141–42
for coal mine health/safety, 157–59
for environmental justice, 251–55
for equitable taxation, 168–70
grassroots organizations, 139–42, 167–68
growth-based development rejected by, 194–95
lobbying efforts, 167
local political backlash against, 143–44, 150–53
against mountaintop removal, 251–52
against political elites/corruption, 140–44
regional consciousness resulting from, 170–76
regional networks for, 139, 157, 165–68, 170
against strip mining, 145–49, 161–65, 167, 195, 196
synchronization of, 168
tactics of, 141
for union reform, 157–61
War on Poverty as catalyst for, 138–39, 170

See also specific activist; organization

adult education, 104, 119–20

adult literacy, 80, 95

affluence, 63–64, 90–91
poverty in midst of, 31–32, 91–93

Affluent Society, The (Galbraith), 63–64, 91–92

African Americans, 20, 25

agriculture
decline of, 28–30, 199, 255
impact of industrialization on, 13–14, 28–29
impact of WWII mobilization on, 11–12
See also farms

AGSLP. *See* Appalachian Group to Save the Land and People

Aid to Families with Dependent Children, 33

Akron (Ohio), Appalachian out-migration to, 22

Alabama, 12, 45

alcoholism, 242

Alice Lloyd College, 173

Alice Lloyd College Outreach Reserves (ALCOR), 113–14

Alinsky, Saul, 99, 108, 131, 137

all-terrain vehicles (ATVs), 256

Almond, Lindsey, 56